Carl Zuckmayer Criticism

HANS WAGENER

CARL ZUCKMAYER CRITICISM:

TRACING ENDANGERED FAME

CAMDEN HOUSE

Published by Camden House, Inc.
Drawer 2025
Columbia, SC 29202 USA

Printed on acid-free paper.
Binding materials are chosen for strength and
durability.

100177491 4

ISBN 1–57113–064–0

Library of Congress Cataloging-in-Publication Data

Wagener, Hans, 1940-
    Carl Zuckmayer criticism : tracing endangered fame / Hans Wagener.
       p.   cm. -- (Studies in German literature, linguistics, and
culture. Literary criticism in perspective)
    Includes bibliographical references (p.   ) and index.
    ISBN 1-57113-064-0 (acid-free paper)
    1. Zuckmayer, Carl, 1896-1977--Criticism and interpretation.
2. Criticism--Germany--History--20th century.   I. Title.
II. Series: Studies in German literature, linguistics, and culture
(Unnumbered). Literary criticism in perspective.
PT2653.U33Z9425   1995
832 ' .912--dc20   95-9743
                                          CIP

Contents

Title Translations

Since the following Zuckmayer titles occur frequently in the text, a translation is provided here:

Als wär's ein Stück von mir (1966; translated as *A Part of Myself,* 1970)

"Aufruf zum Leben" (1942; translated as "Appeal to the Living," 1942)

Ein Bauer aus dem Taunus und andere Geschichten (A Farmer from the Taunus and Other Stories, 1927)

Der Baum (The Tree, 1926)

Die Brüder Grimm (The Brothers Grimm, 1948)

Die Fastnachtsbeichte (1959; translated as *Carnival Confession,* 1961))

Der fröhliche Weinberg (The Merry Vineyard, 1925)

Gedichte (Poems, 1960)

Der Gesang im Feuerofen (The Song of the Fiery Furnace, 1950)

"Die Geschichte vom Lappenvogt Bal" (The Story of Bal, Governor of the Laps, 1927)

"Die Geschichte vom Tümpel" (Story of a Pond, 1927)

"Geschichte von einer Geburt" (Story of a Birth, 1927)

Der Hauptmann von Köpenick (1930; translated as *The Captain of Köpenick,* 1932)

Herr über Leben und Tod (Master of Life and Death, 1938)

Das kalte Licht (The Cold Light, 1955)

Kiktahan oder Die Hinterwäldler (Kiktahan or The Backwoodsmen, 1925)

Kranichtanz (Dance of the Herons, 1976)

Kreuzweg (Crossroad or The Way of the Cross, 1921)

Die langen Wege (Long Walks, 1952)

Das Leben des Horace A. W. Tabor (The Life of Horace A. W. Tabor, 1964)

Eine Liebesgeschichte (1934; translated as "A Love Story," 1937)

Pankraz erwacht (Pankraz Awakens, 1978)

Der Rattenfänger (The Pied Piper, 1975)

Rivalen (Rivals, 1929)

Salwàre oder Die Magdalena von Bozen (1935; translated as *The Moon in the South*, London, 1937; republished as *The Moons Ride Over*, New York, 1937)

Der Seelenbräu (The Soul Brew, 1945)

Der Schelm von Bergen (The Knave of Bergen, 1934)

Sitting-Bull: Ein Indianer-Roman (Sitting Bull: An Indian Novel, 1952)

Ein Sommer in Österreich (A Summer in Austria, 1937)

Des Teufels General (1947; translated as *The Devil's General*, 1962)

Die Uhr schlägt eins (The Clock Strikes One, 1961)

Ulla Winblad oder Musik und Leben des Carl Michael Bellman (Ulla Winblad or Music and Life of Carl Michael Bellman, 1953)

"Die wandernden Hütten" (The Walking Huts, 1948)

Introduction

WITH THE FIRST performance of his drama *Der fröhliche Weinberg* in 1925, Carl Zuckmayer (1896–1977) was catapulted to a fame that was to last throughout the years of the Weimar Republic. It was sustained by such plays as *Schinderhannes* (1927) and *Katharina Knie* (1928) and reached renewed heights with *Der Hauptmann von Köpenick* (1931), making Zuckmayer, next to Bertolt Brecht, the most recognized playwright of the Weimar Republic. All the above plays have one thing in common: they are *Volksstücke* (folk plays) that derive their success from their rootedness in a particular region and its dialect. With the exception of *Der Hauptmann von Köpenick*, which takes place in and around Berlin, the action of all these plays is set in or close to Zuckmayer's home region, the Rhineland, Rhenish Hesse, or the Palatinate. Because of this regional rootedness, their appeal was limited to German tastes, and thus Zuckmayer never became internationally famous. There are few English translations of his works, and they generally drew little international attention from newspaper and magazine reviewers. After the Second World War, however, he again quickly managed to become one of the most frequently performed dramatists in Germany with plays such as *Des Teufels General* (1947), and he scored perhaps his greatest success with his autobiography *Als wär's ein Stück von mir* (1966).

Zuckmayer's themes were German, and his being a German with a half-Jewish background, which he had never paid attention to before the advent of Hitler, determined his fate. Zuckmayer was born on 27 December 1896 in the village of Nackenheim in Rhenish Hesse. He was the son of the owner of a small factory for wine bottle caps. His mother was the daughter of a Protestant church councillor who had converted from Judaism. When Zuckmayer was four years old, his family moved to the neighboring city of Mainz, where he lived and went to school until the outbreak of the First World War. Like everyone else in his class, he volunteered for the army in 1914. He graduated early by means of a simplified emergency exam and spent the next years in the front lines of the Western front serving in field artillery, ultimately as a lieutenant. His initial enthusiasm for war soon gave way to total disillusionment. He expressed his pacifist and leftist leanings by writing for Franz Pfemfert's avant-garde periodical *Die Aktion* (Action). At war's end, he was elected to a soldiers' council and led his men back to Germany. During the period of 1918–20 he was a student at the universities of Frankfurt and then Heidelberg, majoring first in the humanities, then in biology. But rather than concentrating on the subjects he pretended to be studying, he spent much of his time writing. After his first drama, the expressionist *Kreuzweg* (1921), had been accepted by Leopold Jeßner's Staatstheater in Berlin, he quit the university, moved to Berlin, and experienced his first great failure. After an early marriage to his childhood sweetheart, Annemarie Gans, failed in 1920, he spent the next two years with the young actress Annemarie Seidel, trying to publish and to work in any available job just to survive. Then, after Zuckmayer spent a summer in Norway, an old acquaintance from Mainz got him a position as dramaturge or theatrical consultant at the municipal theater in Kiel, where he helped stage a number of modern plays, slowly moving away from expressionism. His days in Kiel were cut short by a theater scandal that ensued after his liberal redaction of Terence's comedy *The Eunuch*. Zuckmayer was fired as a result, purportedly because of total artistic ineptitude. But he did not give up and managed to get a position as second dramaturge at the Schauspielhaus (Playhouse) in Munich, together with Bertolt Brecht. In 1924, they both became dramaturges at the Deutsches Theater in Berlin. Under Brecht's influence, Zuckmayer wrote *Pankraz erwacht* (1925), his second failure as a dramatist. With *Der fröhliche Weinberg* (1925), however, his luck changed and he found his dramatic medium of expression: the folk play. Even before its first performance, the play was awarded the prestigious Kleist Prize. In 1929 Zuckmayer was awarded the Georg Büchner Prize and the *Dramatikerpreis* of the Heidelberg Festival.

Since the tremendous success of the play also made him financially independent overnight, Zuckmayer bought a small country estate in Henndorf, near Salzburg, where, during future years, he spent the summer months with Alice Herdan, whom he had married in 1925 and with whom he had had a daughter, Winnetou, in 1926.

In addition to plays, Zuckmayer published a collection of poetry, *Der Baum* (1926), as well as a collection of stories, *Ein Bauer aus dem Taunus und andere Geschichten* (1927), and he worked as a scriptwriter for the movie *Der blaue Engel* (*The Blue Angel*, 1930). Zuckmayer's meteoric career as a playwright was cut short, however, by the Nazis' rise to power in January 1933. Soon none of his plays could be performed in Germany, and his books were also banned. For personal safety, the writer and his family moved permanently to Austria. His historical play *Der Schelm von Bergen* (1934) premiered at the Burgtheater in Vienna, and his novel *Salwàre oder Die Magdalena von Bozen* (1936) was published there as well. To survive, however, Zuckmayer had to turn to writing for film, an activity with which he was familiar from his work on the script for *The Blue Angel*. His peaceful existence was cut short by the German annexation of Austria in March 1938. Zuckmayer and his family narrowly escaped to Switzerland and, in 1939, moved to Hollywood. At first it seemed as though fortune was smiling on him, supplying him with a well-paid job as a scriptwriter for Warner Brothers. But Zuckmayer found neither the rigidity of script production nor the lifestyle of Hollywood to his liking. There was an interlude in New York, where he briefly taught a course on humor in drama in Erwin Piscator's Dramatic Workshop, a branch of the New School for Social Research. He also exhausted all attempts to succeed as a dramatist in the United States, where, with his old friend Fritz Kortner, he had written an unsuccessful play, *Somewhere in France* (1941). He similarly failed as a prose writer with the autobiography *Second Wind* (1940). Finally he decided to try his luck as a farmer, leasing the Backwoods Farm near Barnard, Vermont. The hard life as a farmer in a harsh climate left him little time for writing; he simply had to attend to physical survival during the Nazi period.

The one play that was to recapture the German audience for him after the collapse of Hitler's Germany, *Des Teufels General*, was about the life of a Nazi general and the German resistance during the Nazi period. The play premiered in Zurich in 1946 and in Germany in 1947. *Der Gesang im Feuerofen* (1950), which dealt with resistance among the Germans and French, was also successful; but neither with the historical dramas — *Barbara Blomberg* (1949), *Ulla Winblad* (1953), *Das Leben des Horace A. W. Tabor* (1964) — nor with his contemporary plays, in which he dealt with topical issues — in particular the atomic espionage drama *Das kalte Licht* (1955), *Die Uhr schlägt eins* (1961), and the legendary *Der Rattenfänger* (1975) — was he able to repeat his old success. Zuckmayer succeeded instead as a prose writer with the idyllic novella *Der Seelenbräu* (1945), in which he pays homage to his home in Austria; with the tightly woven novella about guilt and atonement *Die Fastnachtsbeichte* (1959); and with his autobiography *Als wär's ein Stück von mir* (1966). During these years, many honors were bestowed upon the grand old man of German theater, including the Goethe Prize of the City of Frankfurt (1952), the Great Austrian State Prize (1960), and the Heinrich Heine Prize of the City of Düsseldorf (1972). He became an honorary citizen of his native Nackenheim (1952), of Mainz (1961), and of Saas-Fée (1961). In 1956 Zuckmayer returned to

Europe from the United States; in 1957 he settled in the mountain village of Saas-Fée in Switzerland. He died in Visp, Switzerland, on 18 January 1977.

Zuckmayer's work is biographically subdivided into three periods: the years of the Weimar Republic; his exile years, including his stay in Austria; and the postwar period. The seeming paradox is that, although in many respects his work of the Weimar Republic is the most important, there is absolutely no scholarly secondary literature dating from this period. For this reason, I consider important reviews of first performances during these years. The same dearth of secondary publications exists for Zuckmayer's period in exile, since he was persona non grata in Germany during this time. And since, in contrast to Lion Feuchtwanger, Thomas Mann, Erich Maria Remarque, Vicky Baum, and Franz Werfel, he was not successful in the United States, nothing of note was published on him here either. As an exile, Zuckmayer was known within the circles of German exiles only, consigned to oblivion in his country of refuge as well as his country of birth. Thus only scholarly criticism published after 1945 is available. Moreover, since there is just as much criticism written and/or published in the United States as there is in Germany, it is fairly difficult to assign various schools of thinking or trends in criticism, particularly regarding the lesser works, on which fewer critical voices exist to be classified. Nevertheless, the attempt will be made wherever possible to trace critical developments, particularly with respect to Zuckmayer's two most successful dramas, *Der Hauptmann von Köpenick* and *Des Teufels General.*

The discussion will begin with two short general chapters. The first will deal with biographical and general studies, many of which were written for specific reasons: Zuckmayer's great popularity; his extremely interesting life; and, with regard to the period from 1933–45, because of recent scholarly interest in exile studies. In the second chapter, specialized studies, many of them book-length, and dissertations will be characterized with regard to their scholarly approach so that interpretations regarding individual works discussed in them can be taken up later within the framework of the discussion of these specific works. I decided to include unpublished doctoral dissertations since they constitute a considerable part of the research conducted, particularly in the United States, and since published research makes frequent reference to them.

In the discussion of the individual works it seemed advisable to proceed according to genre and, within each genre, in chronological order of first appearance. It seemed practical to begin with drama, since this is the genre in which Zuckmayer celebrated his greatest successes during the Weimar years and in which the greatest continuity of productivity is noticeable. Since most of Zuckmayer scholarship is devoted to this genre, it was necessary to subdivide this chapter chronologically according to the various types of drama. This will be followed by a chapter on lyric poetry and on prose and films, culminating in the success of Zuckmayer's autobiography of 1966. Because of the dearth of studies on lyric poetry, it seemed ill-advised to devote a separate chapter to it. By structuring this study according to works, I tried to make it possible for the reader to look up the criticism on a particular work without having to read through the entire book. In doing this, however, I was unable to avoid a certain repetitiveness within the individual subchapters.

Since there are such quantities of material on Zuckmayer, a study such as this cannot include all aspects of the field and must be selective. The main criterion for selectivity was to focus on those works by Zuckmayer in which there has been at least a reasonable amount of critical interest.

Two terms that are used rather frequently must to be defined here: *positivistic* is always used to denote the kind of literary research that relies on positive, observable, and proven facts; *textimmanent* is used to denote the type of interpretation that was dominating in Germany after 1945 for almost twenty years. It concentrates on the individual work of art and tries to understand it on its own premises and its own laws, using only the information contained in work of art to contribute to its deeper understanding.

One final note: Since I have contributed fairly extensively to Zuckmayer research during the past eleven years, I will avoid referring to my own research in the first person and refer to myself, like everyone else, by name.

1: Biography and General Assessments

CARL ZUCKMAYER'S LIFE during the Weimar Republic era is at least partially reflected in Helmut Mathy's (1978) article on Zuckmayer's judgment of Rhenish separatism and the French occupation of the Rhineland from 1918 to 1930. When French troops withdrew from the Rhineland on 20 June 1930, Zuckmayer wrote an article for the *Vossische Zeitung* in Berlin in which he displayed a sophisticated view of the French occupation; this article stands out among the general enthusiasm about the final withdrawal. Zuckmayer's original article is reprinted in the same issue of the journal before the one by Mathy. The latter actually says very little about Zuckmayer's essay itself; rather, Mathy has written as a historian who places Zuckmayer's opinions into the larger context of the history of Rhenish Hesse and of Franco-German relations over the centuries. Zuckmayer's article is seen as a valuable historical document for middle-Rhenish history in the Weimar Republic.

Richard Albrecht's (1984) article on the friendship between Zuckmayer and Erich Maria Remarque also uses short publications as historical evidence. Not only had Zuckmayer written a review of Remarque's famous antiwar novel *Im Westen nichts Neues* (*All Quiet on the Western Front*, 1929) that was published in the popular *Berliner Illustrierte*; at the end of 1930, he had also delivered a speech in the Prussian Upper House in favor of the release of the censored American movie made of the novel. This speech, originally published in the *Vossische Zeitung*, is reprinted in the same issue of the *Blätter der Carl-Zuckmayer-Gesellschaft*, after Albrecht's article and after the review of the novel. The article itself says little about Zuckmayer that is not already known either from *Als wär's ein Stück von mir* or from a short article on Remarque's famous book contained in the collection of essays *Aufruf zum Leben* (1976). It merely repeats Zuckmayer's remarks about his friendship with Remarque from *Als wär's ein Stück von mir*, but it does place Zuckmayer's speech within the political context of the final, crisis-ridden phase of the Weimar Republic and the fight that his friends Theodor Haubach and Carlo Mierendorff waged against the rise of National Socialism. It is thus an example of the kind of historical and sociological research applied to literature in the 1970s and 1980s. Regarding Zuckmayer's speech itself, Albrecht points out two strands of argumentation: the emotional appeal to the intellectual members of the "front" generation, who enthusiastically went into war but returned as pacifists and defenders of the democratic Weimar Republic; and arguments of the "other Germany," the Germany of humanistic intellectual giants to which Zuckmayer was going to refer during his exile, against those who identified Germany solely with the Nazis and their followers.

In his miscellany of 1986, Albrecht points out that in the two-volume *Reichshandbuch der Deutschen Gesellschaft* (1930–31), with an introduction by Ferdinand Tönnies, Zuckmayer figures prominently with an entry of thirty-one lines and a photo. Second, Albrecht has discovered that in 1929 Zuckmayer appeared in an advertisement for Adler typewriters, referring to his dramas *Der fröhliche Weinberg, Schinderhannes*, and *Katharina Knie*. This commercial appearance testifies to his prominent status at this time. All these short articles are purely historical and factual in nature, filling minor gaps in our knowledge of Zuckmayer's life during the Weimar Republic.

Zuckmayer's years in exile were treated comprehensively for the first time in a series of articles by Henry Glade in collaboration with Andreas Strenger. In two articles about the European years, Glade (1981a and b) describes the writer's years in Henndorf. He hesitates to call this time an exile because from 1926 on, Zuckmayer had regularly spent eight months out of the year in his Austrian domicile, where he wrote all his works from that period. Nevertheless, the permanent separation from Berlin and his Berlin apartment was emotionally hard for Zuckmayer. Before 1936 he made several trips to Berlin, so his "exile" of 1933–35 was restricted to a feeling of being excluded. From 1935 on, however, he was not permitted to publish in Germany anymore. For Glade, Zuckmayer's literary exile begins with the confiscation of the entire edition of his novel *Salwàre* in 1935 at the Bibliographisches Institut in Leipzig. His romantic desire for freedom and his feeling of responsibility as an author determined his fate as an exile. Since during this time in Austria and Switzerland he was unwilling to accept the artistic constraints of the film industry, as he was later in the United States, this first period of exile anticipates the main problems of the American years. Glade reports all the facts of exile, particularly Zuckmayer's futile attempts to establish himself as an author in the United States, up to the point when he leased the Backwoods Farm in Vermont.

Glade's (1983) article on Zuckmayer's time in Vermont (1941–56) continues the above essay. In Glade's view, Zuckmayer's work as a farmer proved to be a counterweight to his frustrations as a writer and thus helped him maintain his inner equilibrium. Glade lists all the people Zuckmayer had contact with during the period 1941–45; for example, people he met at weekend parties on Dorothy Thompson's country estate. Being an exception among German exiles because he believed it was necessary to distinguish between Nazi and non-Nazi Germans, he also tried to stay out of political infighting among various groups of exiles. Glade reports on Zuckmayer's writing activity during the war years. Zuckmayer wrote over a hundred biographical portraits for the Office of Strategic Services; the so-called *Vermonter Roman*; and a large prose piece on Helene (Lenchen) Demuth, Karl Marx's housekeeper. He also worked on an anthology of fairy tales. None of these projects resulted in publications; only a few short stories, written for American magazines, were published from this period. After an interlude in Woodstock in spring 1945, Zuckmayer returned to the farm and devoted himself almost exclusively to writing, completing *Des Teufels General*, the novella *Der Seelenbräu*, and the essay *Die Brüder Grimm*. Glade points out that *Des Teufels General* contains a number of autobiographical features. He describes Zuckmayer's stay in Vermont and his travels between Europe and the United States from 1951 to June 1956. According to Glade, Zuckmayer's greatest achievement during his time in exile was overcoming a justifiable anger, by means of his deep belief in destiny, against the "tormentors and executioners" (115) of the German people and against the fate that gave his life a different direction. Glade's two essays are based on conversations with the Zuckmayers and on exacting archival work. Their merit lies above all in their factuality; thus they deviate substantially from the stylized account of this time that Zuckmayer himself gave in *Als wär's ein Stück von mir*. Glade's essay of 1989 is a verbatim combination of the above two essays.

In his afterword to the chapter "Austreibung: 1934–39" (Expulsion: 1934–39) from *Als wär's ein Stück von mir*, which was published separately by Philipp Reclam, Jörg von Uthmann (1983) still subscribes to the popular, though highly debatable, thesis that Zuckmayer survived the forced emigration better than many of the so-called rootless asphalt writers (128). Such well-traveled world citizens as Stefan Zweig and Kurt Tucholsky despaired and took their own lives during emigration. Others were broken to such an extent that after the war they were unable to continue working. But Zuckmayer's exile was, in Uthmann's view, only a temporary episode that he apparently survived without bitterness.

Jochen Becker (1986a) builds on Glade's essays, reporting all relevant facts and taking into consideration additional original documents such as Zuckmayer's letters from this time. Contradicting the opinion of Uthmann (1983) and others, Becker poses the central thesis that it is wrong to assume that Zuckmayer weathered the period of exile well; indeed, he posits, next to the First World War, exile constituted the greatest crisis of Zuckmayer's life. Like Glade, Becker believes that the Austrian period (1933–38) only conditionally constituted exile. Furthermore, like many other emigrants during the first phase of exile, Zuckmayer falsely evaluated the political conditions in Germany, assuming that only a temporary aberration was taking place that would soon be ended by the victorious "better forces" (139). During this first period, Zuckmayer concentrated exclusively on his work and shunned politics, as did many other exiles and the members of the so-called "inner emigration" — those intellectuals who were opposed to the Nazi regime but chose not to emigrate. With few exceptions, the works written in Henndorf served solely to secure his material existence. As historical dramas, Becker believes, *Der Schelm von Bergen* and *Bellman* belong to an important genre of exile drama. Following an opinion that was widespread among intellectuals, Zuckmayer considered the Austro-fascism of Chancellors Dollfuß and Schuschnigg the lesser of two evils. Becker sees Zuckmayer's flight to Switzerland in 1938 as the existential break of his exile years, the point at which the futile hopes and illusions of the years since 1933 finally gave way to a forced realism regarding his own situation. Becker reports in detail all the difficulties Zuckmayer encountered in his attempts to break into the American publishing scene. In his report about the controversy with Erika Mann in 1944, he stresses that Zuckmayer was on the side of the other, better Germany, coming out against the thesis of "collective guilt." Becker describes in detail Zuckmayer's moves back and forth between the United States and Germany after the war. In his view, the exile period did not end until Zuckmayer bought his house in Saas-Fée in 1957.

Jeffrey B. Berlin's (1988) publication of the letter Zuckmayer sent to Zweig's (and his own) publisher, Ben Huebsch, after Zweig's suicide, followed by Huebsch's answer, demonstrates how upset Zuckmayer was about Zweig's untimely death.

New stimuli for biographical research into Zuckmayer's exile years were provided by Richard Albrecht (1988). His well-documented essay goes beyond Glade's (1981a and b, 1989) and Becker's (1986a) works. Taking into consideration the special sociohistorical and individual situation of exile, Albrecht utilizes a considerable amount of archival materials not previously considered by Zuckmayer's biographers. He characterizes the writer during the Weimar Republic as a prominent but essentially apolitical author. He shows that the Nazis criticized his plays, from *Der fröhliche Weinberg* to *Der Hauptmann von Köpenick*, not only for racial reasons but, because of the author's distinctly antimilitaristic tendencies, also for political ones. (In Nazi newspapers Zuckmayer was always referred to as a half-Jew.) When the Nazis took over, they considered Zuckmayer a representative of the hated so-called system theater of the Weimar Republic. Because of his publications in Germany and his attempts to retain the large German market, Albrecht — with reference to Döblin — counts Zuckmayer during his Austrian years (1933–38) among the half-emigrants, or authors who were not completely banned in the Third Reich. By quoting letters to the Swiss Social Democrat Josef Halperin, Albrecht documents that Zuckmayer tried to maintain a morally intact attitude between the political fronts. During his time in Austria, Zuckmayer was no emigrant in the literal sense of the word. As Jochen Becker (1986a) had pointed out, the decisive break did not come until his flight from Austria in March 1938. At this point, the Zuckmayers were now *heimatlos* (without a homeland), and the questions of a valid passport, visas, and economic survival were of foremost importance to them. Albrecht describes the author's American years and points out that the Zuckmayers' literary rendition of their life as farmers in Vermont (Herdan-Zuckmayer 1949) is idealized because Zuckmayer not only did physical work as a farmer but also participated in political and literary events. Albrecht sees this time as one in which Zuckmayer became more political. He wrote "Aufruf zum Leben" (1942), *Carlo Mierendorff: Portrait eines deutschen Sozialisten*" (Carlo Mierendorff: Portrait of a German Socialist, 1944), and an open letter to Erika Mann. The tremendous success of *Des Teufels General* immediately after the war was, according to Albrecht, the basis for Zuckmayer's reception and activity in the Federal Republic. Albrecht argues that Zuckmayer's time in exile should be viewed not merely as an interlude but as a serious break, which was not without consequences for his personal development. The particular value of Albrecht's article lies in its exactness and its inclusion and firsthand examination of private and official archival materials. It is indispensable as the basis for all later biographical research on Zuckmayer.

Having gained access to Carl Zuckmayer's FBI dossier, Albrecht (1989) devoted a separate study to this document. However, at the beginning of his essay he comes to the conclusion that, with one exception, these papers do not shed new light on the author's years in the

United States but merely prove that Zuckmayer, like many other German exile authors, was under surveillance by the FBI. Albrecht believes that he had been sent at least four-fifths of the entire file, with many names blacked out, that the publication of "Aufruf zum Leben" in the New York exile weekly *Aufbau* in March 1942 triggered the FBI investigation, and that from fall 1942 to spring 1943 all mail to and from Zuckmayer was checked by the Bureau. The dossier contains fifteen reports mentioning Carl Zuckmayer during the years 1941–49, mostly in connection with publications or endorsements of various exile organizations. In particular, Albrecht interprets Zuckmayer's endorsement of the Moscow Nationalkomitee Freies Deutschland (National Committee [for a] Free Germany) of 1 September 1943 to confirm his thesis of Zuckmayer's politicization during the Second World War. Though its author admits it yields only meager results, the article continues Albrecht's careful, positivistic work on Zuckmayer's life.

In an article of 1985 Hans Wagener deals only indirectly with biographical questions by examining the influence of exile on Zuckmayer's work written during that time.

Zuckmayer's great popularity brought about the publication of a number of biographies for the general public, among them one by Ludwig Emanuel Reindl (1962). The text has the advantage of relying by necessity on Zuckmayer's older autobiographies, in particular *Pro domo* (1938) and *Second Wind* (1940), and is thus not misled by the creative features of *Als wär's ein Stück von mir*. On the other hand, Reindl's uncritical attitude and his abstract and sometimes inflated style prevent an objective assessment. He concentrates on the honors that were bestowed upon Zuckmayer, particularly during the 1950s, and says little about Zuckmayer's life. But as a pictorial presentation, the book is unsurpassed; it also contains many facts and names not found anywhere else. However, its opinions about Zuckmayer's works, particularly the *Zeitstücke* (topical plays) of the 1950s and early 1960s, show a lack of historical perspective.

Arnold Bauer's (1970) monograph is written for a wider, general audience and is introductory by nature. It gives an account of Zuckmayer's life based on a critical reading of *Als wär's ein Stück von mir* and short characterizations of the author's works, dealing with the most successful ones in greater detail and mentioning very briefly the late plays. In accordance with the series in which the booklet appeared, Bauer's style is essayistic and at the same time informative, but he adds nothing to our knowledge about Zuckmayer. In contrast, Thomas Ayck's (1977) biography, which appeared in the popular series

Rowohlt's *Monographien* and contains many photos, is much more critical of Zuckmayer's work. From the beginning, Ayck makes it clear that he wants to approach Zuckmayer objectively. On the one hand, he sides with sociocritical authors; on the other, he stresses Zuckmayer's idealistic search for harmony. In his opinion, the author's unpolitical attitude made it possible for him to return to Germany right after the Second World War and to talk to the young people about National Socialism. Ultimately, however, the sociopolitical tone of Ayck's approach demonstrates that the student revolt of 1968 and the concomitant ideological discussions were still very much on his, Ayck's, mind.

Jochen Becker's 1984 "biographical essay" constitutes the most comprehensive and balanced description of Zuckmayer's life to date. Although it is written from a sympathetic point of view and lacks footnotes, it takes into consideration all important secondary material on biographical matters, quoting unpublished letters that contain important statements of the author. The thread running through the book is *Heimat* (homeland, home region) — Zuckmayer's various *Heimaten* as well as the meaning of the concept of *Heimat* for him. According to Becker, Zuckmayer's *Heimat* of birth, Rhenish Hesse, is superseded by an inner *Heimat* that he seeks in art (1919–25), followed by a new, self-chosen *Heimat* in the "paradise" of Henndorf (1926–33). Becker states clearly that Zuckmayer's exile started in Henndorf, and he therefore treats under "Heimat im Exil" (*Heimat* in Exile) the time period from 1933 to 1945. He shows that in 1933 Zuckmayer concentrated solely on his work as a writer, exercising complete political abstinence. His consciousness of being an exile did not develop until National Socialism further established itself in Germany, leading eventually to the author's feeling of being locked out. When he had to work for the movie industry, Zuckmayer's inner *Heimat* underwent a crisis. His American period of exile became a struggle for survival, with Zuckmayer creating his own *Heimat* in Vermont. Becker, like some earlier biographers, points out that the two most upsetting breaks in Zuckmayer's life were the First World War and exile, disputing the commonly held view that he survived his exile without psychological damage.

The letters between Zuckmayer and his many friends that have been published so far are also significant biographical sources. Probably the most important collection is Hinrich Stoevesandt's (1977) edition of the correspondence between Carl Zuckmayer and Carl Barth, which contains Zuckmayer's Barth obituary as well as a letter to Eberhard Busch. It is a monument to Zuckmayer's late friendship with the famous Swiss theologian. The correspondence between the author and Gustav Gründgens, the most important letters of which were edited by Rolf Badenhausen (1979) with explanatory notes, are interesting for theater historians. As director of the municipal theater in Düsseldorf and, later, the Hamburger Schauspielhaus, Gründgens had performed four of Zuckmayer's dramas. The correspondence contains interesting comments on Zuckmayer's dramas, particularly on cuts suggested by Gründgens. In 1980 Gerald Martin published the correspondence between Zuckmayer and his bibliographer Arnold J. Jacobius, which spans the years 1953–76. Unfortunately, only Zuckmayer's letters are quoted verbatim; Jacobius's letters are summarized by the editor. The letters (several facsimiles are included) not only give insight into the working habits of the author but include a lot of biographical material, particularly chronological notes from 1896 to 1925 that Zuckmayer had sent to Jacobius.

The clearest testimony to Zuckmayer's expressionist spirit during the First World War is contained in his letters to Kurt Grell (1981), son of an old Hanseatic Hamburg family, whom he had befriended during the summer of 1915 in northern France. The letters, which are interspersed with many previously unpublished poems, cover the years 1915–20 and show Zuckmayer's personal and literary development during this time. The correspondence came to an end in 1920 because the "red lieutenant" Zuckmayer and the monarchist Grell went in different directions politically.

In 1982 five letters to the theater director Boleslaw Barlog (Zuckmayer 1982a) and five to Henry Goverts (Zuckmayer 1982b) were published, and Winrich Meiszies (1982) edited Zuckmayer's correspondence with Louise Dumont and Gustav Lindemann, who from 1905 to 1932 served as directors of the Schauspielhaus Düsseldorf. In the same year, Gerald P. R. Martin published Zuckmayer's correspondence with Günther Niemeyer about *Der Rattenfänger* (1982a) and his correspondence with Gottfried von Einem, the composer of the music for *Der Rattenfänger* (1982b). In 1984 Martin dedicated one issue of the *Blätter der Carl-Zuckmayer-Gesellschaft* to the friendship between Carl Zuckmayer and Fritz Usinger, a lyric poet from Hesse. The bulk of the issue is the correspondence (including some facsimiles) between the two friends, who met in 1918–19 in Heidelberg and carried on a correspondence of which twenty-three letters and postcards from Zuckmayer to Usinger and seventeen letters from Usinger to Zuckmayer have survived. The correspondence was interrupted by the war but began to flourish again in 1965. As Martin points out, the amazing thing about it is that Usinger does not talk about Zuckmayer's stage characters. Being a lyric poet, he appreciated Zuckmayer as such. Similarly, Zuckmayer does not talk about Usinger's essays but is enthusiastic about his poems. In 1985 Martin published, with detailed commentary, two letters from Zuckmayer to Hans Cleres, whom he probably had met as a student in Frankfurt am Main and with whom he had been at least periodically in contact from 1930 to 1955.

Personal memories supplement the correspondence. Nino Erné (1985) reports four encounters with Zuckmayer: the first in 1948, when Zuckmayer was discussing *Des Teufels General* with former soldiers; in 1956, when Erné was putting together the *Festschrift Fülle der Zeit* for the S. Fischer publishing company; in 1964 at a performance of *Der Hauptmann von Köpenick* in Berlin; and in 1975 for a television interview with the writer. These are personal, anecdotal remarks — memories that contribute to a portrait of Zuckmayer but are of little or no scholarly value. The same is true of a 1980 book by Christine and Piltti Heiskanen. Günther Fleckenstein's 1986 essay, in which he remembers his work with Zuckmayer's dramas, includes a number of hitherto unpublished letters in which Zuckmayer makes statements regarding his plays. Apart from that, what Fleckenstein has to say does not merit scholarly consideration.

Three personal interviews deserve particular mention because both the questions and Zuckmayer's answers are of importance to research. The interview in the collection *Werkstattgespräche mit Schriftstellern*, which Horst Bienek (1962) conducted in 1961 in Saas-Fée, deals mainly with Zuckmayer's work habits and creative process. Zuckmayer talks especially about *Die Uhr schlägt eins*, then his latest play. The second interview was conducted by Ben Witter (1969), who visited Zuckmayer in Saas-Fée in October 1967 and took long walks with him. Though he asks few questions, Witter succeeds in showing how Zuckmayer lives and behaves and thus gives an accurate portrait of the writer. Adelbert Reif (1977) interviewed Zuckmayer on 25 November 1976 in Zurich. It is the last detailed interview the author gave before his final illness, and it demonstrates not only his humane attitude but also his interest in political issues.

Along with the prizes and honors Zuckmayer received, a number of *Festschriften* and other commemorative writings were published. These contain biographical material, congratulatory letters, and essays on the author's works. *Fülle der Zeit* (1956) is the first and most significant *Festschrift* published on the occasion of Zuckmayer's important birthdays — in this case his sixtieth. In contrast to other volumes published on similar occasions, it contains several articles of scholarly value, such as Luise Rinser's "Porträtskizze" and Alfred Happ's essay "Dichterisches Theater." It also includes congratulatory essays by Zuckmayer's friends, critics, and directors, among them Theodor Heuss, Nino Erné, Paul Friedrich Weber, Siegfried Melchinger, Gertrud von le Fort, Friedrich Bischoff, Ludwig Berger, Friedrich Torberg, Hanns W. Eppelsheimer, Boleslaw Barlog, Ulrich Kühn, Johannes Urzidil, Alexander Lernet-Holenia, and Bruno E. Werner, and previously unpublished pieces by Zuckmayer, including an autobiographical sketch.

Carl Zuckmayer in Mainz, edited by Walter Heist (1970), documents Zuckmayer's visit in Mainz during May 1970, stressing his close relationship with the area. It also contains Zuckmayer's speech on his old friend Ludwig Berger as well as many photos. The little book *Der helle Klang: Zu Carl Zuckmayers 75. Geburtstag in Amriswil* contains a letter from Carl J. Burckhardt to the editor, Dino Larese (1972), on the occasion of Zuckmayer's seventy-fifth birthday; a letter from Zuckmayer to Burckhardt on the occasion of Burckhardt's eightieth birthday; three unpublished poems by Zuckmayer and photos of Zuckmayer and his homes. It does not, however, pretend to have any scholarly value. Similarly, *Carl Zuckmayer in Saas-Fee: Ein Album* (1976) by the Saas-Fée local historian Werner Imseng is a photo documentation of Zuckmayer's life at his last home. The many photos of the house, of Zuckmayer and his family, of the surrounding landscape, and of occasions when the writer was honored make the book an interesting album. It has no scholarly value; nor was it the author's intention to make such a contribution.

The *Festschrift für Carl Zuckmayer* (Glauert, Martin, and Heist 1976), which was published for his eightieth birthday, contains addresses and tributes from the author's friends and a report by Barbara Glauert on the holdings of various archives that contributed materials to the Mainz exhibition *Carl Zuckmayer auf der Bühne* (Glauert 1976a). It also contains Zuckmayer's bibliography for 1971–76, compiled by Harro Kieser. The scholarly value of most of the contributions is negligible. The volume, edited by Walter Heist, includes correspondence between Zuckmayer and the governing mayor of Mainz, Jockel Fuchs, but the letters say little about either the people or Zuckmayer's work. The commemorative volume *Abschied von Carl Zuckmayer* (Glauert and Roland 1977), which also makes no pretense of scholarship, includes twenty-two speeches and reminiscences as well as thirty-six pages of photos.

Many general essays and monographs on Zuckmayer also contain biographical facts. In some cases they are organized according to the author's life, but the emphasis is more on his work. Bauer's (1970) and Ayck's (1977) biographies could easily be included in this category also; and Mews's (1981a) and Wagener's (1983a, 1987, 1989) introductions could be included among the biographies per se.

In 1947 a general article on Zuckmayer was written by Axel Eggebrecht, who shows special appreciation for the prose of *Ein Bauer aus dem Taunus* and the lyric poetry of *Der Baum*. He also remarks expectantly on *Des Teufels General*, the first performance of which was about to take place in Germany at that time. The article talks about Zuckmayer's relation to the Nazi period and reflects on the position he had taken in his speech commemorating Carlo Mierendorff. In his popular handbook on contemporary German authors, Franz Lennartz (1959) celebrates Zuckmayer as the most successful living German dramatist, using numerous quotes from the author's own writings and those of his critics. In 1960 Otto Basil published a well-written character study of Zuckmayer in the context of twentieth-century literary history. However, his judgments repeat established opinions; for example, that Zuckmayer had the rare and fortunate gift to write solidly constructed and effective plays that also had a conspicuously artistic basis and that his characters were realistic. More journalistic than scholarly, the article tries to introduce Zuckmayer to a wide audience with cultural interests. H. F. Garten's 1964 essay surveys Zuckmayer's dramas from *Kreuzweg* to *Der Gesang im Feuerofen*. Sheila Rooke's 1964 article is not quite reliable in its biographical data, but it contains original observations regarding Zuckmayer's works that will be discussed later. Ingeborg Drewitz's (1966) portrait of Zuckmayer attempts to characterize him as an apolitical author who has "stood up to the challenges of the twentieth century," always "remaining true to himself" (21).

Another general characterization of Zuckmayer and his works is Wolfgang Paulsen's 1967 essayistic article. Basing his assessment on an intimate knowledge of the history of German literature, Paulsen is able to show the tradition in which Zuckmayer stands. The article is in the best tradition of German intellectual history. Paulsen establishes connections between Zuckmayer and nineteenth- and early-twentieth-century literature that few other Zuckmayer scholars would have been able to make. According to him, Zuckmayer's beginnings are in the naturalistic tradition, but Zuckmayer distinguishes his work from naturalism by abandoning any sociocritical moralism in favor of stressing the human. Out of naturalistic categories he created new objectivity, but he always remained conscious of its origin. The advent of Hitler challenged his principally positive view of life. Paulsen stresses that the author is continually concerned with nature from an nonmetaphysical and affirming standpoint. Reality never became questionable to him. He does not celebrate nature and does not treat it with inappropriate reverence, which can so easily lead to a "pseudoreligious blackout" (332). The special attraction of Zuckmayer's nature descriptions is his interweaving of reason and feeling. In his dramas, which take the form of biographical theater, Zuckmayer depicts human beings as products of their milieu. He focuses on the individual, but he knows that the individual is part of the world.

In its biographical account, Rudolf Lange's 1969 introductory book on Zuckmayer the dramatist relies heavily on *Als wär's ein Stück von mir*, quoting it extensively and uncritically. Lange gives short outlines and interpretations of the dramas with few new insights. In the last part of his book, he merely quotes reviews of the plays' first performances. He points out that in the pre-1933 dramas Zuckmayer deals not with problems but primarily with people, less in their development than in their current behavior. Thus Lange contradicts Ingeborg Engelsing-Malek (1960), whose *amor fati* idea, to be discussed later, always involves the characters' development. According to Lange, at an early stage Zuckmayer developed a kind of broadsheet technique, presenting his action in form of significant scenes or "stations" (91). He maintained this technique even in his late dramas, without allowing post-Second World War formal innovations or new ways of theatrical presentation to influence him. He is a humanist who wants to bring out timeless elements in topical situations. His theme is man in his connection with earthly and metaphysical orders, in the German classicist spirit of self-realization.

Siegfried Sudhof's general article "Carl Zuckmayer" (1973) is biographically structured, with remarks about the writer's works embedded in a chronological context. Sudhof's general characterization stresses three points: 1. Although Zuckmayer never pursued narrow topical ideas, his goal was to protect man, to formulate the claim of humaneness (64). In this manner he tried to transfer the traditions of German classicism into modernity. 2. The landscape of Rhenish Hesse was an important element stressing ties to his home region in almost all of his works. 3. His work is not prophetic in character; it does not intend to proclaim any particular political or philosophical teaching but rather attempts to mirror his time, though not masking the positive. He is an optimistic author who believes in man's inherent good.

The first complete scholarly introduction to Zuckmayer's works in English was written by Siegfried Mews (1981a). Mews concentrates less on the author's life than on his works, giving a balanced evaluation of the plays, poetry, and prose. In case of the plays, he often relies heavily on the reviews of their first performances. Many comparisons with other German writers, especially Brecht, make the reading interesting to students of German literature. Though Mews makes careful interpretations, his book is based primarily on facts. Considering his prospective American audience, he stresses all aspects of Zuckmayer's relationship to America, both biographically and creatively. At the end, he concludes that Zuckmayer "falls ultimately short of the genuine accomplishments in the realm of world literature by the likes of Rilke, Kafka, Thomas Mann, and Brecht. At the same time, on the basis of those same criteria, Zuckmayer deserves a wider recognition in this country than he has been accorded so far" (140).

Hans Wagener's introductory book on Zuckmayer (1983a) is a kind of German pendant to Mews's work, in contrast to which it deals with Zuckmayer's life in an introductory chapter and then presents interpretations of Zuckmayer's works according to genre. Wagener's point of departure is often Engelsing-Malek's 1960 concept of *amor fati* as underlying the development of Zuckmayer's dramatic heroes, but he also incorporates other significant research literature into his evaluations. In a final chapter on Zuckmayer's theory of drama that continues many of Henry Glade's (1960) considerations, Wagener points out the religious elements in Zuckmayer's worldview that also form the basis of his aesthetics. Wagener's later, shorter characterizations of Zuckmayer (1987 and 1989) are both encyclopedia articles giving biographical data and briefly characterizing his works. This is also true of Blake Lee Spahr's article of 1992, though Spahr brings to his observations the specific perspective of an American.

2: Specialized Studies

SCHOLARLY PREOCCUPATION WITH Zuckmayer's work did not begin until after the Second World War, when it was no doubt stimulated by the success of his novella *Der Seelenbräu* and even more by his dramas *Des Teufels General*, *Der Gesang im Feuerofen*, and *Der Hauptmann von Köpenick*. Dissertations and other specialized studies were not written until this time, and only a few appeared in Germany; American and German scholars working at universities in the United States were soon taking the lead in Zuckmayer scholarship. This may be due to the fact that the study of German literature in Germany was still focused primarily on traditionally highly regarded and philosophically probing literature, whereas Zuckmayer's work was easily relegated to the twilight of folk literature.

The first dissertation to break the silence was Wolfgang Teelen's (1952), written at the University of Marburg. Teelen's goal was to interpret Zuckmayer's dramas and thus to trace his development as a dramatist over a time span of thirty years (1920–50), from *Kreuzweg* to *Der Gesang im Feuerofen*. Teelen attempted to uncover the creative laws (Gestaltungsgesetze; 1) in Zuckmayer's work, to describe their specific nature in comparison with other dramatic laws, and to test their ability to produce theatrical effects. His main interest is in the language structure and the stagecraft of the individual plays, though he also discusses possible interpretations. He gives special consideration to the peculiar relationship between form and message (*Gestalt und Gehalt*; 1), which in his view is a special problem in Zuckmayer's plays.

The terminology he applies (*Gestaltungsgesetze*, *Gestalt* and *Gehalt* [1]; *Organismus* [12]) is inherently fuzzy and indicates his reliance on close textual reading for his judgments. He uses the Swiss scholar Emil Staiger as his authority in the application of terms such as *lyric*, *epic*, and *dramatic*, to which in the course of the investigation he adds the term *filmic*. Ultimately, his conceptual grid, which he applies uniformly to all of Zuckmayer's dramas, serves to limit the scope of his conclusions.

Paul Meinherz's dissertation, published in 1960, was written under the direction of Emil Staiger himself. Not surprisingly, it is also influenced by his teacher's textimmanent interpretive method and concern for form. Meinherz tries to determine the epic and lyric elements in Zuckmayer's dramas and thus to determine the essence of his plays (3).

Like Engelsing-Malek (1960), but closer to Teelen in his methodology, he interprets Zuckmayer's works as an attempt to bring theater and drama closer together. In this endeavor Zuckmayer is forced to make compromises, but it becomes obvious that the theatrical aspect of the form is closer to his heart than strict drama is. His work did not originate from the spirit of dramatic literature but rather from older enjoyment of masks and mimics and the inner need to present them in the form of a play. He renounces dramatic tension in favor of a more traditional German play. In order to demonstrate his point, Meinherz devotes separate chapters to *Katharina Knie, Der Hauptmann von Köpenick,* and *Der Gesang im Feuerofen,* but he does include the other dramas in his discussion as well. In his opinion *Der Gesang im Feuerofen, Ulla Winblad,* and *Der Schelm von Bergen* confirm the impression that Zuckmayer's work is poetic theater, a term first applied by Alfred Happ (1956). According to Meinherz, poetic theater goes beyond the purely dramatic and develops a poetic message (118).

J. Vandenrath's 1960 dissertation was written at the University of Liège. Vandenrath suggests that Zuckmayer's dramas are written for the stage. As such they are works of art that must be examined on theatrical criteria. Vandenrath begins with the plays' form, viewing them in their totality. After discussing the difference between the elements of drama and theater in general, he applies this terminological grid to the individual plays. Vandenrath does not test Zuckmayer's works as documents of the author's worldview but as works of art. In contrast to the Marxist Wilfried Adling (1959), he measures with an artistic yardstick, not an ideological one. His methodology is based on theoretical articles and books by older scholars such as Robert Petsch, Emil Staiger, and Arthur Kutscher. He praises Wolfgang Kayser's *Das sprachliche Kunstwerk* (1948), in which the work of art itself is made the object of consideration and understood according to its own laws.

Vandenrath observes that in the course of his artistic development, Zuckmayer's humanity becomes deeper and nobler. Whereas the theatrical (scenic, mimic) side decreases, the dramatic elements (conflicts, problems, inner development) grow from one play to the next. Not only does the basic situation become more interesting and the action weightier; there are also increasingly bold spiritual discussions.

According to Vandenrath, Zuckmayer had found his basic form in *Der fröhliche Weinberg.* In his later plays he resumed, changed, and further developed this form. Its basic principle is an alternation of group scene and dialogue. Furthermore, there is a development from the farcical comedy to the serious problem drama, from action to dialogue, from the concrete to the abstract. Zuckmayer thus pays for the expansion of his mental horizons with a loss of artistic substance. A negative development in language goes along with a positive development in the spiritual (mental) and dramatic.

It is noteworthy that the above European dissertations are all textimmanent in their methodological approach, thus reflecting the critical methodology prevailing in the study of German literature in German speaking countries at the time. As a result, they are all primarily concerned with the *form* of Zuckmayer's dramas.

The contrast between this approach and the politically oriented approach of contemporary East German scholarship is apparent in Wilfried Adling's dissertation, which was published in 1959 (originally submitted in 1956) and which tries to evaluate Zuckmayer's work in terms of his worldview. Its goal is to render a picture of the author's intellectual and political development, which Adling embeds in contemporaneous political history. Zuckmayer's dramas are therefore examined here in terms of their message; matters of form are only touched upon. Adling's dissertation is the prime example of East German Marxist-Leninist criticism that, because its worldview is fundamentally opposed to Zuckmayer's, results in a total misunderstanding of the author's works and leads to a negative view of Zuckmayer. But, as Vandenrath (1960) later conceded, in spite of his one-sidedness, Adling penetrates deeply into Zuckmayer's oeuvre. His analysis of Zuckmayer's relationship to the bourgeoisie, to the Weimar Republic, to socialism and communism, to the Soviet Union, and to the United States is convincing, albeit written in politically-tinged language. He comes to wrong conclusions, however, regarding Zuckmayer's works because instead of judging them in terms of the author's intention, he critiques them from the view of what *Adling* thought he should have written. Any deviations from the Marxist-Leninist ideological line, which favored so-called socialist realism, are considered aberrations and errors. Thus in Adling's opinion, Zuckmayer's attitude is unrealistic, antiprogressive, and colored by vitalism (254). During the Weimar Republic, Zuckmayer's works supported only indirectly the reactionary circles of the imperialistic bourgeoisie by playing down the fascist danger. His latest works, however, increasingly serve the interests of the most reactionary groups of the present. Thus Adling discovers serious weaknesses in the political message, particularly in *Des Teufels General*, *Der Gesang im Feuerofen*, and *Das kalte Licht*. Their supposedly open support for reconciliation with fascism and their open agitation against the Soviet Union make

Zuckmayer increasingly a Cold War dramatist. After 1945 his works assume traits of grafted, artificial symbolism or crude sensationalism (254). His mastery of dramatic technique and his gift for creating living characters successfully mask the fact that his relationship toward reality makes real creative art impossible. Because of his firm grounding in Marxism-Leninism, Adling is unable to understand Zuckmayer on his own terms, though his line of argumentation is logical and consequent.

The only other book-length investigation of Zuckmayer conducted in the GDR is Werner Lüder's (1987) dissertation on the reception of *Des Teufels General* in East and West Germany. Lüder attempts to penetrate into the questions of the interrelationship between the aesthetics of production and reception. Although he also discusses *Der fröhliche Weinberg, Der Hauptmann von Köpenick, Der Gesang im Feuerofen*, and *Das kalte Licht*, his main attention is focused on *Des Teufels General* and its reviews. While he takes issue with Adling on certain points, Lüder also judges Zuckmayer's works from a Marxist standpoint.

American scholarship, like American criticism in general, has always shown a greater appreciation and understanding of popular literature, whether or not it has philosophical depth. This more open and more positive attitude is also visible in American Zuckmayer scholarship from the 1950s through the 1970s; to a large extent it focuses on Zuckmayer's personal views, the content and message of his works, rather than on the aesthetic aspects of his fiction and drama. This includes Ian C. Loram's (1954) introduction to Zuckmayer. The article contains a sketchy biography, an anecdotal account of an evening at the Zuckmayers' in Vermont, and a few vague remarks about Zuckmayer's works that do not go beyond the scope of an encyclopedia entry. As far as Zuckmayer's personal views are concerned, Loram mentions without elaboration "the relationship of the individual to the world around him, especially to the natural world," (148) and "an almost pantheistic view of nature, a reverence for the creative process, a love for life in all its manifestations, a belief in freedom, the supreme importance and the ultimate victory of the individual" (149). Loram may have tried to draw attention to the author in the United States, but he does not present new insights or even fulfill the demands of positivistic scholarship.

Much more important is Arnold John Jacobius's 1955 dissertation, written at New York University, together with the first comprehensive Zuckmayer bibliography, which was brought up to date by Harro Kieser (**Bibliographies**: Jacobius 1971). Jacobius tries to extract Zuckmayer's worldview from his plays, narratives, speeches, essays, and letters. He draws on the message and on thematic and stylistic elements in Zuckmayer's dramas, relating them not only to the entirety of the author's work but also to his personality and artistic development. Jacobius considers Zuckmayer's experience of nature to be of fundamental importance for Zuckmayer's worldview. It is based on physical, sensuous contact but also includes mystical insights. Nature in itself is neither good nor bad. In an endless cycle of growth and decay, life triumphs. Man is both the culmination of nature and also its master. He is subject to his own natural order. Man is basically good, and his highest destiny is self-fulfillment, which has been preordained by fate. His work is filled with the idea of *Humanität* (humanity, humaneness), which demands respect and reverence, and the resulting nobility of the personality independent of social nobility. Zuckmayer's drama represents man not as an island but within the context of his environment and time. Regarding subject matter, Zuckmayer's work is concentrated around particular motifs and themes. Jacobius is the first to attempt an extensive discussion of *Heimat* in Zuckmayer's work, a discussion later to be continued by Becker (1984) and Finke (1990). According to Jacobius, the *Heimat* motif runs like a red thread through Zuckmayer's dramas. *Heimat* is not to be understood in a biological or nationalistic sense but rather as an emotional connection. The opposite of *Heimat* — namely, lack of *Heimat*, or *Heimatlosigkeit* — is represented in a number of Zuckmayer's characters, first in Schinderhannes, but even more in the character of Wilhelm Voigt in *Der Hauptmann von Köpenick*. Since *Heimat* plays such an important role in his work, Zuckmayer is considered by many a *Volksdichter* (popular poet), an author who writes about and for the people. His idea of *Volk* has nothing to do with nationalistic or racial ideas. Rather, he interprets the term in the spirit of his own *Humanität* as an association of independent individuals who are bound together by the community of spiritual and emotional experiences. The greatest bond that ties them together is the common language. For Zuckmayer, the opposite of *Volk* is not the individual but the mass, the rowdy, amorphous crowd that is held together by hate and desire and the urge to destroy. The poet's view toward Germany is split between a deep awareness of national weaknesses on the one hand and, on the other, a passionate belief in a German mission with respect to *Humanität*. It is the expression of Zuckmayer's ahistorical and apolitical attitude that is based on and related to things human. In Zuckmayer's work, love of life is complemented by a love of fate, Nietzsche's *amor fati*.

Zuckmayer's dramas are dominated by epic and lyric elements. As Teelen (1952) had already pointed out, in the later dramas the influence of film is particularly obvious. The dominating role of epic elements is the expression of the reciprocal relationship between joy of life on the one hand and the awareness of an unfathomable fate on the other. Both are rooted in Zuckmayer's outlook on life.

Jacobius does not present a textimmanent interpretation. He consciously avoids value judgments of individual works, evaluating them as documents of Zuckmayer's weltanschauung rather than analyzing them as works of art. Jacobius stresses the consistent elements in Zuckmayer's worldview. As a result, he tends to neglect his personal and artistic development. The entire analysis is full of a rather positive assessment of the author's work, adhering to Zuckmayer's intended strategies and thus tending to overlook weaknesses.

Henry Glade (1958) is also in tune with Zuckmayer's stated intentions, investigating his works from the *Humanität* perspective. In contrast to Jacobius (1955), whose study he knew, Glade considers Zuckmayer's works in the sequence of composition with respect to *Humanität*. Like Jacobius, he discusses all of Zuckmayer's writings and gives virtually no aesthetic evaluation. Based on Heinrich Hoffmann's definition in *Die Humanitätsidee in der Geschichte des Abendlandes* (1951), Glade thinks of *Humanität* as "a generalization of the love that is central in Zuckmayer's outlook" (2). Whereas Zuckmayer himself rarely uses the term, "its first explicit formulation [is given] in *Die Brüder Grimm* (1948)" (3), comprising an ethical and a metaphysical component. In Glade's view, Zuckmayer's life and work are devoted increasingly to the realization of the ideal of *Humanität*. Whereas between 1925 and 1933 the author's work displays "spontaneous *Humanität*," which is not conscious of itself but is embodied in the characters and their actions, his later work (1933–56) shows a more self-conscious and reflective type: "tendentious *Humanität*," a term that Glade uses, with reference to Zuckmayer himself, "as a creation of a new moral climate and a quickening of the healing forces that arise from man's recognition of the essential unity of all existence" (4). Glade subdivides Zuckmayer's works into a "realistic-folklore phase (1925–32)" (5) and a second period, which he again subdivides "into an initial phase, characterized by the interpenetration of realistic and metaphysical elements (1933–39) and a later phase (1940–56) in which the vexing present-day problems of a sociopolitical nature are drawn in for subject-matter and in which Zuckmayer tends toward a more complex orientation involving realistic, metaphysical and symbolical elements" (6).

After discussing the concept of *Humanität* with regard to Zuckmayer's individual works, Glade summarizes his findings in a final chapter, "Theory (1933–56)," which is devoted to the relationships between *Humanität* and nature, nature and religion, nature and aesthetics. Here Glade tries to determine Zuckmayer's philosophy, which he finds rooted in "a robust and joyful affirmation of life and a feeling of innate oneness with nature" (156). In the final analysis, Glade views Zuckmayer as "quasi-mystic" because at the core of his nature philosophy he sees "eros or instinctive drive for unitary experience of the life-force" (161). Nature is invested with the attributes of divine immanence. God is "identical with the harmony of the inspired or inspiring order of the universe" (166f.). Zuckmayer believes in the inherent unity of all phases of life, including death. His aesthetic formulations are firmly grounded in his nature philosophy: grounded in the premise of an equation of nature and human nature. It is the writer's task to depict the "deeper reality" of all human actions, the "secret measure of all things," (170) thus reconciling the destructive dualism inherent in all existence. From 1940 on, the aforementioned ethical or humanitarian element is added to these considerations, no doubt under the influence of contemporary history. Zuckmayer becomes especially concerned with the cathartic effects of his dramas. The dramatist becomes "a healer who gives men an insight into their wholeness of selfhood through nature's eros" (176). Glade extrapolates Zuckmayer's philosophy from his poetic and essayistic works without regard for their formal elements or their aesthetic value, in the vein of earlier intellectual history.

Two years later Glade (1960) tried to systematize Carl Zuckmayer's theory of aesthetics, primarily based on his biographical and essayistic writings *Pro domo, Die Brüder Grimm,* and *Die langen Wege* (1952). At the outset Glade admits that Zuckmayer is not a reflective mind and that, in contrast to Brecht, he has not provided a particularly orderly formulation of his ideas. His aesthetics are rooted in his weltanschauung, in his "pantheistic credo in which the eros force plays the key role" (163). By this he means the "instinctive drive for unitary experience of the life-force *per se* [which] constitutes the very core of Zuckmayer's philosophy of nature" (164). Since Zuckmayer tends to deduce his aesthetics from the prevalent tenor of his works, Glade discusses it in relation to the two major periods of Zuckmayer's creativity: a first period, extending from 1925 to 1932, which he classifies as "realistic-folklore" and which does not yield any theoretical treatises; and "a second, deliberate period, from 1933" (165) to the writer's present, which in turn he subdivides into an initial phase, 1933–39, characterized by a mixture of realistic and metaphysical elements, and a later phase, 1940 to the present. During the period of 1933–39 he considers the artist's highest task "to make of art a reflection of nature-life through a creative reconciliation of the destructive dualism inherent in all existence" (166). This reconciliation is achieved through beauty or eros in nature, with nature symbolizing the incommensurable and ultimately the divine essence. The essence of *Humanität* during this period is a loving acceptance of destiny — in other words, a challenge to self-fulfillment.

Zuckmayer's theoretical writings during the phase from 1940 to the present provide a more rounded and detailed aesthetics. His most prominent concern became the realization of his *Humanität* ideal, which comprised both ethics and a transcendental or eros force. He believed in the ability of the dramatist to change not the course of history but rather the moral climate. Correspondingly, his great concern over ethical and humanitarian considerations became an important part of his postwar dramas. He wanted to continue the cathartic tradition of drama. Glade sensitively summarizes and paraphrases Zuckmayer's views from his theoretical writings, trying to bring into a system what Zuckmayer stated in a number of different contexts. There is no further analysis and no attempt to place his remarks in the history of aesthetics or philosophy. But in spite of Glade's abstract language, Zuckmayer's views become clearer in his study than in any earlier one.

Like Glade, Ingeborg Engelsing-Malek (1960) undertakes a straightforward examination of Zuckmayer's works. It is no wonder that Zuckmayer was impressed with her work and provided a short introduction to it. Her book-length study, originally an American Ph.D. thesis, provided stimuli for future Zuckmayer research. Considering the author's entire dramatic oeuvre up to that time, she convincingly shows that Nietzsche's *amor fati* (the love of one's destiny) is the unifying idea of his dramas. Zuckmayer's use of *amor fati* is somewhat different, however. In contrast to Nietzsche's *amor fati*, which originated from longing, Zuckmayer's view of life is Dionysian; he tries to achieve harmony between personal freedom and the higher meaning of world affairs, between Dionysian freedom and law. *Amor fati* for him always includes a belief in the constructive forces of life: self-awareness, ability to love, belief in God, and recognition of life. It has been shaped by a loving contemplation of nature. According to Engelsing-Malek, the basic fable of Zuckmayer's plays is as follows: the hero wrestles with his fate, which he does not know yet but of which he has a presentiment.

At times he tries to outwit it with rational arguments, and he is not re-deemed until he recognizes it and accepts it. In her impressive book Engelsing-Malek analyzes the dramas in terms of these basic premises, without, however, going beyond the dramas themselves, except for brief references to the works of Nietzsche and Driesch.

At the beginning of the 1960s, the kind of textimmanent interpre-tation exemplified by Teelen (1952), Meinherz (1960), and Vanden-rath (1960) gave way to the view that an author be evaluated primarily as a social critic. This shift occurred in both West Germany and in the United States. Thus Robert Kafka Lehrer (1962) investigates what he calls social awareness in the folk plays Zuckmayer wrote between 1925 and 1931: *Der fröhliche Weinberg, Schinderhannes, Katharina Knie,* and *Der Hauptmann von Köpenick.* Lehrer's contention is that Zuck-mayer had more in mind than the production of sad or amusing folk plays to delight his spectators. Rather, he wanted to communicate his "social awareness" as a citizen of the Weimar Republic. The last three of the four plays in question are therefore only ostensibly folk plays; in reality they are "parables in the format of the folk play," whose format was designed to contain those philosophical expressions — that social awareness — which comprised Carl Zuckmayer's attitude toward the intellectual, political, economic, and social problems of the Weimar Re-public" (15). Thus in form and content Zuckmayer's folk plays closely approach the German *Zeitstück.* Lehrer then tries to prove that in *Kreuzweg* and in *Pankraz erwacht* Zuckmayer had used expressionist and Brechtian techniques to communicate his social criticisms and ideas; his switch to the folk play was just a continuation of his search for the most socially effective form for this purpose. In his detailed discus-sion of the four plays, Lehrer uses the critical reaction as a measure of Zuckmayer's effectiveness in accomplishing this goal and is forced to concede that the reviews "tended to conceal rather than reveal Zuck-mayer's responsibility, his mission as a writer of documents of social criticism, of *Zeitstücke*" (344). Although this conclusion compels us to ask to what extent a socially critical aim is indeed present in the folk plays, Lehrer's dissertation must be viewed as part of the trend of the 1960s to see the communication of social and political criticism as the writer's main obligation.

Raymond Erford Barrick's dissertation (1964) also looks at Zuck-mayer's works as the expression of specific ideas. It clarifies and expands on a point that was only hinted at in Jacobius's investigation (1955), namely Zuckmayer's mystical philosophy as revealed in his life and works. Barrick tries to describe the main characteristics of what he calls the philosophical mysticism of Carl Zuckmayer by referring to his works, particularly the essayistic and autobiographical writings *Pro domo*, *Die langen Wege*, and *Die Brüder Grimm*; the novel *Salwàre oder Die Magdalena von Bozen*; and the drama *Der Gesang im Feuerofen*. According to Barrick, Zuckmayer emphasizes personal, mystical intuition as the principal source through which man comes to know truth. "The goal of human reason is, in Zuckmayer's view, an awareness of the spiritual nature of the universe" (12). There is, however, "no clear-cut technique or method of procedure which might guarantee the revelation of the secrets of existence. Only by living and growing through hard-won experience does one become ripe for the attainment of mystical insight" (172). Such insight offers not certainty but hope. The central feature of Zuckmayer's philosophy is the belief in the essential oneness of all things. Zuckmayer regards every individual as a unique microscopic representation of the universe, related to every other human being as well as to the entire cosmos. At the end of man's endless striving stands the reunion with the all-embracing primal spirit. Zuckmayer clearly takes a positive view of the material world and earthly existence. He is a positive type of mystic as defined by William Pepperell Montague in *The Ways of Knowing* (1925). Throughout Zuckmayer's dramas and other works, there are recurring attempts to harmonize the divine will he detects in creation with the will of the individuated being. The purpose of life is to temper and purify the soul in preparation for its reunion with God. True internal harmony can be won by pursuing one's destiny boldly.

It is difficult at times to follow Barrick's train of thought because, in his fervor to prove that Zuckmayer is a positive mystic, he sometimes goes beyond what can be shown in the text. But the ideohistorical grid that he superimposes upon Zuckmayer and his works does illuminate a number of the writer's qualities and clarify meanings of passages one might otherwise pass over.

The dissertation by Marvin Robert Maddox (1975) examines the intellectual kinship between Gerhart Hauptmann and Zuckmayer, analyzing the extent to which this kinship may be attributed to Hauptmann's influence on Zuckmayer. The friendship between Zuckmayer and his teacher definitely influenced Zuckmayer's literary production, although it is difficult to determine the exact nature and extent of this influence. The dissertation proceeds chronologically from *Kreuzweg* through Zuckmayer's revision of Hauptmann's drama *Herbert Engelmann* in 1952, with emphasis on Zuckmayer's literary development between 1920 and 1931. The many parallels in theme and theatrical technique in the two men's work are attributed to similarities in their worldviews, their common perception of the nature of man, and the central position they both accorded man in their dramas. Both dramatists present heroes whose problems are caused by their grappling with their fate, and they acknowledge the influence of strong metaphysical forces on their heroes' fate. Both concentrate on human beings, relegating social problems to the background. Neither believes that such problems can be eliminated by revolution or different social or political systems. Both advocate the manifestation of a Christian attitude of brotherly love as the key to a satisfactory solution of social conflicts. Both possess an unusual ability to capture the spirit of the German *Volk*, which is enhanced by their use of local dialect dialogue.

In her dissertation "The Central Women Figures in Carl Zuckmayer's Dramas" (1976), Ausma Balinkin starts with the premise that the major female roles have been largely neglected in the scholarly discussion of Zuckmayer's plays, except for their relationships with the male characters. She defends her approach by stating that it is crucial to a thorough understanding of Zuckmayer's works because "the ideas of interdependence, of reciprocity, of love, trust, and harmony, especially between the sexes, are fundamental to Zuckmayer's life-view" (1–2). Moreover — and this confirms that there are autobiographical elements in Zuckmayer's plays — many of the female figures "resembled the author in their attitudes and traits, others originate in his experiences and encounters" (3). Consequently, Balinkin first discusses Zuckmayer's relationship to women, based on his autobiographical writings, concluding that the author's early experience of nature shapes his concept of the female and that "his multi-dimensional women figures frequently reflect many of the physical and psychological concepts of the women who attracted him and whom he loved in his adult life. These vibrant stage characters interact in the same way as did he with the women who shared his life: the men and women are equal partners in relationships of reciprocal love and understanding, of trust and respect for each other's individuality" (11). For example, Zuckmayer's friendly separation from Annemarie Gans and from Mirl Seidel is reflected in Harras's relationship to his former lover Olivia in *Des Teufels General*. Similar separations occur in several other plays. After they part, the lovers' affection for each other remains intact. In Zuckmayer's work, women figures play increasingly commanding roles in their relationship with men. They move from spontaneous, resilient figures to more complex, emancipated, but simultaneously more vulnerable personalities. Approximately midway in his career, the women figures reach parity in this respect with their male counterparts. After that, "the central female roles tend to overshadow those of their male counterparts" (26). Balinkin traces this development, referring to and interpreting the women figures in Zuckmayer's dramas according to the author's intentions. Her approach is feminist in its title only, as she states: "It is not the intent of this monograph to view Zuckmayer's dramatic work from either the feminist or the anti-feminist perspective (to do either would be to distort the view of the humanist Zuckmayer)" (179). Her interpretations are textimmanent rather than based on to social-historical or sociocritical investigation. Thus her approach in her dissertation is rather old-fashioned for the time it was written.

It is appropriate to contrast Balinkin's study with Sonja Czech's (1985) M.A. thesis, written at the University of Mainz and inspired by Dieter Kafitz's 1983 article on women figures in *Salwàre*. In contrast to Ausma Balinkin's 1976 approach, Czech's is ideological; she uses criteria from the history of the women's movement, although her argumentation is not feminist by current standards. She judges the female character in Zuckmayer's dramas by the state of the discussion of women's questions at the time of his writing. She discusses select dramas under the headings "Die Frau in der Rolle der Geliebten" (The Woman in the Role of a Lover), "Die Frau in der Rolle Gefährtin" (The Woman in the Role of a Companion), "Die Frau in der Rolle der Mutter" (The Woman in the Role of the Mother), and "Die Frau als 'Dirne' " (The Woman as a "Whore"). In all four cases, it becomes evident that Zuckmayer idealizes women, pointing out their closeness to nature and their intuitive ability to rely on their feelings. He declares qualities such as capability for devotion, readiness to make sacrifices, and motherliness to be natural, though in reality they are the result of social roles imposed upon women. Zuckmayer's view of women is, without a doubt, influenced by the vitalistic philosophy of Ludwig Klages and Hans Driesch, who also influenced him in many other respects. He was not aware that by reducing women to creatures of nature he was at the same time depriving them of their individuality. Women in Zuckmayer's works, Czech contends, are thus not elevated but are categorized in traditional sex roles. Czech demonstrates that there are clear parallels between Zuckmayer's women characters and the conservative views of the majority of the women's clubs of the Weimar Republic, particularly its Catholic wing. As Kafitz points out in his introduction to Czech's study, Zuckmayer cannot be blamed for the fact that similar views were subsequently introduced into the mother cult of National Socialism, but they indicate the dubiousness of a blindly accepted vitalistic worldview. Consequently, Czech does not criticize Zuckmayer's view of women but only his unconsciousness of the discussion of their position at the time of writing. In its critical consideration of Zuckmayer's male and female characters and its placement of Zuckmayer in the conservative currents of the Weimar Republic, Czech's study definitely gives new stimuli to Zuckmayer research by applying at least some tenets of modern critical theory to his work.

Gabriele Lindner's M.A. thesis, written in 1982 (a year before Sonja Czech's) and published in 1986, also treats women in the work of Carl Zuckmayer, using *Katharina Knie, Ulla Winblad,* and *Barbara Blomberg* as examples. Whereas Sonja Czech views Zuckmayer's women in light of the women's movement, Lindner rather gives textimmanent interpretations of the works she analyzes. She judges Zuckmayer's characters by comparing them with the historical models in the case of *Ulla Winblad* and *Barbara Blomberg* and only partly refers to positions of the women's movement. Regarding methodology, her thesis lies between Ausma Balinkin's and Sonja Czech's. She also treats the *amor fati* of the title characters, thus showing her deep indebtedness to Engelsing-Malek (1960). Her consideration of the structure of the dramas elucidates striking similarities among the various types of women figures, but because of Lindner's methodology, Czech is clearly two steps ahead of her.

Other aspects of Zuckmayer's work have received scholarly attention. Siegfried Mews (1973b) has investigated his view of America, pointing out that it is, "to a large extent, determined by his fascination with the frontier world of the American Indian" (477). James Fenimore Cooper's *Leatherstocking Tales* (5 vols., 1826–41) and the much admired Karl May in particular shaped Zuckmayer's view of this continent, as is evident in *Pankraz erwacht* and *Sitting Bull: Ein Indianer-Roman* (1952). "It can be said then that during the first phase of the writer's creativity (from approximately 1920 to 1933) Karl May remained virtually unchallenged as the main source for Carl Zuckmayer's notions concerning the New World" (483). After going through Zuckmayer's works in which America plays a role, Mews concludes that he "deeply believed in the fundamental strength of the American society, which would enable it to return to the virtues of the past and eventually to overcome all ills besetting it" (494). Mews's article is a successful motif study in that it considers the treatment of America in all of Zuckmayer's writings.

In his 1985 article, Hans Wagener investigates the influence of exile on the author's exile work. He points out that Zuckmayer's concentrated film writing during his time in Austria and Switzerland resulted in the creation of naive regional literature (*Ein Sommer in Österreich*, 1937) or colportage-type novellas (*Herr über Leben und Tod*, 1938), prose without reference to the present (*Salwàre* and, later, *Der Seelenbräu*), and self-reflective essays and autobiographical writings (*Pro domo*, *Second Wind*). Zuckmayer thus reacted to his exile by trying, on the one hand, to escape reality and, on the other hand, to come to terms with his own time through the use of new literary forms. In his plays, he continued for a while dramatizing historical subjects. *Der Schelm von Bergen*, *Bellman*, and *Barbara Blomberg* were all begun in Vermont, and all three have strong lyric elements and few allusions to the author's present. Under the influence of political events, however, Zuckmayer turned toward the *Zeitstück* (*Somewhere in France*, 1941; *Des Teufels General*). In his poetry Zuckmayer made his nature poems the allegorical carriers of political meaning with occasionally defiant optimism. Finally he turned to the elegy, in which he reflected upon his personal exile.

Margot Finke's 1990 dissertation is similar to Wagener's approach in that she investigates Zuckmayer's work "in relation to various historical events which play a role in his works, especially during the period 1915–1970" (ii); and, like Becker (1984), she discusses Zuckmayer's concept of *Heimat*. After an introductory biographical sketch, she shows the role the various German regions play in Zuckmayer's works, the perception of German culture as reflected in his work, and his perception of German history and society (1900–70). As she states in her introduction, "*werkimmanente* (new criticism) analysis will be the thesis' basic approach, [while] autobiographical, historical (*werktranszendente*) aspects will also be employed in order to obtain the most complete picture of Zuckmayer's image of Germany and German society as expressed in his work" (iv). The result is meager in that the long thesis adds little on the works themselves. Finke has simply put together, summarized, and paraphrased Zuckmayer's statements and characterizations regarding the topic at hand without adding much of her own interpretation. Methodologically, the thesis does not go beyond the early 1960s.

William Grange (1991) approaches Zuckmayer from the perspective of the theater historian, investigating in detail the collaboration between Carl Zuckmayer and his director Heinz Hilpert, who between 1925 and 1961 directed nine Zuckmayer plays. Grange wants the book to serve as "a lens through which the reader may view the German theatre in the middle of the twentieth century" (xv), sweeping across the Weimar Republic, the Third Reich, and the Cold War period. He divides the productions into three "trilogies": the "German trilogy" (*Der fröhliche Weinberg, Der Hauptmann von Köpenick*, and *Des Teufels General*), the "metaphysical trilogy" (*Der Gesang im Feuerofen, Ulla Winblad*, and *Die Uhr schlägt eins*), and the "amorphous trilogy," plays united by nothing thematic or even intentional (*Pankraz erwacht, Kat*, and *Barbara Blomberg*). This subdivision applies solely to the collaboration of the two artists, leaving out all other plays that may or may not belong to any of these groups. Zuckmayer wrote plays with Hilpert in mind as the director, and often their final printed version was the result of Hilpert's extensive cuts and other suggestions. Zuckmayer's strength was writing dialogue, sometimes at the expense of tightly focused plot construction; but Hilpert was able to remedy this flaw by skillful cutting.

It is noteworthy that, with the exception of the theses by Teelen, Meinherz, Vandenrath, Adling, and Czech, all the above studies were written by Americans or Germans working in the United States; this testifies to the enormous impetus Zuckmayer research received from this country.

There are several studies that reflect Zuckmayer's reception in Germany and abroad. Since the Zuckmayer bibliography by Jacobius (1971), continued and updated by Kieser, lists only a limited number of translations — probably because of the "German" character of many of Zuckmayer's works — it is not amazing that so far only two studies have been devoted to Zuckmayer's reception in other countries: In the *Festschrift für Carl Zuckmayer* (ed. Glauert, Martin, and Heist 1976), Gustav Korlén reports briefly on Zuckmayer's reception in Sweden, including two productions of *Der Hauptmann von Köpenick* in 1931 and productions of *Des Teufels General* and *Das kalte Licht*. These were the only three Zuckmayer plays performed in Sweden. Several Swedish literary critics pointed out that the reason no Swedish theater performed *Ulla Winblad* was probably that the play violated historical accuracy; and since this gaffe was committed by a foreigner, the play would be considered sacrilegious by Swedes. Swedish radio played an important role in presenting Zuckmayer's *Der Hauptmann von Köpenick* and *Des Teufels General* after the Second World War. The prose works *Eine Liebesgeschichte* (1934) and *Die Fastnachtsbeichte* were translated in Sweden, but *Als wär's ein Stück von mir* was not.

Zuckmayer's reception in the United States was the subject of a detailed article by Siegfried Mews (1981b). Mews points out that there were only three independent American book translations that appeared in the United States: one of *Salwàre oder Die Magdalena von Bozen* under the title *The Moons Ride Over* (1937), one of *Second Wind* (1940), and a translation of *Als wär's ein Stück von mir* under the title *A Part of Myself* (1970; abbreviated version). Thus the prose and memoir writer rather than the dramatist was in the foreground; the translations of two dramas, *The Devil's General* (1962) and *The Captain of Köpenick* (1974), appeared only in anthologies. Mews delineates three phases of reception. During the first, before 1933, Zuckmayer was not completely ignored in the United States — the *New York Times* published five reviews of plays he wrote or reworked, but he was branded as a German author. Between 1933 and 1939 he received even less attention in the American press except that between 1937 and 1939 a number of English translations of his works appeared. The number increased after the author's arrival in the United States in 1939, thus affording him a chance to establish himself as a writer. *Second Wind* was at least a small success; the drama *Somewhere in France*, written jointly with Fritz Kortner, was a total flop. Several short stories were published in American magazines, but with too much time between them to boost Zuckmayer's recognition. From 1950 on, Zuckmayer received somewhat more attention in the United States, but almost exclusively because of the success of his dramas in Europe. Although some of his dramas were later sporadically performed in America, the film versions had more of an impact. More important to his recognition than performances or the publication of translations was the scholarly work on Zuckmayer, which, beginning in 1947, soon surpassed that conducted in Europe. Ironically, the fact that Zuckmayer is still well-known in the United States rests on his uncertain contribution to the script for *The Blue Angel*.

In what was originally an oral presentation, Wolfgang Mettenberger (1992) ponders about the reasons for Zuckmayer's great theatrical success during the Weimar Republic. He believes one major factor was Zuckmayer's instinctively correct analysis of sociocultural changes. Timing was another: during the second half of the 1920s, the Germans were able to laugh again for the first time after the First World War because the economic situation had stabilized. A third factor was the revitalization of the German folk play. Hans Wagener (1983c), on the other hand, deals with the reasons for Zuckmayer's lack of success as a dramatist in Germany from 1950 on (*Der Gesang im Feuerofen*). In his opinion, there are many reasons, including the thematic and formal weaknesses of individual plays and a discrepancy between Zuckmayer's drama and contemporary theater, of which he was not a part. Until

3: Drama

Expressionism and Wild West

ZUCKMAYER'S FIRST DRAMA, the expressionistic *Prometheus*, which was written by the twenty-two-year-old author in 1918 but not published until 1981, was first performed under the direction of Günther Fleckenstein at the Deutsches Theater Göttingen on 3 November 1984. Gerhard P. Martin (1985a) has edited the reviews, which are, for the most part, negative.

Kreuzweg, the first drama that was performed during Zuckmayer's lifetime, premiered on 10 December 1920 at Leopold Jeßner's Staatstheater in Berlin. It was directed by Ludwig Berger, Zuckmayer's childhood friend from Mainz. The largely conservative audience hissed and laughed at the serious scenes of the play. After only three performances, the last two of which were poorly attended, the remaining scheduled performances were canceled. In *Als wär's ein Stück von mir*, Zuckmayer admitted that it was not a good play. It did receive, however, relatively favorable reviews from some professional critics: Emil Faktor (1920) praised the surging beauty of the verses, and Herbert Ihering (1920) lauded Zuckmayer's poetic calling, which he perceived as founded in *Humanität* and not falsified by intellectualism. Of the bourgeois reviewers, on the other hand, Alfred Kerr (1920) was more critical, castigating the drama as one more work from the big factory of redemption literature. Later the Zuckmayer enthusiast Arnold John Jacobius (1955) adopted this view, declaring that the theme of the play is the redemption of man through the power of love. The question of the drama's classification as part of expressionist literature was rightfully taken up by Siegfried Mews (1981a). Mews concludes carefully that "there can be little doubt that Zuckmayer's first drama is indebted to expressionism. Its central theme — the quest for man in the abstract — the dramatic structure in which the causal interrelationship between the individual scenes is missing, the lack of convincing psychological motivation, and the shadowy, ill-defined characters indicate that the playwright was following a contemporary trend" (24).

It was not until 1952 that the play received scholarly attention. In his dissertation on Zuckmayer's stage works, Wolfgang Teelen (1952),

applying Emil Staiger's terminology (lyric, epic, and dramatic) to
Kreuzweg, concludes that the mostly lyrical character of the individual
scenes runs counter to the "law" of drama that demands that individual
action result from the context of the totality of events. By making use
of "station technique" and expressionist language, Zuckmayer has created individual scenes with persons who are merely bearers of ideas and
not human beings. Thus, in Teelen's view, the drama cannot be termed
dramatic since there is no meaningful goal, no social message. The play
focuses on Christa Kutter and her path through the various situations of
her life following her encounter with the Brückenmann, a superhuman
being who has entrusted her with a redemptive mission. Teelen, like Jacobius (1955), sees the motif of love, which ultimately suppresses that
of the peasants' revolt, as all important. The second most important
motif is the affirmation of life, evident in the optimistic ending of the
drama. (The result of the confused conditions and events is probably
the overcoming of hatred by the happiness of pure love.) Teelen thus
applies the Staigerian grid and comes to his conclusions within this
terminological framework.

    Also from a textimmanent perspective, the only detailed interpreta-
tion devoted solely to *Kreuzweg* was published in 1957 by J. Vandenrath. The views he expressed here were later confirmed and expanded in
his dissertation of 1960. For him, the play is of interest because it fur-
thers our understanding of Zuckmayer's total oeuvre and because it is a
work typical of German expressionism. Vandenrath points out that the
action is unimportant; it merely provides the playwright an opportunity
to bring characters to the stage, lead them to each other, and have them
present themselves with plastic postures, expressive gestures, and expressionist poetry. The action is almost hidden under lyric poetry. The
work's abstract wordiness precludes the presentation of concrete social
facts, results in vagueness, and generally typifies standard expressionism.
In Vandenrath's view, the play is weak. Although it is not worth trying
to make sense of the action, it should be kept in mind that in spite of
the fuzziness of the often-used term *Mensch* (man, human being), this
first work of Zuckmayer's pronounces his humanist ideal. This ideal is
seen in connection with nature. Salvation is possible through sexual
love. In the feeling the author conveys of nature and country life,
Kreuzweg transcends expressionism, Vandenrath believes, pointing
ahead to traits of Zuckmayer's future plays. The play marks Zuckmayer's liberation from three pressing experiences of his life: religion,
sexual love, and, most importantly, the 1918 revolution. The peasants'
revolt portrayed in the play has no concrete goals in terms of effectuat-

ing social change but rather adds a religious, mystical touch. Zuckmayer uses it to help himself come to terms with the revolution at the end of the First World War, a point later taken up by Rudolf Lange (1969). The question of playability was later pursued by the theater historian William Grange (1991), who judges the play to be "a mishmash of noble sentiment and youthful expostulation, neither of which proved effectively structured for performance" (14–15).

Ausma Balinkin (1976) points out that *Kreuzweg* establishes Zuckmayer's practice of viewing people not as isolated beings but rather as interdependent, interacting individuals. Women play crucial roles in these relationships, as is evident in *Kreuzweg*. On the one hand there is Christa, an uncomplicated girl who is free from inner conflict and who accepts her destiny, which demands that she carry out a selfless mission of love. She clearly consents to serve as an instrument of salvation: "In fulfilling her mission she finds her own fulfillment in the perfect peace and harmony of death" (28). The second type of woman — as personified in Madelon — is the complex, flawed personality whom inner discord directs inward and toward self-isolation: "She reaches out not to give, but to receive" (28). The third type, such as the witch Julle Rothendel, is the atavistic, paganistic vixen who espouses chaos and destruction. *Kreuzweg* thus foreshadows later characterizations and relationships.

Later criticism has pursued different paths. In his investigation of Zuckmayer's plays, Robert Kafka Lehrer (1962) focuses on his social awareness and concludes that *Kreuzweg* fails by this standard. Consequently, Lehrer considers the play "an amorphous compound of all the elements of playcraft" and finds that "the yield of this compound was lyric monologue rather than dialogue, was harangue instead of drama" (43). In his view, Zuckmayer tried to portray his "humanistic concept of the relationship between man and nature" (75) through the genre of expressionist drama and failed in communicating his ideas to his audience.

In his rather conservative investigation of the relationship between Zuckmayer and his teacher Gerhart Hauptmann, Marvin Robert Maddox (1975) selects *Kreuzweg* as one of the dramas for discussion because it is the only one of Zuckmayer's plays on which the author himself specifically acknowledges Hauptmann's influence. Maddox points out the similarity between the character of Christa and that of Rautendelein in Hauptmann's *Die versunkene Glocke* (*The Sunken Bell*, 1897). The peasants' revolt bears several similarities to the weavers' revolt in Hauptmann's *Die Weber* (*The Weavers*, 1892). But only part of the peasants' unhappiness and discontent in *Kreuzweg* is due to social and economic factors, whereas in Hauptmann's work, these factors are central. In some respects, however, *Kreuzweg* is closer to the spirit of Gerhart Hauptmann's works than any of Zuckmayer's later plays, particularly because of its prevailing atmosphere of suffering and pessimism. In Maddox's opinion, the fact that Madelon is left at the end to begin a new life elsewhere hardly mutes the pessimistic tone.

The political left, personified by Oskar Kanehl (1920), had immediately rejected Zuckmayer's play when it was first performed because of its lack of concreteness and its failure to demonstrate proletarian mass consciousness and the pathos of class struggle. For Kanehl, Zuckmayer was another example of a merely literary revolutionary, and his play should be forgotten with others that are similar. Later, socialist realism became Marxist critic Wilfried Adling's critical tool (1959). Admittedly, he was the first critic who made sense of the double action of the revolution on the one hand and of Christa Kutter on the other. According to Adling, the work depicts persons who are under some kind of yoke; at the same time, however, it depicts persons who are searching for a true human being (*Mensch*). Thus Christa, like Madelon and Hilario, ultimately finds her way to abstract man through her love for mankind. But Adling criticizes this split of the action, calling it a discrepancy. He feels that the play falls apart as a result. Whereas the objective and real conflict that forms the basis of the peasants' revolt allows for real drama, the conflict governing Christa Kutter's fate is subjective and abstract. She has the mystical task of helping abstract man out of his abstract trouble. Instead of objectively changing historical conditions, Zuckmayer sees in the subjective change of individual human beings the decisive means of creating a better world. For the Marxist Adling, anything abstract and subjective is automatically bad. Realistic art is his ideal, and Zuckmayer's intention cannot be reconciled with his demands.

Zuckmayer's second drama, *Kiktahan oder Die Hinterwäldler*, which takes place in the American Wild West, marks the beginning of Zuckmayer's move away from the expressionism of *Kreuzweg*. The play premiered on 15 February 1925 under the new title *Pankraz erwacht* in a matinée performance of the experimental Junge Bühne in the Deutsches Theater. Since this premiere performance remained the only one — the play was not taken over by the regular program of the Deutsches Theater — it marks Zuckmayer's second official failure as a dramatist. The play was included neither in the *Gesammelte Werke* of 1960 nor in the *Werkausgabe in zehn Bänden* of 1976; it was first printed in *Carl Zuckmayer '78: Ein Jahrbuch*, where Barbara Glauert (1978) reports on the two different versions, its origins, and the editorial principles underlying its first edition. A number of reviews of the first performance are also included.

The lack of scholarly interest in this drama is probably due to the fact that the text was not available until it was reprinted in 1978. The only scholars who have taken a closer look at *Pankraz erwacht* are Siegfried Mews and Raymond English in a joint study of 1974. In his later book (1981a) Mews repeated some of the views expressed in this article. Mews and English point out many parallels between *Pankraz erwacht* and Bertolt Brecht's *Im Dickicht*, the first version of *Im Dickicht der Städte* (*Jungle of Cities*, 1924). These parallels — among them milieu, themes and motifs, depiction of characters and character constellation, and the use of songs and ballads — may be attributed to Brecht's direct influence. But there are also important differences between the two dramatists in their depiction of nature and man. Whereas Brecht compares the existence of the individual to the struggle for physical survival in a desolate jungle, for Zuckmayer man can be redeemed. For him the antagonistic powers of nature represent the life principle itself, the constant cycle of life and death within a vaguely sensed divine order. Ultimately, Zuckmayer was able to extricate himself from Brecht's fascination and to find his own style. In comparison to *Kreuzweg*, *Pankraz erwacht* displays stronger elements of realism. The raucous, boisterous drinking scenes and songs, on the other hand, foreshadow the uninhibited enjoyment of life portrayed in *Der fröhliche Weinberg*.

William Grange (1991) deals with the first production of the play under Heinz Hilpert's direction. As a result of his point of departure, he tries to play up Hilpert's contribution to shaping the play. In his opinion, "given the nature of Hilpert's contributions in subsequent work together one may assume that Hilpert's influence rivaled that of Brecht" (181).

Folk Plays

Because *Der Hauptmann von Köpenick* and *Der fröhliche Weinberg* are still Zuckmayer's most successful plays, his popularity rests largely on his reputation as an author of folk plays. This term is precarious, however, and has therefore been the subject of a number of articles on its relation to Zuckmayer's works. In his review of *Schinderhannes*, Alfred Kerr (1927) warns of the dangers in Zuckmayer's overly close ties to the soil, stating that while Zuckmayer's power lies in its indigenous freshness, it is limited by this same quality. Marianne Kesting (1969) feels that after his brilliant comedy *Der Hauptmann von Köpenick*, which is a true folk play, Zuckmayer turned to more questionable versions of folk drama. He was pursuing, in his own words, healthy fun, the genuine *Volkstum*, the sincere love for one's *Heimat* — values that totalitarian governments on the right and the left were later praising to their citizens in the industrialized countries as "natural." His folk plays contained a concentration of all romantic clichés that exist about folksiness.

In 1977, Thomas Ayck commented that, in contrast to Brecht's politically oriented folk plays, Zuckmayer's were not political. To him, the genre was a vehicle for dealing with the existence and problems of broad strata of society and characterizing people without political action or exotic milieu. He provided theater *about* but not *for* the people. Unfortunately, Zuckmayer's interest in the people was often expressed in idyllic elements, superficial gaiety, folklore, and the depiction of a romantic milieu.

Other critics took a more positive attitude toward Zuckmayer as an author of folk literature. In his generally positive account of Zuckmayer's life and works, Arnold Bauer (1970) points out that what is lasting in literature does not always meet aesthetic criteria. Zuckmayer's works may be counted among great literature, but a popular author often finds greater and more lasting resonance than an esoteric one. Zuckmayer often returns to motifs of folk art: song, fairy tale, chronicle, and anecdote. Yet he successfully combines love for his native land with a world citizenship that affirms friendship among peoples.

Other critics not only labeled Zuckmayer an author of folk literature but tried to evaluate him as such. After noting the multiple associations of the word *Volk*, Martin Greiner (1958) treats Zuckmayer's and Brecht's renewal of the folk play and, by comparing the two, shows that Zuckmayer's limits and strengths are also the limits and strengths of the folk play. This strength unfolds in the homelike, indigenous, and familiar and abates when faced with the unfamiliar. The folk play is the close-to-nature realm between art and kitsch, the realm of popularity. Where others move about only hesitatingly, Zuckmayer gains his freedom and surefootedness in dealing with everyday problems. Zuckmayer puts crude, natural things on stage, but in this respect he never transgresses the limits set by the convention of the folk play. In his dissertation of 1962, Robert Kafka Lehrer advances the thesis "that the epithet 'folk dramatist' did not entirely do justice to the playwright. It did in no way indicate that behind a folk play lay points of view which revealed

Zuckmayer to be not only a man of conscience, but a man with a mission as well" (334). For this reason, Lehrer introduces the term *social awareness* to demonstrate how Zuckmayer had transcended the traditional folk play. Erwin Rotermund (1970) attributes Zuckmayer's and Horváth's renewal of the folk play during the Weimar Republic to a decline of the utopian and ideological in conjunction with the economic boom after 1924. A turn to new objectivity is concomitant with this change. In Hans Poser's 1978 view, however, such a sociologically reasoned interpretation implies the reproach that Zuckmayer's turn away from expressionism toward the folk play signals an increasing lack of political interest on the part of the bourgeoisie, which fled from the utopian realm into the crude comedy and realism of the folk play.

The reasons for the popularity of Zuckmayer's early folk plays were discussed publicly at the tenth anniversary of the Carl-Zuckmayer-Gesellschaft on 7 July 1982 in Mainz. The proceedings were published under the title "Zuckmayers Werk zwischen Volkstümlichkeit und Realismus" (Zuckmayer's Work between Popularity and Realism) in the *Blätter der Carl-Zuckmayer-Gesellschaft* ([Anonymous] 1986). The panel chair was Anton Maria Keim, the cultural affairs officer of Mainz. Panelists were the theater directors Georg Aufenanger and Günther Fleckenstein, the GDR writer Rolf Schneider, and Professors Dieter Kafitz, Horst Meixner, Siegfried Mews, and Willy Michel. In Mews's opinion, Zuckmayer creates characters from a particular geographic region in a specific historic situation, ultimately expanding the term *Heimat* from the local to the national level. In Kafitz's view, Zuckmayer's plays meet the audiences' traditional expectations. His popularity is based on sticking to the classic-humanist ideal of human personality. For Meixner, Zuckmayer's *Volkstümlichkeit*, or popularity, results from creating characters with whom the audience can identify. His social criticism is always restricted to the criticism of symptoms. His weakness is his inability to penetrate to deeper analyses. Schneider believes that Zuckmayer's popularity rests on the fact that he excludes those intellectual elements that were always considered suspect in Germany. His characters are nice fellows, but they never analyze a situation. His idea of civilization is romantic; he is a "green" writer, for whom city and countryside are hostile opposites. If the discussion demonstrated anything, it was that, as Meixner put it, the term Volk is a "puffy" one that has a different meaning for everyone and that Zuckmayer is great where he knows what kind of characters he must create so that the audience can identify with them.

Der fröhliche Weinberg

The uninhibited joy of life that permeates *Der fröhliche Weinberg* (1925) is present earlier in the songs of *Pankraz erwacht.* But only with the later play, which he wrote in Berlin in the Wannsee villa of a distant relative, was Zuckmayer able to achieve his great breakthrough as a dramatist. Written in his native Rhine-Hessian dialect and playing in his home region, this comedy was in the genre most closely akin to Zuckmayer's nature: the folk play. The remainder of the plays he was to write during the Weimar Republic period would be folk plays. After Zuckmayer had been awarded the prestigious Kleist Prize for the play by the critic Paul Fechter, the first performance took place on 22 December 1925 at Berlin's Theater am Schiffbauerdamm under the direction of Reinhard Bruck. For many critics, including Alfred Kerr (1925), it marked the end of expressionism in literature.

Der fröhliche Weinberg did not receive scholarly attention until after the Second World War. Several studies of the play approach it from the textimmanent method of interpretation, trying to determine its value for the theater, its realization of a certain structure, or its expression of certain ideas. Thus, applying his Staigerian terminological grid to *Der fröhliche Weinberg*, Wolfgang Teelen (1952) comes to the conclusion that the play at no point goes beyond the depiction of a motley group of people and a merry colorfulness. The play is epic — that is, without individualization of action, presenting rather a state of existence (127). Teelen believes that Zuckmayer succeeds in presenting real people on a simple level and providing the viewer a genuine theater experience — though spectators may later become disillusioned when they realize the play's events fail to develop toward an important goal.

The critic Alfred Happ (1956) is in principle not far from Teelen. He calls Zuckmayer's dramatic works "poetic theater," a concept that goes back to Zuckmayer himself. Happ's remarks about the various dramas are intended not as interpretations but as analyses of effects. He sees *Der fröhliche Weinberg* not only as a work born out of Zuckmayer's love for his home region but also as a satirical work in which the author pokes fun at the clichés of language that in many segments of society replaced genuine feeling. Despite the play's satirical elements, however, Zuckmayer's humor remains humane.

In his dissertation of 1960 J. Vandenrath also discussed matters of style and genre. Whereas we may laugh at the positive, natural Rhenish characters, only the ungenuine ones are grotesque, he says; they are characterized by means of satirical realism. The war veterans are an example. *Der fröhliche Weinberg* is above all a farcical comedy meant to give viewers a laugh. Viewing the play by this standard, Vandenrath applies Teelen's textimmanent method and arrives at an assessment similar to Teelen's. As late as 1993, Siegfried Sudhof is interested in the play's importance for theatrical style: the unaffected adoption of traditional forms and a sympathetic renunciation of stylistic originality. At the same time, he sees the play as a renunciation of the militant type of theater that promotes a particular philosophy of life.

Other interpreters looked at the play in terms of its expression of Zuckmayer's worldview. Thus in his 1958 dissertation on the concept of *Humanität* in Zuckmayer's dramas, Henry Glade sees the substance of the play in Annemarie's "belief in the primacy of the genuine heart and of true free love as contrasted with any other dictates, whether secular or ecclesiastic" (11). The play "reveals Zuckmayer's primal experience ('Urerlebnis'): Nature in the Rhenish-Hessian perspective" (12). His *Humanität* reveals itself in the equation of life-nature. In his article "The Motif of Encounter in Zuckmayer's Dramas" (1963), Glade merely confirms that the drama is a superb demonstration of Zuckmayer's primal experience of nature, framed in a Rhenish-Hessian perspective. His concept of life and its ethos is derived from this nature-life equation. It is in *Der fröhliche Weinberg* that "nature as the ultimate criterion of human integration furnishes the fundamental dichotomy of the play in terms of the natural vs. unnatural which is embodied in the grouping of Gunderloch-Annemarie-Klärchen-Jochen vs. Knuzius" (183).

Ingeborg Engelsing-Malek (1960) successfully applies her structural model of *amor fati* to the drama. In her eyes Zuckmayer's hero, Gunderloch, is struggling with his fate; reason becomes the adversary of his soul, but ultimately the elementary powers of nature turn out to be stronger than scheming reason, so Gunderloch accepts his fate. Engelsing-Malek demonstrates that within twelve hours Gunderloch undergoes an inner transformation that leads him to new insights and finally to the recognition of his own nature. His rational considerations and plans for his life turn out to be wrong. After the brawl, he feels born again and no longer too old to fall in love with Annemarie. Engelsing-Malek also recognizes that Zuckmayer wanted to satisfy the curiosity of his spectators and to share his high spirits with them; but, to her credit, she points out that even this comedy contains Zuckmayer's underlying basic philosophy.

Her view is confirmed by J. Vandenrath (1960), for whom the message of the play is that even natural, healthy people may be in danger of becoming unfaithful to their nature. *Der fröhliche Weinberg* sees man as part of nature and subject to its laws. It is man's task to heed these laws and to live according to them. Otherwise he leaves the order of nature and becomes spurious. Thus Gunderloch's decision to retire was against the law of nature, as was Klärchen's engagement to Knuzius (the main representative of ungenuine man). Zuckmayer's treatment of sexual matters in this play is also an example of his worldview. In *Der fröhliche Weinberg*, sexuality appears as the expression of a positive attitude toward life and its joys.

Other interpretations, typical of the late 1950s and early 1960s, concern the social and political elements of the play. The Marxist Wilfried Adling (1959) criticizes its conciliatory ending, which Teelen (1952) had already objected to. Adling feels that Zuckmayer is so caught up in his folksy atmosphere that he neglects the more important possibilities of rendering a political message. Adling reproaches him for insufficient penetration of reality, for not going beyond the *beginnings* of artistic realism. In 1987, Werner Lüder continued Adling's Marxist criticism, focusing on Knuzius as a caricature of fascism, a vehicle through which Zuckmayer could show the absurdity of national clichés. By making light of national ideology, Zuckmayer reveals that he did not recognize clearly enough the threat the times posed to his humanistic ideas.

Tracing the development of social awareness in Zuckmayer's dramas, Robert Kafka Lehrer stresses in his 1962 dissertation that Zuckmayer, in recreating a naturalistic picture of a Rhenish community, also tried to cast light upon such issues as anti-Semitism, political reaction, petty bureaucracy, and graft in German life. Zuckmayer used mild irony, caricature, and a strong comedic sense in his depiction of the characters, language, mores, and manners of the simple country folk. The fact that the National Socialist Party, some members of the Jewish community, the inhabitants of Zuckmayer's native Nackenheim, and officials of the Catholic Church reacted very critically demonstrated that he had successfully used the genre of the folk play to communicate his "social awareness."

Coming from the social-critical stance of the generation of the 1968 student rebellion, Thomas Ayck (1977) emphasizes that Zuckmayer does not clearly stress the social differences between the characters in the play. Though he shows a group of people from various social classes and professions who have come together at a vintner's estate at the time of the grape harvest, money interests and the political reality of the Weimar Republic figure in the play, thus restricting the idyllic frame.

Zuckmayer's use of dialect does not mark a retreat from dealing with the sociopolitical experiences of the Weimar Republic but rather voices a protest against the political jargon of the nationalists, the political trespasses of the veterans, the empty talk of the civil servants and the traveling merchants. In using regionalism this way, however, Zuckmayer risks eliciting only an emotional response from the audience and excluding rational argumentation.

Zuckmayer's first biographer, Arnold Bauer (1970), studies the play's success. After all the exaggerated language of expressionism and the problem plays of the first postwar years, the theatergoing public was starving for freshness and reality. Furthermore, the play addressed a number of different social groups within the audience, combining farcical effects with social satire. Thus, in spite of their many reservations, it also satisfied the needs of intellectuals. Contributing to the success also was the fact that Zuckmayer focused not on social satire but on the earthy characters of his home region. In *Der fröhliche Weinberg* as well as in the author's other early dramas, Bauer sees a conscious continuation of the naturalist tradition expanded by topical insertions of quotes and typically neorealistic passages. In 1981, Siegfried Mews (1981a) pointed out that the realism of *Der fröhliche Weinberg* is not the naturalism of yesterday: "Rather, Zuckmayer availed himself of time-honored comedy traditions to induce laughter and create merriment" (35). Although he presents a detailed account of the reception and criticism of *Der fröhliche Weinberg* as well as a comparing it with Brecht's *Herr Puntila und sein Knecht Matti* (*Mr. Puntila and His Man Matti*, 1948), he fails to attempt an interpretation of his own.

The question of the play's affiliation with a particular literary movement was also discussed in three articles that treat it within the genre of the folk play. Martin Greiner (1958) shows that the dramatist has parodistically turned around the old rural custom of making sure before the wedding that the bride is able to bear children. But Zuckmayer is not concerned about old customs and the honor of an academician; his aim is to unmask a shabby fortune hunter who is thinking of money when he talks about honor. In Greiner's view, *Der fröhliche Weinberg* is no problem play, and it contains no bitter social criticism. Its important aspects are the vineyard itself and its many different types of people. In an article that comes to very negative conclusions, Erwin Rotermund (1970) cites the drama as exemplifying Zuckmayer's intentions to revive the folk play during the Weimar Republic. He identifies several features that are characteristic of the folk play. The action is promoted by the comic intrigue of the two main female characters. A skillful distribution of individual and crowd scenes heightens the effect of the play on the spectators. Animal and plant symbols and metaphors interpret the human sphere, in particular the vineyard, the privet bower, and the sow that, although doomed to die, becomes a symbol of life. Zuckmayer presents a naive apotheosis of nature. There is no discrepancy between speaking and acting. The positive characters are able to communicate their feelings, but the negative characters are not: Knuzius and Bruchmüller speak in an artificial, nationalistic jargon. Sentimentality and crude obscenity are only nuances of the same vital consciousness, demonstrating an affinity to Ludwig Klages's vitalistic philosophy that cannot be overlooked. Yet the success of the play was far greater than its importance. Its reception demonstrates the disappearance of utopian thinking, a thinking that goes beyond the social reality of the Weimar Republic. It should not be overlooked, however, that topical issues are represented in the play: the infamous *Dolchstoßlegende* (legend of the "stab in the back"), problems concerning the assimilation of Jews, the fate of the veterans, the excesses of nationalistic pathos, and bureaucratic corruption. But at the end, the satire on representatives of the politically conservative forces of the Weimar Republic changes into comical caricature; after their humiliation they are ultimately integrated into the affirmative, Dionysian context. By making the Dionysian, carnal sphere absolute and by glorifying nature, the playwright fails to effect a penetrating analysis of concrete constellations of the postwar period. In Rotermund's opinion, Zuckmayer's naive trust in nature, which renders all social differences and political conflicts unimportant, cannot be justified by writing in the genre of the folk play. He poses the question whether or not *Der fröhliche Weinberg* really goes beyond crude jokes and cheap sexuality (Brecht). Moreover, Gunderloch, the main representative of the Dionysian, is not a man of the *Volk* but the rich owner of an estate. Zuckmayer fails to reflect upon this monopolization of the Dionysian in the bourgeois society of the Weimar Republic. Thus Rotermund's sociologically motivated criticism ultimately questions Zuckmayer's contribution to the renewal of the folk play.

In an article surveying the renewal of the folk play in Zuckmayer, Horváth, and Brecht, Hans Poser (1978) goes a step further than Greiner and Rotermund. First he points out that in *Der fröhliche Weinberg* all elements of the folk play are united: the space of a concrete, limited landscape; the motif of inheritance, closely connected with that of the wedding, in this case of several couples; the drinking and brawling, interspersed with songs and crude eroticism. On the one hand, such elements portray man's sexuality and physicality; on the other hand, they satirize current politics. Zuckmayer satirizes representatives of various social groups and exposes them to the laughter of the spectators. Through Knuzius and Bruchmüller he demonstrates to what extent the bourgeoisie of his time had already adopted anti-Semitic and fascist ideas. In Poser's view this mixture of crude comedic elements and ideological issues moves the work away from the pure folk play and closer to satirical comedy. The political elements of *Der fröhliche Weinberg* turn it from mere folk play into a work of literary dimension. The comical effects in *Der fröhliche Weinberg* are not only derived from the situation; they are also brought about by the unmasking of political catchwords. The victims of this type of comedy are finally included in the happy end. But in contrast to Rotermund (1970), Poser doubts that they are included in the affirmative, Dionysian communion. Using Schiller's terms, he calls Zuckmayer a "naive" poet and renewer of the folk play, whereas Horváth could be called a "sentimental" poet. Whereas Zuckmayer's characters are able to realize their natural humanity within a particular landscape, Horváth's characters hide their egotistical drives and meanness behind their environment. Zuckmayer's characters are able to follow their true feelings and their nature; Horváth's do not have true feelings. Brecht, in turn, intended not only to renew the folk play but to use it for didactic purposes by writing parables. Poser thus places Zuckmayer's folk plays into the general context of the renewal of the folk play in German twentieth-century literature. He shows that Zuckmayer had transcended the folk play genre, though differently from the ways his fellow writers Horváth and Brecht had done so.

The relation of the play to the work of another dramatist is also Marvin Robert Maddox's 1975 topic. He feels that *Der fröhliche Weinberg* put Zuckmayer firmly into the tradition of Gerhart Hauptmann — in for example, *Die Jungfern vom Bischofsberg* (*The Maidens of the Mount*, 1907). One of the characteristics both dramatists have in common is their use of dialect to make their characters realistic. And like Hauptmann, Zuckmayer advocates that man must live in harmony with himself, with other human beings, and with nature.

The women figures in *Der fröhliche Weinberg* became the subject of two studies. In her textimmanent reading, Ausma Balinkin (1976) calls the women in *Der fröhliche Weinberg* and *Schinderhannes* "completely integrated personalities. Free from inner conflict themselves, they play traditional catalytic roles" (29). They are attuned to nature in a direct and personal way. This is particularly true for Annemarie whose mode of thinking, like Gunderloch's, is rooted in nature. Her outward appearance is the expression of her attitude. The women of the drama distinguish themselves from the men by their uniquely feminine characteristics of intense and reliable intuition. Annemarie and Julchen in *Schinderhannes* are the most intuitive and uncomplicated of all of Zuckmayer's women figures. Their psychological makeup is completely free of conflict.

In her methodologically more sophisticated study, which considers the state of discussion on women's issues in 1925, Sonja Czech (1985) analyzes *Der fröhliche Weinberg* from the premise that Zuckmayer venerated women as part of nature, as different from males, but on the basis of male superiority. She demonstrates that, apart from endorsing sexuality as an important part of the male role, Zuckmayer does not make a contribution to the analysis of sexual problems as seen during the Weimar Republic. His advocacy of drastic sexuality is solely an absolutizing of the Dionysian human drives. The figure of Klärchen is included in the action solely for her love relationship with Jochen; her one-sided function does not leave room for individuality, so she is reduced to the status of an exchangeable object, the attraction of which is exhausted when it is no longer young. In Zuckmayer's ideal of the sexes, there is a contrast between male and female, with Gunderloch embodying the classical male attributes: power, wealth, knowledge, victory, rudeness, cruelty, violence, activity. Next to such male qualities, women can have only a subordinate, complementing function, as exemplified in Klärchen and Annemarie.

A big success when it was first performed, the play still draws audiences in summer theater performances. But it was later eclipsed by another comedy, *Der Hauptmann von Köpenick*.

Schinderhannes

Zuckmayer did not try to capitalize on the success of *Der fröhliche Weinberg* by immediately writing another such comedy. His next drama, *Schinderhannes*, was not completed until 1927. Set in Rhenish Hesse, it is the story of a German Robin Hood type, the robber Johannes Bückler, who was known as Schinderhannes. He and his gang roamed the Hunsrück mountains during the Napoleonic era. In 1803 he was beheaded in Zuckmayer's native Mainz, together with nineteen members of his gang. As early as 1922, during his time at the municipal theater in Kiel, Zuckmayer had composed a ballad about Schinderhannes on the basis of legends and songs that were popular in his home region.

The play was first performed on 13 October 1927 at Berlin's Lessing-Theater under the direction of Reinhard Bruck. Eugen Klöpfer played Schinderhannes; Käthe Dorsch played Julchen. Max Liebermann designed the stage settings. Although this was not a comedy but rather a romantic Storm and Stress drama, it was as successful as *Der fröhliche Weinberg* had been. A phenomenon occurred with the play, however, that was to happen again in Zuckmayer's career. Whereas the audience liked it, the reviews were mixed. Paul Fechter (1927) felt that Zuckmayer had confirmed the expectations raised by *Der fröhliche Weinberg*, but he criticized the lack of active dramatic elements after Schinderhannes is defeated by the French troops. At that point lyric elements prevail; the play becomes too long and lacks concentration. Zuckmayer's colleague Erich Kästner (1927), at that time theater critic for the *Neue Leipziger Zeitung*, noted the same lack of dramatic action. In his opinion, Zuckmayer created local color in lusty hues, but instead of staging the fate of a rebel, he only showed the unusual private life of a haunted creature. Thus the play is popular entertainment and a tragic revue, but not a tragedy — a theatrical mosaic, but not a drama. Felix Holländer (1932) criticized the artificial simplicity and sentimentality of the play as well as its lack of revolutionary decisiveness and poetic power.

The first scholarly evaluation of the play, like that of *Der fröhliche Weinberg*, was a textimmanent reading concerned primarily with genre and aesthetic form. It is interesting to note that most of the scholarly assessments presented arguments similar to those of the initial reviews. Thus Wolfgang Teelen (1952) points out that, in contrast to the situation comedy *Der fröhliche Weinberg*, Zuckmayer wanted in this play to bring the character of a folk hero on stage within the context of a full story. Yet instead of portraying Schinderhannes as an individual, Zuckmayer endowed him with epic qualities and "colors" (128). As a result, the play presents not the conflict between society and Schinderhannes but solely a flat characterization of a man who tries to remain faithful to himself in spite of adverse conditions.

In his similar investigation J. Vandenrath (1960) sees two happenings in *Schinderhannes*: a demand for social justice and the unfolding of a unique individual. It is based on a dramatic situation: a man clashes with the social order of his time. But, as Wilfried Adling (1959) also points out, Zuckmayer focuses not on criticism of social injustice but on the strength of Schinderhannes. The play is a celebration of a life that ultimately triumphs even over death. In Vandenrath's view, the play has more drama elements — in Staiger's terminology — than *Der fröhliche Weinberg*. In addition, it is important even today as Zuckmayer's contribution to the folk play form. Rudolf Lange (1969) too is primarily concerned with the question of genre, of epic versus dramatic. He stresses the ballad-like character of the play, which Zuckmayer derives from the original form of the material, the *Moritat* (broadside ballad). This source material inclines the play toward the epic rather than the dramatic.

Other interpretations concentrate on Zuckmayer's realization of a particular theme, motif, or structure. In his 1958 dissertation, Henry Glade shows that the high point of *Humanität* in the drama is the hero's encounter with his beloved Julchen when she points out to him his reckless defiance of the law of nature and the senselessness of his plan to attack the French army. In his article of 1963, he adds that the encounter motif, which is most commonly found in the union of two persons, inevitably leads to the recognition of a higher mode of existence. The essence of the drama is therefore not in the conflict between characters but in what takes place when the two primary characters come together. As is evident in Schinderhannes, the encounter motif "precipitates the dramatic goal which the hero or heroine tends to reach at the very end of the dramas: a symbolical recognition through the encounter-phenomenon of the life-force per se" (188). Through what happens in the crucial encounter, "the individual's potentials are quickened to an attainment of a sense of belonging, a trust-in-life and a metaphysical knowledge of wholeness" (189). Glade's idea of the importance of the encounter motif was taken up by E. Speidel (1968) in an article in the British periodical *Modern Language Review*. Speidel cites *Schinderhannes* and *Der Hauptmann von Köpenick* to show how "the relation between individual and community, between *Einzelweg* and *Begegnung*, forms the basic structure of these plays, and how, for Zuckmayer, the stage thus becomes a metaphysical institution" (426). Speidel then interprets *Schinderhannes* as a drama of class struggle between exploiters and exploited, between whom Schinderhannes stands as someone who has rejected the standards of society. Although he denies the values of the community, he acts to impress other people and to show off his own strength and vitality. He is a loner who clashes with the world around him. The encounters between him and the community stimulate the action of the play. His function is to render the community conscious of itself and its problems. Although socialist ideas are present in this play, Schinderhannes rebels not as a revolutionary but unconsciously, simply by succumbing to his fate, to "the metaphysical forces to which man is subjected" (430). Schinderhannes's death and the triumph of the reactionary powers do not spell a victory for these forces: Schinderhannes is not fighting for a better world but simply following his calling. The play thus ends with a victory of the life force.

Helen Swediuk-Cheyne (1980) analyzes the characters of Zuckmayer's dramas through another recurrent motif: the motif of "starting
over from the beginning," which in her view is based on Zuckmayer's
positive attitude toward life and all of creation and on his premise that
the goal of all drama is the transformation not of environment but of
man's attitude. Schinderhannes is a prime example of this kind of
change. After Julchen has borne him a child, he wants to start all over
again. It is not important that he is unable to do that in this life. At the
end he finds himself and can be certain of eternal life.

There is no question that Swediuk-Cheyne's view is indebted to the
earlier dissertation of Ingeborg Engelsing-Malek (1960), who sees
Schinderhannes as a complement to *Der fröhliche Weinberg*. Whereas
Gunderloch is a man of action who finds his way back to inner harmony
with nature, *Schinderhannes* shows what happens if this harmony does
not exist. Whereas Gunderloch was merely *endangered* by hubris, hubris
is the main theme in the later play. Schinderhannes tries to fight against
individual cases of injustice, but he fails to see that he is fighting against
a general order that ultimately overcomes him. In contrast to Schinderhannes, Julchen is one of Zuckmayer's women figures with a healthy
instinct that borders on a superhuman prophetic gift. Unlike Peppard
(1952), who sees the "moment of moral decision" only in the later
dramas *Des Teufels General, Der Gesang im Feuerofen*, and *Barbara
Blomberg*, Engelsing-Malek points out that this element is present in
Zuckmayer's earlier dramas, though it is understood more subjectively
in them. Thus Schinderhannes, against Julchen's advice, takes on the
French troops, acting out of hubris. He is beaten and feels depressed,
but he returns to his true self after he has been arrested, and he dies as
the braggart he has been throughout his life. His actions originate from
an inner compulsion even against the voice of reason. His inner conflict, in terms of *amor fati*, remains unresolved in the end. In contrast
to Engelsing-Malek, Paul Meinherz (1960) fails to see that Schinderhannes undergoes an inner development from hubris to defeatism to a
life-affirming attitude. In his view, Schinderhannes always remains
faithful to himself and does not invite spectators to identify with him.
His infallibility rather reminds us of elements of the puppet play.

Literary tradition is the focus of Siegfried Sudhof (1973) and
Marvin Robert Maddox (1975). Sudhof points out that in *Schinderhannes* the tradition in which Zuckmayer writes becomes obvious: it is
that of Schiller, Hauptmann, Büchner — all names that Fechter (1927)
had mentioned in his early review. Maddox investigates in detail Zuckmayer's indebtedness to Hauptmann. In *Schinderhannes* he sees con-

firmation of both dramatists' unusual ability to capture the spirit of the German *Volk* and to reproduce their various regional dialects. The social protest in *Schinderhannes*, which culminates in a rebellion of the *Volk*, bears many characteristics of the rebellion in Hauptmann's *Die Weber* and, to a lesser extent, of *Florian Geyer* (1896). The stress is, however, on timeless individual problems rather than on social ones. Schinderhannes is not pitted against any specific foe. His personal problems are created by his intense desire for unlimited personal freedom and his struggle to remain true to his own nature even in the face of his impending execution. He has become a social outcast because he enjoys this role. Blake Lee Spahr (1992) too stresses the folk hero's dependency on Hauptmann's dramas.

Still other assessments place greater value on the political and social aspects of the drama. The Marxist Wilfried Adling (1959) praises Zuckmayer for trying to capture the situation and the mood of the lower social classes and to concentrate on them, but in his opinion he failed to use them as the basis for a realistic drama. Zuckmayer's attention is exclusively focused on the question of whether Schinderhannes remains faithful to his "miserable individualism" (76). Instead of judging in concrete terms, Zuckmayer interprets in abstract terms; he thus obscures the facts and makes Schinderhannes practice the playwright's own brand of late-bourgeois vitalistic thinking. This unrealistic glorification of a miserable character into a naive, tragic, romantic hero is irreconcilable with the concrete social elements in the depiction of the time. Robert Kafka Lehrer's (1962) sociocritical approach considers *Schinderhannes* the product of the author's first "conscious resolve to cast his social awareness into the format of the folk play" (149). Zuckmayer has chosen for his setting a period of German history that bore many similarities to the political and social conditions of the 1920s, which enables him to comment on the political, social, and economic tribulations of the Weimar Republic. The main political parallels consisted in the occupation of the Rhineland by the French, both during the Napoleonic era and following the First World War, as well as similar social grievances and the need for a strong German leadership. But, in Lehrer's opinion, Zuckmayer was not successful in accomplishing his goals. He "failed to supply reasonable motivation for his central figure, failed to provide him with a tangible opponent, failed — or was not interested — in fully documented references, other than generalities, to the specific injustices which pertained either to historical or contemporary times. As a consequence, *Schinderhannes* did not appeal to its audiences so much as a play of social criticism as it did as a charming folk play" (150–51). It achieved its popularity because of its language, its lyricism, and its minor characters — all elements of a folk play — but failed as a parable for dramaturgical reasons. Lehrer believes that Zuckmayer's friend Carlo Mierendorff, who spoke before admiring crowds in the manner of a folk hero, served as a model for the character of Schinderhannes. Since the contemporary reviewers provide little evidence of Zuckmayer's proclaimed "social awareness," one must ask whether it was present in the play in the first place.

Thomas Ayck (1977) characterizes *Schinderhannes* as a ballad about a social revolutionary, a fighter for social justice and national liberty, a German Robin Hood who wants to introduce an order in which wealth and power are more equitably distributed. It appears almost as an afterthought when Ayck, like Lehrer (1962), concludes that in spite of its sociocritical accusations, the drama does not give a basic analysis of historical conditions but concentrates on the vital character of Schinderhannes, who is fighting for good against evil. Toward the end of the drama Zuckmayer increasingly loses sight of the social aspects. Since the social and economic experiences become secondary, Zuckmayer thus rejects the definition of man as a historical being. Because of his concentration on the question of social criticism versus the vitality of the title character, Ayck totally ignores Schinderhannes's inner conflict and character change.

In contrast to Ayck, Siegfried Mews (1981a), like Adling (1959) and Lehrer (1962), negatively critiques the treatment of political and sociocritical aspects. He points out that Zuckmayer rejected two allegedly prominent traits of Schinderhannes: his enmity toward the French and his anti-Semitism. "At the same time, he did not endorse the cause of the separatists and thus displayed a conciliatory attitude toward the enemy whom he had fought in World War I" (41). Like Lehrer (1962), Mews draws attention to *Schinderhannes's* failure to communicate its author's increasing social awareness, particularly in the hero's conversation with Julchen. In his actions, Schinderhannes is not primarily motivated by social compassion. Rather, his role "must be ultimately interpreted in a metaphysical context" (43). Mews thus also treats ideas Speidel (1968) had expressed before him.

Two studies have focused on the women figures of *Schinderhannes*, particularly Julchen Blasius. In the opinion of Ausma Balinkin (1976) Zuckmayer portrays her as having no life of her own without Schinderhannes. Her "completely integrated personality" (29) acts as a counterforce to his violently rebellious nature. Sonja Czech (1985) discusses Julchen under the heading of "Die Frau in der Rolle der Gefährtin"

(The Woman in the Role of a Comrade), a role that in her view automatically entails a reduction of Julchen's personality, since her existence
is restricted to that of a complementary character and her aspirations are
not directed toward the development of self-realization in the modern
sense. Julchen bears certain similarities to the women in *Der fröhliche
Weinberg*: she is subject to the hero's sphere of influence and has a
complementary existence. The reason for the different weight accorded
to the male and the female protagonists is Zuckmayer's strong interest
in Schinderhannes, who from the first scene is characterized as an arrogant show-off. Thus all Julchen can be is the dependent comrade who
provides emotional support. In Julchen's intuitive decision to stay with
Schinderhannes and her failure to contemplate the practical social and
legal implications of being left behind pregnant, Zuckmayer again ro-
manticizes intuitive forces. Julchen accepts her fate at the side of her
beloved man even during the evening prior to Schinderhannes's execution.

Katharina Knie

Zuckmayer's next folk play, *Katharina Knie*, was first performed on 20
December 1928 in Berlin's Lessing-Theater, with Elisabeth Lennartz in
the title role and the famous Albert Bassermann as Father Knie. In spite
of, or maybe because of, the play's strong sentimental bent, it was, like
Schinderhannes, a smashing success with the audience but not with the
critics. Paul Fechter (1928) praises the first two acts as among Zuckmayer's best to date because of the atmosphere they depict, but he
criticizes the undramatic elements of the play's structure, its epic qualities that, in the second part, dangerously change into the lyrical. Alfred
Kerr (1928) calls it a pretty genre painting of the home region but
notes that it fails to depict contemporary issues; the play could have
taken place fifty years earlier. In several sentimental scenes, he states,
Zuckmayer is close to kitsch.

This criticism permeated most later interpretations. In Arnold
Bauer's (1970) view, the characters and their conflicts are far too ro-
manticized; Zuckmayer sees the world of the traveling show people
through the eyes of a boy. Hans Wagener (1983a) believes that the
conflict of the play is covered up by the sentimentalized milieu and the
idealized depiction of Father Knie.

The scholarly discussion of the play concentrates either on form (in
most cases from a textimmanent perspective) or on content. In the latter case, the interpreters focus either on Katharina's decision between
two worlds (the itinerant world of the tightrope walkers and the seden-

tary world of the farmers) or on the problems of social and economic change: the decline of the old-fashioned circus entertainers in face of the inflation of 1923 and the emergence of new entertainment industries such as radio and film.

Scholarly discussion of the play's form occurs first in Wolfgang Teelen's dissertation of 1952. According to Teelen, *Katharina Knie* hardly constitutes progress in Zuckmayer's work. Zuckmayer now clearly pursues dramatic goals, but not effectively. The characters remain portraits who act not to demonstrate character developments but to make their own and others' movements and circumstances visible. Katharina's conflict between love and the group of tightrope walkers, which Fechter (1928) had already identified as the play's most important conflict, is almost covered up by descriptions of milieu and specific situations. The weakness of the play is that the character of the farmer Rothacker is so conventional that it is difficult to imagine how Katharina feels such a close bond to him. It is therefore not surprising that at the end she stays with the performers. Teelen stresses that Zuckmayer's original intention is not a skillfully arranged plot or far-reaching conflicts. He thus continues his discussion of Zuckmayer's plays in terms of the prevalence of lyric, epic, and dramatic qualities.

Arguing along Teelen's lines, J. Vandenrath (1960) notices an increased importance of dramatic elements in *Katharina Knie*. He sees this importance as the logical consequence of the play's dramatic conflict, Katharina's decision, which is not just between father and fiancé but between two different forms of life: the wandering circus artists and the sedentary farmers. After the father's death, an ethical conflict is added: duty versus inclination. Realism, humor, and sentimentality are combined in this play even more fully than they are in *Schinderhannes*.

In contrast to Teelen and Vandenrath, Paul Meinherz (1960) perceives in this play a renunciation of dramatic effects, a predominantly epic character. This is confirmed by Rothacker's mother's appearance as his representative in the final act. The epic quality is enhanced by her late introduction shortly before the end of the drama. The focus is not on dramatic dialogues but on reflective monologues, on Father Knie's memories, and on eulogies on the art of tightrope walking. Meinherz anticipates Lehrer's (1962) main point, that Father Knie's fight for his life is at the same time a fight for his art.

Ingeborg Engelsing-Malek (1960) continues the genre discussion as well as the characterization of the main conflict as one between inclination and duty. For her the drama is an undramatic psychological character study of Katharina, who lacks the quiet self-confidence of

Annemarie and Julchen. She is torn between two feelings, favoring both the vagrant life of the circus artists, as personified by her father, and the sedentary life of the farmer, as personified by Rothacker. She does not make a pact with reason, as Gunderloch does, but ultimately she goes where she feels she is needed more, sacrificing her inclination for her duty and thus accepting her fate in brave resignation. Along the same lines, Rudolf Lange (1969) pronounces that Katharina's final decision to continue her father's work makes the play an *Entwicklungsdrama* (developmental drama) in terms of German classicism, with its ideal of self-realization. Katharina has found her personal destiny and her obligation toward society.

Arnold John Jacobius (1955) adds a new twist to the discussion of the main dramatic conflict, seeing it as one between inner and more objective values and thus introducing a series of interpretations concerned with meaning rather than form. He distinguishes between two forms of *Heimat* that are opposed in *Katharina Knie*: the exterior, biological, local *Heimat* of the Palatinate and the inner *Heimat* of the mind, the *Heimat* of art. In this case it is the *Heimat* of the acrobats that is endangered by progress and changing tastes. In this respect art and *Heimat* are synonymous. Jacobius's views are not far from those of Alfred Happ (1956) in *Fülle der Zeit* who discusses the play as "poetic theater." Like Jacobius, he perceives a dichotomy by identifying the acrobat's migrant life as an existence in the service of art. He points out that the play does not just paint colorful scenes of the artists' life but derives its actual tension from the old conflict between staying put and migrating, between the nourishing existence of the farmer and a self-sacrificing life in the service of "art." Henry Glade (1958) goes another step further by raising this conflict to a metaphysical level. He suggests that, in *Katharina Knie*, Zuckmayer has introduced the dichotomy of fate and freedom. Katharina must "fulfill her destiny by belonging to the greater whole or by bringing her life into harmony with the transcendental pattern. Therein resides freedom" (17). In his article of 1963 he similarly sees in the play "a first indication of the later and more explicitly stated view of an inescapable event which links man to the larger unitary pattern, comprising all existences" (184).

Other critics ignored such lofty possibilities, concentrating solely on the here and now of economic realities. The first to focus on the economic developments of the early 1920s and their implications for plot development was the GDR critic Wilfried Adling (1959). In his opinion, Zuckmayer failed to interpret the situation of the Knie enterprise in terms of capitalist production during the Weimar Republic and thus created a drama that ends in a utopia. Knie's anachronistic enterprise cannot be saved by the energy of an individual; it can at best be held together for a short while before it falls victim to the laws of the capitalist order. By glorifying the world of the Knie troupe as connected to free, organic life, Zuckmayer defends a late-bourgeois vitalistic romanticism, in Adling's view. Vandenrath (1960) had said in Zuckmayer's defense that the play's sentimentality does have a place in a folk play. Thus this minor point alone demonstrates the different conclusions that can be reached by a sympathetic, textimmanent interpretation and a Marxist one that tries to find fault with a bourgeois author.

Martin Greiner (1958) had already come to the conclusion that the play should rather be be called "Father Knie" because Katharina's story is actually only an appendix to the fate of the grand old man and his faithfulness to art and trust in life in spite of the decline of his profession. Continuing this train of thought, Robert Kafka Lehrer (1962) regards Katharina's defection from the troupe as symbolic of the defection of Knie's audiences, who are forced to find cheaper means of entertainment because of economic necessity. Katharina's dilemma becomes subordinate to Zuckmayer's main theme: the decline of the old folk art of funambulism as a result of economic problems and changes in public taste and the place and pride of the artist of a dying profession, symbolically revealed in the tragedy of Father Knie. Zuckmayer intended his drama as a paean and final tribute.

Two studies are devoted to the play's women figures. For Ausma Balinkin (1976), the heroine Katharina Knie signals the beginning of a new phase in Zuckmayer's characterization of women including figures in *Ulla Winblad, Barbara Blomberg, Der Schelm von Bergen,* and *Des Teufels General.* In these dramas the women, while still vigorous, resilient, and energetic, "reflect more and more the writer's own nonconformist views with regard to such issues as religion, pompous authority, social conventions, and power" (31). The central women figures of this period are conspicuous for their deficient insight, as the male characters had been previously. They are self-centered and make erroneous, egocentric decisions. Through an initial lack of instinctive perception of their roles in life, they commit errors in judgment as they search for their predestined place or pursue personal happiness. Balinkin thus applies the *amor fati* concept, first applied to Zuckmayer by Engelsing-Malek (1960), to the central women characters. She sees Katharina Knie as "the first of Zuckmayer's realistic women figures undergoing a maturation process, in which she realizes that the individual does not lead an isolated existence" (33).

In her M.A. thesis on Zuckmayer's women figures, Gabriele Lindner (1986) interprets Katharina's doubts about her wishes and goals as a postpubescent developmental stage, pointing out that Zuckmayer's heroines rarely show inner disintegration. In accordance with Engelsing-Malek's (1960) concept of *amor fati*, which ultimately becomes the underlying principle for her decision, Katharina's conflict consists in her inability to accept her fate and her desperate search for a point of gravity. Rothacker's mother, a mother figure for Katharina too, facilitates her decision and opens up the way for her to go back to her father. She and the earthy cashier Bibbo serve to familiarize her with the principle of *amor fati*. The example of Katharina Knie shows what happens when insight into this principle is lacking. For her father, Katharina is still an object whose function it is to bear many children, to enlarge and perpetuate the family business. Her initial passivity and resignation are traditional qualities of women, like a willingness to make sacrifices and to show devotion. These qualities that are expected of women increase their general conflict between duty and desire, between self-determination and acceptance of a predetermined fate. Like the new, modern type of woman that had become popular in the Berlin of the 1920s, Katharina thus does not correspond to the bourgeois expectations of the woman as a homemaker but displays modern behaviors, such as making an independent choice of a marriage partner and — although this is not shown explicitly — living with him first in a kind of trial marriage. Thus Lindner's line of argumentation, although still text-immanent in her approach, succeeds in elucidating aspects of Katharina's character and development that had escaped earlier interpreters.

The French study by Marie-Odile Blum (1993) uses a more modern critical approach that may be termed interdisciplinary. Blum quotes from the works of psychologists and philosophers to characterize Zuckmayer's personal philosophy and to show his deep understanding of the world of the funambulists. She characterizes it in terms of "the risk and the game" (261) and "the habit and the experience" (263). In her opinion, *Katharina Knie* is a drama about the circus world, not about father fixation or the choice between a vagrant and a sedentary life. In writing about the funambulists, Zuckmayer adhered to the medieval idea of the human life as a permanent spectacle.

Der Hauptmann von Köpenick

Zuckmayer's greatest and most lasting success was *Der Hauptmann von Köpenick* (1931). In the view of all modern critics, this is the author's best play, and it is one of the few successful German comedies ever. The play premiered on 5 March 1931 at the Deutsches Theater, Berlin, under Heinz Hilpert's direction. Werner Krauss played Wilhelm Voigt. It has, not surprisingly, received more critical attention than any other Zuckmayer drama, but since it came out only a few years before Hitler's rise to power (from 1933 on it was not permitted to be performed) there was no scholarly response to it until after the Second World War. Therefore, as in the case of *Schinderhannes* and *Katharina Knie*, reviews of the first performance must be considered. Later, in *Als wär's ein Stück von mir*, Zuckmayer pointed out that it was meant to be a highly political drama; it was indeed already considered such at its first performance. In Herbert Ihering's (1931) review, for example, it is pointed out that Germany was laughing on the political right and on the left. In Ihering's judgment, the humor is rooted in the use of dialect, but the play lacks a firm point of view, a Weltanschauung from which the events are presented. Consequently, it remains unclear whether the drama is to be viewed as a farce about the military, as lighthearted social criticism, or as a satire. Bernhard Diebold (1931) stated that Zuckmayer had written not only the fable about the false captain but also the countermyth, the tragedy of the real captain in civilian clothes and the history of the uniform itself. In his opinion, the characters are not well-rounded beings but types. Zuckmayer's satire does not attack people; he sees only victims of a system and mocks only circumstances. These views would be restated in several scholarly interpretations after the Second World War.

Since the Nazi era demonstrated again the German respect for uniforms, the play not only returned to popularity after the Second World War; it also became mandatory reading in secondary schools. As a result, commentaries and interpretations came out, designed to aid teachers and/or students. Paul Riegel's 1960 interpretation is directed toward secondary school teachers. Riegel sees Zuckmayer's dramatic theory in contrast to Brecht's, whose "Anmerkungen zur Oper Aufstieg und Fall der Stadt Mahagonny" (Remarks on the Opera *Rise and Fall of the Town of Mahagonny*) — his program for an epic theater — was published in the same year Zuckmayer's "German fairy tale," *Der Hauptmann von Köpenick*, premiered. Riegel recommends that secondary teachers use Zuckmayer's drama as a picture of the time it depicts, the Wilhelminian Empire before the First World War, as interpreted by its author. According to him, Zuckmayer has condensed actual events and shed light on the historical background. He acts not as a polemic satirist but as a reasonable observer who does not pass judgment on his people. Riegel also gives concrete hints on how to introduce the text to students in the upper classes of the German Gymnasium. The language of the characters shows that they appear as representatives of certain social classes and types, often suffering a resulting loss of individuality. When Riegel pronounces that his intention is to show how Zuckmayer has depicted the character of the era before the First World War and its people by means of their language, he seems to step back again from his earlier intention of making history come alive and falls back into the then fashionable textimmanent methodology. With its primary concern for form and language and its neglect of political and social implications, Riegel's interpretation shows the characteristic shortcomings of this approach.

Wolfgang Butzlaff's pedagogical article of 1964 follows the same methodological approach. Proclaiming a "key word method" for the interpretation of literature, he interprets Zuckmayer's drama by pointing out the use of key words such as *Mensch* and *menschlich*, *Ordnung* and *ordentlich*. In this case these words do suffice to characterize the most important figures in the play.

Commentaries that are specifically designed for use by students and/or teachers are not included here as they do not contain new scholarly insights. The following two general interpretations, though written specifically for use by pedagogues and students, are an exception. The first one is Werner Frizen's 1986 interpretation, which appeared in the series Oldenbourg Interpretationen. It constitutes the most detailed and comprehensive interpretation of the play available to date. Although it is clearly directed at teachers of secondary schools and thus contains detailed suggestions on how to deal with the play in the classroom, it satisfies all scholarly demands. A detailed discussion of the structure of the play is supplemented by graphs. Particular stress is placed on the historical Voigt and on a comparison of his account and Zuckmayer's version. An interpretation of the language used by Zuckmayer's characters is found nowhere else in such minute detail. Yet in spite of its scholarly acumen, Frizen's terminology betrays its origin: a leftist view that was characteristic of representatives of the 1968 student revolt. Thus Emperor William II is depicted as a confidence man on the throne and Mayor Obermüller as a caricature of the adaptive behavior of the high civil servants to the *Ungeist*. There is talk of *Klassenjustiz* (class justice) and the *Sprache der Herrschenden* (language of the ruling classes; 82), revealing a Marxist line of thinking. Thus the Wilhelminian era appears in Frizen's description a lot worse than it does in Zuckmayer's play where conciliatory, idyllic features are included. Nevertheless, no scholarly treatment of the drama can ignore this exacting interpretation.

Hans Wagener's 1988 interpretation of the play, which largely follows that of his Zuckmayer monograph of 1983, is politically neutral in spirit. In accordance with the editorial guidelines for the essays of the volume in which it appeared, the article treats the origin and writing of the play as well as its place in literary history. It also considers structure and genre, message (*Mensch* and *Menschenordnung*), and reception. Like the other essays of the volume, the interpretation is aimed at the university student and secondary school teacher.

Some literary historians placed the play in various traditions and identified its parallels to works by other German authors. E. Speidel (1968) feels that the contrast between Voigt's humaneness and the abstractness of the rest of society is similar to the one between Büchner's title character in *Woyzeck* (published anonymously in 1879) and the unfeeling people surrounding him. But whereas in Woyzeck's case this realization leads to his increasing isolation and loneliness, Voigt derives courage from it that results in his salvation. Rudolf Koester (1970) places Zuckmayer's play in the context and tradition of the German comedy, namely Kleist's *Der zerbrochene Krug* (*The Broken Jug*, 1811) and Hauptmanns *Der Biberpelz* (*The Beaver Coat*, 1893), each of which features a lawbreaker as its main character and a breach of the law that generates all the action and conflict. By comparing the heroes of the three plays, Koester comes to the conclusion that there is an increasing humanization of the criminal in German literature since the eighteenth century, a fading in the belief that their offenses show moral turpitude, "in inverse ratio to the legal gravity of their crimes" (378). In all three comedies, a subversion of justice is promoted by certain custodians of the law who become increasingly loathsome. Whereas in Kleist's drama justice is restored at the end by a representative of the state, in Hauptmann's and Zuckmayer's dramas, the world remains in its unjust state. The social context accounts for the different treatment of the criminal's problems in society. In contrast to the limited focus of Kleist and Hauptmann, Zuckmayer portrays a kind of injustice that is "an inevitable by-product of a mentality which pervades the whole society" (384). His criminal hero is characterized by extraordinarily positive humanity and a sense of fair play. Having evolved into a champion of human dignity and justice, he has the true and just perspective on the world and thus assumes the function of Gerichtsrat Walter in Kleist's comedy. Koester sees an evolution of the criminal in the German comedy "from a deviate individual in a justice-seeking society to a justice-seeking individual in a deviate society" (388). His study is of interest not so much because it traces a development of questionable logic; rather, it is the only one that places Zuckmayer's drama in the history of German comedy.

After stating that *Der Hauptmann von Köpenick* is the most ingenious drama Zuckmayer has written, Siegfried Sudhof (1973) praises the historical ambivalence of the play that it shares with Heinrich Mann's *Der Untertan* (*The Patrioteer*, or *Little Superman*, 1918). In contrast to Wilhelm Schäfer's novel about the captain, an important element of Zuckmayer's play is the combination of the historical with the general, the personal with the factual. Furthermore, Zuckmayer has added a moral component that was not entirely missing in the earlier plays but that is of prime importance in this one: he is concerned with man's responsibility toward a higher law, his connection with a higher order. This adds a new, deeper dimension to his drama. As a result, it becomes an accusation against suppression, a defense of humane behavior in general. Finally, Jürgen Hein (1977) sees the play in the tradition of the folk play as we know it from Marieluise Fleißer and Ödön von Horváth, allowing for the combination of heterogeneous elements.

William Grange's (1991) study of the collaboration between Zuckmayer and the director Heinz Hilpert is also historically and factually oriented. In Grange's view, the published version of *Der Hauptmann von Köpenick* was the result of their collaborative effort. Trying to create the illusion of real human life on stage, as Otto Brahm had wanted to do many years before, Hilpert cut Zuckmayer's script extensively, according to Grange, and "formed it from an inchoate collection of scenes . . . into something performable . . . . The changes Hilpert made later appeared in the published versions of the play and indicate that Zuckmayer was in agreement" (88).

The scholarly discourse of the 1950s and early 1960s is characterized by the textimmanent approach with its primary concern about generic form. Thus in Wolfgang Teelen's opinion (1952), *Der Hauptmann von Köpenick* is not a drama but rather the high point of Zuckmayer's character portraits. There is no dramatic tension that leads to a final resolution. Only the "road" is important: the playwright establishes Voigt's portrait by presenting the stations of this road and the final scene, which for Teelen resembles a picture. Next to this series of stations portraying Voigt, the portrait of the uniform evolves in a similar series. The people who become visible in these stations are important for the moment only. The basic concept of the play is epic. Teelen sees the work not as a social critique but as the strange, sad, sympathetic story of an oddball. The most important quality of the play is humor.

Using the same Staigerian concern and generic grid as a point of departure, as Teelen does, Paul Meinherz (1960) sees in Zuckmayer's shaping of his historical material a renunciation of the dramatic as such. In his view, the playwright did not depict the conditions in the German Reich but showed Wilhelm Voigt as a human being. The unity of the play lies not in the observation of the three classical unities, in his opinion, but in the unity of the central character. The play is entirely epic, with scene after scene strung together as independent parts. Unlike Riegel (1960), Meinherz believes that the play fulfills the criteria of Brecht's epic theater despite its outward dramatic form. Since Zuckmayer does not employ an artificial alienation effect, he is able to linger between play and reality, fairy tale and satire. *Der Hauptmann von Köpenick* was Zuckmayer's best character portrayal, but the character depicted does not have a relationship with his environment. The portrait has been placed, so to speak, into a frame, and consequently it endangers the drama. The other figures of the play serve only to characterize Voigt.

At first glance J. Vandenrath (1960), also part of the textimmanent school, seems to be addressing the question of the social message, but he comes to conclusions similar to those of Teelen and Meinherz. He states that Zuckmayer has now finally left the Rhineland and spiritually conquered Berlin. As in *Schinderhannes*, here a man is pitted against the society of his time; Zuckmayer shows how "genuine" life defends itself against the inhumanity of the power institutions of artificial people. The depiction of the history of the uniform and of the coup in Köpenick, and the rendition of a social picture of the entire Wilhelminian state are all strong dramatic ("theater") elements of the play. Zuckmayer's sympathy and compassion are clearly on the side of the genuine people: Voigt, Wabschke, the sick girl, and Voigt's sister. Zuckmayer defends the humaneness of the poor and the weak against an almighty state. He satirizes the representatives of the Wilhelminian state but limits his attack by immersing the entire play in an atmosphere of humor. The ending exposes the military state to ridicule. In Vandenrath's opinion, the play represents the high point of Zuckmayer's characterization of people by means of their language.

In several other textimmanent interpretations, the play's message and key concepts clearly assume importance over its form. The question of *Humanität* in the drama was taken up by Henry Glade in 1958. He points out that in *Der Hauptmann von Köpenick* "the concept of *Hu-*

manität . . . pivots basically on the distinction between a human and divine order. The human order within the historical context is revealed as violating Zuckmayer's natural law, due to its inhuman fixities and absurdities" (22). Voigt rebels from the noblest motives of *Humanität*, which Glade equates with the divine order. In his article of 1963, Glade combines this view with his theory of the importance of encounter in Zuckmayer's works and arrives at the conclusion that "Voigt's encounter with the tubercular seamstress on the threshold of death provides the turning point of this drama. For it is only through this encounter in purest humanity that Voigt subsequently is receptive to the discovery of divine authority through his inner voice — an encounter which leads to the recognition of the ultimate law of life as man's responsibility to God in terms of fullest self-realization" (184).

Dealing with Zuckmayer as the author of folk plays, Martin Greiner (1958) sees *Der Hauptmann von Köpenick* as a German fairy tale, true to its subtitle, in which a man sets out to find his *Heimat*. At the same time it is a fairy tale about the force of the uniform that maintains its magic even in the state of misery and humiliation, giving its wearer power over the hearts and minds of man. The play marks the high point of Zuckmayer's development as a dramatist. From now on his creativity shifts to the *Zeitstück*.

Glade's interpretation is not far from that of Ingeborg Engelsing-Malek (1960), who incorporates the question of man's relation to God in her *amor fati* model. Agreeing with most other interpreters, she sees the problem of the play in the fight of the human beings against the letter of the law. Voigt conducts this fight without any allies, as an individual against the prevailing order, without vengeance and viciousness, following the inner voice that makes him responsible for his life. As is typical in Zuckmayer's works, *amor fati* is in the center of the play. The hero becomes conscious of it through his inner voice. *Amor fati* becomes identical with *amor dei*; the inner voice communicates God's will. Following Greiner's lead, Engelsing-Malek interprets the story as a fairy tale. As in a fairy tale, the fate of one person determines the epic content of the play, which assumes a dramatic character in a few scenes only. Thus, on the matter of form, Engelsing-Malek adheres to Teelen's (1952) views.

Greiner's and Engelsing-Malek's fairy-tale interpretations of the drama were taken up and questioned by a number of scholars. Rudolf Lange (1969), for example, believes that Zuckmayer uses the term ironically. Thomas Ayck (1977) agrees. For him, Zuckmayer reached a high point with *Der Hauptmann von Köpenick* in combining *Zeitstück* and folk play. But although the term *Märchen* (fairy tale) in the subtitle must be understood ironically, it also characterizes an apolitical German's view of history. Moreover, the fairy-tale structure is a basic element of Zuckmayer's folk plays, which are characterized by the clear separation of good and evil, the temporary disturbance of the human order, and dealings with miraculous powers (Zuckmayer calls them life, love, nature, and God) that are not questioned by the main character. Ayck believes that Engelsing-Malek's interpretation of the play overlooks the tension between fairy tale and sociopolitical reality. Ayck sees this tension as the center of the satirical play and suggests that, with this comedy, Zuckmayer has succeeded in writing one of the great dramas of parodistic, sociocritical literature.

In an article published in 1972, Mews (1972) also takes up Engelsing-Malek's interpretation. He points out that while the play belongs to the tradition of German fairy-tale dramas, it is based on a documented historical event and thus fits neither category. The timeless elements lend the drama a dimension of universal validity that Mews sees, for example, in the proverb "Kleider machen Leute" (The tailor makes the man). Apart from its concrete function of indicating the wearer's rank in the military order, the uniform has almost magical attributes, again suggesting the fairy tale.

Jürgen Hein (1977), on the other hand, believes that the play goes far beyond a fairy tale, that the fairy-tale mold is fractured, indicating the historical reality of the Wilhelminian era, in which it originates. Hein also points out the ambiguity of the play. On the one hand, it is the critical rendition of a historical case; on the other it is the illumination of a Prussian idyll. It also allows the transferral of meaning to similar cases in history, like the anecdote. (The play can thus be called a dramatic anecdote.) Hein thus accepts and combines all the preceding interpretations.

As far as structure is concerned, the play has a pronounced cinematic quality. The character constellations correspond to the basic dramatic principles of contrastive, additive, and differentiating. The dialect becomes a metaphor for Prussia and at the same time allows for a differentiation of the characters according to rank and social standing. Language reveals the characters, particularly Wormser. The history of the play's reception — two years after its first performance it was banned by the National Socialists — proves that its political and sociocritical aspects were not eclipsed by trivial theatrical effects. Hein concludes that the play cannot be one-sidedly interpreted as either humanistic or political. Although he critically reviews the most common and plausible interpretations, he ends by adding his own idea: *Der Hauptmann von Köpenick* is to be seen as a dramatic anecdote.

The most recent critic to stress the fairy-tale character of the play is Helen Swediuk-Cheyne (1980). She points to the importance of the theme of starting over, which is contained in a quote from the Grimms' fairy tale "The Bremen Town Musicians" in which a rooster urges others to follow him and his friends because "something better than death we will find everywhere." For Wilhelm Voigt it marks the beginning of the insight that man has to master his life by using his inner powers.

Engelsing-Malek (1960) addresses the question of the play's sociocritical and political significance, an issue that became the focal point of a number of subsequent interpretations. She accepts Zuckmayer's own statement in *Als wär's ein Stück von mir* that he wrote the play as a warning following the National Socialists' victory in the September elections of 1930. She comes to the conclusion that Zuckmayer does not ignore social problems but tries to present them without tendentiousness, taking away their pungency with a conciliatory ending. The question of the play's social significance is Robert Kafka Lehrer's (1962) primary concern. He regards *Der Hauptmann von Köpenick* as "the culmination in Zuckmayer's attempt to express his awareness of social conditions through the medium of the folk drama" (246). His main purpose was to satirize German militarism, authoritarianism, nationalism, and the evils of bureaucracy in general. Voigt's tragedy is the tragedy of an individual "for whom it is made impossible to become a law-abiding citizen (his greatest desire) in the country of his birth" (265).

The German-American Germanist Wolfgang Paulsen (1967) agrees that the play's problematic and moving element is the homeless man without a passport. But in his opinion, the political aspects are the weakest part of the play, and they remain at its margin. Wilhelm Voigt is attractive to the audience as a human being and because he is so obviously stronger than any of the other characters. We resist the fact that someone so valuable can be mechanically ground up by society. The dramatic tension thus results from the aesthetic structure of the play, not from the political issue.

During the 1960s, the emphasis in scholarly discourse shifted back and forth between the social and political aspects of the play and the aesthetic ones. E. Speidel (1968) lays greater stress on the sociocritical. For him *Der Hauptmann von Köpenick* shows the same division in society as *Schinderhannes*, except that here social weaknesses are revealed only to the audience and not to Voigt's fellows in the drama. Instead of

the division between rich and poor, here society is divided into those
who are part of or respect the army and its ranks and those who are social outcasts. In contrast to Schinderhannes, however, Voigt, an outcast
because of his violation of the law, desperately tries to conform to accepted standards of society. He fights for his rights, and as in *Schinderhannes*, the encounters between the protagonist and society fuel the
action. The events of *Der Hauptmann von Köpenick* can all be reduced
to an abstract principle, the ideas of *Pflicht* and *Ordnung* (duty and order) — a reduction that, according to Zuckmayer's *Pro domo*, is an
eminently German quality. These concepts, however, are taken so absolutely that they endanger the fullness of human existence. In contrast to
all the other characters of the play, Voigt is concerned only with simple
and concrete matters, thus embodying the "unity of all living things"
(434) that Zuckmayer demands. Voigt sees the unity of everything living; he "feels his own existence to be part of a universal life-force"
(434). The juxtaposition of the individual and the whole is thus the
cornerstone of Zuckmayer's dramatic art. Speidel's article is distin-
guished from many others by its interpretation of the dramas through
Zuckmayer's essayistic statements, such as *Pro domo* and *Die langen
Wege*.

For Arnold Bauer (1970), *Der Hauptmann von Köpenick* is a mas-
terpiece of parodistic and sociocritical literature and perhaps even a pre-
figuration of theater of the absurd. Siegfried Mews (1981a) is more
critical of Zuckmayer's attempt at social criticism. In his opinion, the
satire of the Wilhelminian military and bureaucratic establishment is
blunted by the final reconciliation. "Second, in the final analysis it is not
men acting in a clearly definable context who are responsible for the
injustices that are committed in the name of law and order but rather
the irrational, almost magical powers emanating from the uniform"
(50). Zuckmayer's conciliatory and subtle approach is evident everywhere. In being directed not against specific social institutions or individuals — we are reminded of Bernhard Diebold's 1931 review —
functioning in a social context but rather against underlying ideas and
assumptions, the play "constitutes 'metaphysical' theater rather than
'littérature engagée' " (52). Blake Lee Spahr (1992) sees the sociocritical intent of the play in the allegorical proportions the uniform pro-
gressively assumes: "The progress of this symbol . . . reflects the fate of
German militarism" (463).

Leftist critics view the work differently. In a review of the later play
Des Teufels General, the Marxist critic Paul Rilla (1950) also addresses
Der Hauptmann von Köpenick, seeing the dramatic annihilation of the

protagonist in both plays as a dubious matter. *Der Hauptmann von Köpenick* is not a satirical picture of the times but the illumination of the Prussian idyll. Zuckmayer is not a satirist, and consequently he misses the point, distributing light and shadow too evenly and thereby doing injustice to the subject matter. Zuckmayer is politically ignorant in this view. Similarly, Wilfried Adling (1959) writes that Zuckmayer's critical depiction fails to probe the depth of the historical and political problems inherent in his subject matter. His positive depiction of Schlettow and Obermüller makes us forget the dangerous political roles the arrogant, militaristic Prussian nobility and the postrevolutionary liberal, bourgeois compromisers have historically played. Zuckmayer is too concerned about the façade of the Wilhelminian era and neglects to focus on the so-called ideals of the nobility and the liberal bourgeoisie. Instead of depicting the uniform as part of the imperialistic militarization, Zuckmayer isolates it and makes it the main problem. Neglecting to depict the social forces that have brought about the fetish uniform, Zuckmayer becomes a victim of the very fetishism he wants to fight. Voigt's role in objectively serving the Wilhelminian system is less important than his worldview. Wolfgang Karalus (1989) tries to see the historical Wilhelm Voigt as a victim of the Wilhelminian society he interprets from a Marxist point of view. For him the literary subject matter has class character; Voigt is a representative of the *Lumpenproletariat* (proletariat in rags; 839). Zuckmayer has not only unmasked the almightiness of the uniform but — albeit unintentionally — glorified it. Karalus thus merely echoes Rilla's 1950 verdict.

But not all Marxist critics took such a negative view of the drama. Werner Lüder (1987) remarks that Zuckmayer tries to draw attention to the dangers threatening the Weimar Republic — a blind trust in a rigid bureaucracy and the latent danger of militarization and "fascistization." Irony and satire are employed much more here than in *Der fröhliche Weinberg* to develop characters out of their social determination. But since Zuckmayer does not analyze the social forces that are pushing toward fascism, his warning remains intuitive. As a result, the drama ends with a conciliatory break from its basic premise as satire.

Rainer Zimmermann's 1989 attempt at a new interpretation is in a group by itself. For him *Der Hauptmann von Köpenick* is a typical drama of the 1930s. Zimmermann sees the uniform not as an allegory of militarism, Prussianism, or the principle of authority but rather as an allegory of convention that has been rendered absolute. The play works because of the tension between the two allegorical levels, between what the uniform actually represents and its dramatic function. There is a connection between the uniform as the representative of uniformity and the conventionality of the characters' language. This interpretation helps us understand Voigt's development as "desubjectivization," "conventionalization," and adaptation, pointing to the fact that the mere means (the uniform and the passport) become independent. In Zimmermann's view, the uniform is a typical symbol for the 1930s because it illustrates the confusion of convention and meaning, of appearance and actuality. Conventional reception of the drama considered what the uniform represented on the "outside," namely militarism, Prussianism, bureaucracy, and order. Thus the symbol tends to displace its meaning. This process, Zimmermann feels, is exactly what characterizes the 1930s. He gives examples of the uniformity and conventionality of language, the loss of communication and longing for immediacy, the "instrumentalization" of speaking and the displacement of subjectivity, the dominance of the means and their latent violence, adaptation as a form of settling conflicts — all characteristic features of the 1930s. Zimmermann's ideological criticism, especially in its linguistic insights, is at the cutting edge of postmodern criticism of the 1980s. The question arises, however, whether his highly abstract considerations do not tend to argue away the obvious.

Reviews of recent productions of the play in Mainz, Berlin, and Munich collected in *Blätter der Carl-Zuckmayer-Gesellschaft* ([Anonymous] 1984) illustrate that some aspects of the play have not survived the last fifty years well: the uniform is of no great importance today, and some reviewers criticize Zuckmayer for not acknowledging the upcoming First World War (at the time of the play's action) or the threat from the Nazis (at the time of Zuckmayer's writing). These voices demand that literature be relevant and topical, thus asking of Zuckmayer the kind of political engagement that he simply was not concerned about. In the same issue of the *Blätter der Carl-Zuckmayer-Gesellschaft*, Boy Gobert, the director of the 1983 Berlin production, and Claus Engeroff (1984) talk about this staging by the Berlin Schiller-Theater. In their view, the drama deals with German history, German identity and attitude, and German failure. It would be easy to change the play to depict Voigt as an asylum-seeking Turk, Pakistani, or Chilean who despairs when faced with German bureaucracy; but making the subject topical would be a mistake. Therefore the production must stick to the specific historical time and leave the characters in that milieu. To be sure, the argument that the characters in Zuckmayer's play stand for militarism and state control is correct, but the article lacks logical argumentation and does not rise above feuilletonistic self-defense.

Adaptations

Zuckmayer's folk plays during the Weimar Republic era are supplemented by two adaptations of American literature for the German stage. His loose adaptation of Maxwell Anderson and Laurence Stalling's *What Price Glory?* (1926) under the title *Rivalen* — the German title of the American film version of 1927 — opened on 20 March 1929 in the Theater an der Königgrätzer Straße. Erwin Piscator directed the play; Fritz Kortner and Hans Albers played the leading roles.

Pauline Steiner and Horst Frenz (1947) were the first critics to deal with *Rivalen*, writing for the American periodical *German Quarterly*. These authors point out the great differences between the two versions, stating that "although Zuckmayer has written a play which closely resembles the American play in action, he has changed the spirit of the play and, to attain this, has altered the characters, language, and structure of the original" (240). Zuckmayer used the American play as a vehicle for expressing his own bitter feelings about war and militarism. In contrast to *What Price Glory?*, his adaptation reveals a tendency to reproach the military officers in the rear, the *Etappe*, and to glorify the front-line soldier who actually fought the battles. Zuckmayer thus prepared the audience for the attack on militarism that he would launch about a year later in *Der Hauptmann von Köpenick*. To achieve this goal, he changed the characters, which in the American play were individual personalities, to types, symbolic representations. He changed their language, making it much stronger than in the original version, adding exaggerations and crass jokes. He also lengthened many speeches and expanded the play by adding a prologue and a scene at the end. "This results in retarding the action and weakens the dramatic structure considerably," Steiner and Frenz decree (250). They compare the texts of the American and German plays to underpin their conclusions. Typical of the spirit of 1947 America is their surprise at the crassness of Zuckmayer's language.

Like Steiner and Frenz, J. Vandenrath (1960) sees the adaptation as an *Etappendrama* (drama of the rear). He feels that Zuckmayer was particularly attracted to the American play by its image of war, which is presented entirely from the point of view of the front-line soldier. The brutality of the fighting is contrasted with scenes featuring the generals and the headquarters. Ingeborg Engelsing-Malek (1960) agrees with

Vandenrath. She argues that Zuckmayer has used the material to convey his memories of the First World War and his view of war in general. Thus the language becomes more exuberant, the sexual element is stressed, and the character of the Jew Lipinsky is clearly emphasized.

Several critics took issue with some of Steiner and Frenz's views. J. Vandenrath (1960), for example, disputes the assertion that Zuckmayer had changed the individual personalities of the play into types. Siegfried Mews (1981a) takes issue with the assertion that "Zuckmayer had made use of the Americans' plot as a vehicle for his own feelings against militarism" (241), calling it an "overstatement." In Mews's opinion, "the atmosphere of 'war, wine and women' evokes *The Merry Vineyard*, if we disregard the element of war" (55).

Wilfried Adling (1959), here, as before, is interested not in form but in the question of the play's antiwar message. From his Marxist point of view, he criticizes the play's objectivistic glorification of crafty mercenaries and of imperialistic war, which at least engenders manly virtues, as Ernst Jünger shows in his works, too. On this point, Mews (1981a) seems to give a modified echo of Adling's ideas. Although the sincerity of Zuckmayer's antiwar sentiments is beyond question, he praises comradeship as a positive aspect of war and thus communicates a somewhat ambivalent message.

The contradictory critical assessment of the adaptation mirrors the first reviews, which are reprinted by Glauert (1977), and explains why the drama was not the smashing success the adapter may have hoped for in light of his friend Erich Maria Remarque's success with *Im Westen nichts Neues* (*All Quiet on the Western Front*, 1929).

Zuckmayer's dramatization of Ernest Hemingway's *A Farewell to Arms* (1929), under the title *Kat* (1931), premiered on 1 September 1931 under Heinz Hilpert's direction at the Deutsches Theater in Berlin. On the playbill, Zuckmayer and Hilpert appeared jointly as adapters. The question of their collaboration was treated in a 1976 article by the American Wayne Kvam. Working with a typescript copy of the German manuscript and Hilpert's original production book, Kvam concludes that Hilpert "may have supplied the initial inspiration and may have aided in culling Hemingway's dialogue from the novel, but he probably made his major contributions in the capacity of director" (195). Comparing the drama to the novel, act by act, Kvam finds that Zuckmayer and Hilpert injected humor, melodrama, and occasional sentimentality into their dramatization while retaining the antiwar message and tragic outcome of the novel. Hemingway's stylistic trade-

marks, however, especially in his descriptive prose, are sorely missing in
Kat.

In Kvam's opinion, Zuckmayer dramatized Hemingway's novel because he and Hemingway had had similar experiences during the First
World War and had responded to the war in similar ways. They wrote
in a similar style: Kvam notes that "the concrete factuality and rapid,
colloquial dialogue in Hemingway's novel are also distinctive qualities
in Zuckmayer's dramas" (200). Kvam sees another similarity between
the works of the two men: in *A Farewell to Arms, Schinderhannes,
Katharina Knie,* and *Der Hauptmann von Köpenick* an outsider determined to defend his integrity is pitted against a system designed to
destroy it. In both authors' works, healing love is a moving force. Kvam
offers a possible explanation for the adaptation. There was at the time a
renewed interest in the war play, prompted by novels about the war,
and Zuckmayer combined elements of their form with the elements of
the then popular *Zeitstück,* reasonably hoping for a commercial success.
Finally, Kvam places the performance of *Kat* in the political picture of
Germany at the time: "Zuckmayer permitted Hemingway's endorsement of individual freedom to come to life on the Berlin stage at a time
when the cause of freedom was under attack as never before in Germany's history" (202). Kvam's article is thus a piece of conventional literary history and a bit of comparative literary criticism mixed with a lot
of conjecture about the reasons for the adaptation. It is the type of socially oriented criticism that had become popular in the late 1960s. In
Mews's opinion (1978) in *Carl Zuckmayer '78,* Kvam probably overes-
timates the political importance of the adaptation.

In his book on the lifelong collaboration between Zuckmayer and
Hilpert, the theater historian William Grange (1991) also takes up *Kat.*
He calls it "a blatant attempt" on the part of Zuckmayer and Hilpert to
capitalize upon their success with [*Der Hauptmann von] Köpenick*"
(37). Judging it from the standpoint of what Zuckmayer referred to in a
letter to the *Vossische Zeitung* (published on 25 August 1931) as "that
law of the theater," he comes to the conclusion that the authors failed
to create a dramatic link between the events that constitute the play:
"The through-line of action in *Kat* was not direct: the progression of
events did not create a logical causality, but seemed to wind meander-
ingly with various stop-offs along the way to its unfortunately obvious
destination" (197).

Historical Plays

Der Schelm von Bergen

Zuckmayer's first historical play, *Der Schelm von Bergen*, deals with the old Rhenish legend of the emperor's wife and an executioner's son. It premiered on 21 October 1934 at the Vienna Burgtheater under the direction of Hermann Röbbeling. At this time Zuckmayer's plays could not be performed in Germany, although at least one friendly review appeared in the *Deutsche Allgemeine Zeitung*, Berlin (See Glauert 1977, 194–95).

As in the case of earlier plays, the scholarly reception did not begin until after the Second World War, and as before, it began with the textimmanent interpreters whose foremost concern was the play's form. The first point that comes up repeatedly in this discussion is Zuckmayer's archaic language. In Wolfgang Teelen's opinion (1952), *Der Schelm von Bergen* is important primarily as an experiment with language. Similarly, Alfred Happ (1956) praises Zuckmayer's ability to endow his characters with an artificially archaic language and defends him against criticism by referring to his poetic license within the concept of "poetic theater." Ingeborg Engelsing-Malek (1960) also judges Zuckmayer's language positively. In her opinion, it takes away the embarrassing elements from the subject matter by removing them from reality and elevating them into timelessness. J. Vandenrath (1960) finds Zuckmayer's experimentation with language interesting, but in his opinion it sometimes goes too far. Nevertheless, it helps create the impression of colorfulness in the operatic character of the scenes staged as tableaus. For Wolfgang Paulsen (1967) Zuckmayer's use of language in *Der Schelm von Bergen* demonstrates the surprising range of his art. Paulsen assumes that a conscious search for new subject matters and forms preceded its writing, an idea Zuckmayer expressed in his autobiographical writings. In *Der Schelm von Bergen* the author becomes a philologist. Whereas before his characters' language was his own, he now speaks through them. *Der Schelm von Bergen* marks the end of Zuckmayer dialect literature. By contrast Martin Greiner (1958) criticizes the artificially archaic language, which he finds disturbing in the play. Similarly, Rudolf Lange (1969) calls the impression of the play ambiguous. In his opinion, Zuckmayer's flight into the past had to fail: you cannot poetize language without having it lose its genuineness.

As far as the play's structure is concerned, Teelen (1960) feels that Zuckmayer applies here the same dramatic method of grouping pictures

that he used in *Der Hauptmann von Köpenick*. The epic is so prominent
that the scenes fail to cohere as drama. Zuckmayer has transgressed the
limit set for the prevalence of the epic in a drama and has thus reached,
and in decisive points gone beyond, the limits of his previous working
method.

For Arnold John Jacobius (1955), *Der Schelm von Bergen* marks a
turning point in that Zuckmayer leaves the unbroken realism of his folk
plays, adjusting the style of the drama to its more subtle psychological
action. This transformation is accompanied and conditioned by his new
outlook on life. Life in its sensuous, enjoyable, and lamentable forms is
at the center, but the question of fatal connections garners increasing
attention. Furthermore, in Jacobius's view, *Der Schelm von Bergen*
demonstrates the importance of the encounter motif. The goal of the
encounter is the fulfillment of the self in the other, in the perfection of
a higher unity. This motif was picked up by Henry Glade (1958 and
1963), according to whom (1958) the concept of encounter plays a
significant role in the play, describing "an inescapable event linking man
to the larger unitary pattern comprising all existence" (31). In his 1963
article Glade reemphasizes that the encounter phenomenon provides
the leitmotif in *Der Schelm von Bergen*. The empress and Vincent, the
executioner's son, embody the expanded concept of encounter that
Glade, like Jacobius (1955), links to the concept of self-realization.
"Furthermore, throughout their encounter they are linked to the transcendental and divinely ordained pattern" (186).

Glade's encounter theory is not far from Ingeborg Engelsing-
Malek's (1960) idea of *amor fati*. In her view, the theme of the play is
Zuckmayer's old one of the right of the individual versus the demands
of the community. In *Der Schelm von Bergen* this problem has a new
interpretation in that love, the most personal of all feelings, is contrasted with law and the divine order. This is Zuckmayer's first play in
which order becomes a decisive factor in the fulfillment of destiny. The
executioner and the emperor both represent the social order in different
ways, and they are unable to escape from it. In the end, the individual
recognizes the necessity of the order, and the order respects the individual.

What Engelsing-Malek refers to as love, Henry Glade (1963) calls
Humanität. For him the play shows a marked development of a more
reflective perspective, a conscious attempt to formulate the rationale for
life in transcendental and ethical terms. In Glade's opinion, the story
centers on the figure of the emperor, in whom the ethical core of the
expanding idea of *Humanität* is embodied. His self-conquest in the

face of his suspicion of his wife's infidelity is a new aspect of Zuckmayer's *Humanität*. The drama thus "initiates Zuckmayer's more tendentiously oriented type of *Humanität*" (39), which combines metaphysical and ethical components.

J. Vandenrath (1960) differentiates between two different areas of action: one governed by politics, the other by love. The goal of the political action is to consolidate the emperor's authority; the goal of the love action is to unite the lovers. At the end, love turns out to be the redeeming power: the emperor forgives his wife in the same manner in which he has forgiven his enemies. Through this ethical act of forgiveness, he becomes the central character of the play. The message of the play is that every man is under the sign of an inescapable fate. He should not try to extricate himself from it but should rather consent to it. Liberation, redemption toward fulfillment of one's own character, can be brought about only by the encounter with love. It is interesting that Vandenrath thus independently comes to conclusions similar to Glade's (1958 and 1963) and Engelsing-Malek's (1960).

It is interesting too that various critics make different assumptions about the paternity of the empress's child. Whereas Teelen (1952) and Meinherz (1960) assume that Zuckmayer leaves it open to interpretation whether or not the child originated from the encounter between the empress and the executioner's son, Wilfried Adling (1959) assumes that the child is the emperor's. Vandenrath believes the executioner to be the father.

Wolfgang Paulsen (1967) draws attention to the play's position in Zuckmayer's development as a dramatist. He points out that whereas the author was earlier at his best writing about recent history, in *Der Schelm von Bergen* history and legend dominate the material. Man becomes a symbol for something outside himself; his humanity dissolves into meaning that must be deciphered. Arnold Bauer (1970) states that Zuckmayer did not intend to condemn moral conditions at an imaginary imperial court; his concern was rather to demand the right of human beings to fulfill their personal goals and wishes.

Whereas the above critics remain more or less within the realm of textimmanent interpretation, others tried to establish a link between Zuckmayer's flight into history and his present political situation. The most extreme example of this type of approach is the interpretation of the Marxist Wilfried Adling (1959), who sees in the emperor Zuckmayer's incorporation of the "other Germany" — in contrast to the fascist dictatorship — uniting power and mild wisdom. On the other hand, the lovers' ultimate acceptance of their different lives, which are determined by their different social positions, is the expression of Zuckmayer's questions, conflicts, decisions, and hopes during his exile. Adling accuses Zuckmayer of a mystification of the Middle Ages into the aristocratic ideal that, in his opinion, is part of the fascist mythology of history and the fascists' plans for a greater Germany through an idealization of medieval German greatness.

For Ingeborg Drewitz (1966), the justice and humaneness of the rulers are the opposite of the contemporary dictatorship in Germany. Rudolf Lange (1969) continues the autobiographical aspects of this interpretation in more general and less radical terms than Adling, claiming that the author's painful experiences had found their way into *Der Schelm von Bergen*. Siegfried Mews (1977 and 1981a) reinforces this view. He points out that, in spite of their seemingly nonpolitical, historical subject matter, *Der Schelm von Bergen* and *Bellman* (1938) reflect subjects and themes of the exiled author's situation. *Der Schelm von Bergen*, however, can be called an exile drama only in a limited sense since the book edition appeared in 1934 from Ullstein's Propyläen Verlag in Berlin. However, because Zuckmayer's plays were now banned from performance in Germany, its premiere took place in Vienna. In spite of its mythic action and setting, the play confirms the divinely ordained social order and contains a hidden conservative message. Mews even speculates that in the author's glorification of the social "class" one might see a hidden expression of sympathy for Austrofascism and the corporative state advocated by the Austrian chancellor Dollfuß, who had been assassinated on 25 July 1934. Considering the corporate state the lesser of two evils, one might speculate that Zuckmayer consciously adapted to the dominating political ideology of Austria, which was providing him with a home. Becker (1984), in the revised edition (1989) of his essay, cautions that the ideology of a corporate state in *Der Schelm von Bergen* cannot be judged positively without reservation, even if the accommodation to the country of exile played a role in Zuckmayer's drama. Blake Lee Spahr (1992) sees the topicality of the play in its main theme of "an immutable order," which "was pertinent in Germany of the early 1930s" (464).

Ausma Balinkin's (1976) investigation of the central women figures in Zuckmayer's dramas marks a return to textimmanent interpretation at a time when such an approach was considered outdated, both in Germany and the United States. She focusing merely on the women characters, though her conclusions are similar to those of Engelsing-Malek (1960) and Glade (1958 and 1963). She points out that, unlike *Katharina Knie*, the empress in *Der Schelm von Bergen* does not regain her insight into her appropriate role without help. Rather, she must be reminded that to cast off one's duty is to cast off oneself. But, like the later character Barbara Blomberg, she learns to transform personal love into a greater, altruistic love. She makes her decision out of free will and thus adds to her inner strength. "The Empress's willing acceptance of her destined role signals restored harmony and order as it restores her own integrity and benefits the man she loves" (35). In her examination of the image of Zuckmayer's women figures, Sonja Czech (1985) states that the author is concerned not about the emperor's forgiving the empress but about his stressing motherhood as a woman's fulfillment in life. As a result of the unclear circumstances of the motif of encounter and the stress on the motif of fertility, many realistic implications for the image of women are neglected, in particular the position of the woman in marriage. Fertility in its biological character is placed in an almost sacred framework. With his exaggerated endorsement of motherhood, Zuckmayer unwittingly fell in with the expectations of the Third Reich, since the conservative women's movement, to which Zuckmayer's concept of women was close, had been integrated into Nazi Germany. Thus the only interpretation that is influenced by contemporary feminism is in its conclusions close to that of Adling's (1959) Marxist one.

Ulla Winblad (Musik und Leben des Carl Michael Bellman)

Originally, the drama *Musik und Leben des Carl Michael Bellman* was going to be performed in Vienna's Theater an der Josephstadt; the first rehearsals had been scheduled for 11 March 1938, when German troops marched into Austria and all plans for staging the play had to be given up. As a result, the first performance did not take place until 14 November 1938, under the direction of Leopold Lindtberg, at the Schauspielhaus in Zurich, *the* stage of German artists in exile. A new version, titled *Ulla Winblad*, was first staged by Heinz Hilpert on 21 October 1953 in Göttingen.

Since the 1938 version was not published, Wolfgang Teelen (1952) does not deal with it. Ian C. Loram (1955) reports on the historical models for the play and points out how Zuckmayer used only those facts of their lives that suited his intent. Loram makes the most detailed comparison between drama and history. He does not consider *Ulla Winblad* a great drama compared with *Des Teufels General* and *Der Gesang im Feuerofen*. In his opinion, the action involving Gustav III is not convincingly integrated with the Bellman action. On the other hand, he believes Zuckmayer captured the "bohemian" side of Bellman's character to a remarkable degree. The play's worth lies in Zuckmayer's "re-affirmation of his optimistic belief in the essential value of life and a plea for a return to the basically human instincts and emotions" (18) as well as his rejection of cold, hard reasoning that stifles feeling. Apart from this observation and its positivistic comparison between drama and history, however, Loram's article does not go beyond textimmanent examination of the play's characters.

In the *Festschrift Fülle der Zeit* (1956), Alfred Happ praises the beginning of the play as a prime example of "poetic theater" because the poet who depicts human beings and interprets sentiments makes the dramatist wait until he has finished his exposition.

In the following textimmanent interpretations, the authors repeatedly distinguish between political and love action, and they equate the characters with various views of life. In Henry Glade's opinion, Bellman exemplifies the utter freedom of the restless heart, and Lindkrona typifies the conventional desire for security, whereas the king typifies a reckless disregard for it; Ulla Winblad follows Zuckmayer's middle road, the ideal of "living dangerously" (1958: 60), and thus possesses all the attributes of Zuckmayer's ideal woman of this period. She acts in naive response to her own natural instincts or eros. Thus "the most salient aspects of *Humanität* in this drama are revealed through the concept of love or naturalistic eros in its relationship with eros and security" (64). Each major character exemplifies a different facet of these concepts.

Like Loram (1955), Ingeborg Engelsing-Malek (1960) finds the construction of the play dissatisfying. The love story does not mesh with the political action. The characters of Gustav III and Lindkrona remain pale. The chief conflict has its origin in a decision that is incongruent with Ulla's nature. The play shows how she ultimately finds her way back to a form of life she is destined to live. Her fate is her love for Bellman. The attitude of the two main characters, Ulla and Bellman, thus corresponds to Zuckmayer's *amor fati*; Ulla's development is a typical example of the basic structure of Zuckmayer's dramas. J. Vandenrath (1960) also sees two separate actions in this play, as he does in *Der Schelm von Bergen*: the love action and the political action at court. For him, the play shows Zuckmayer as a poet who uses theatrical means. The appearance of Bellman with his friends, which occurs twice, is one of the high points of genuine theater in Zuckmayer's work, Vandenrath believes. The play has many operatic features. Zuckmayer has successfully communicated the Bellman songs to a German audience.

Arnold Bauer (1970) characterizes the drama in terms of genre. In his opinion *Ulla Winblad* is Zuckmayer's first play that is more ballad-like and epic than dramatic. Its true poetry consists in the playwright's fantastic depiction of the characters, which are taken from Bellman's *Fredmans Epistlar* (1790).

Several interpreters have tried to account for the play's lack of success. For Wolfgang Paulsen (1967), a character like Ulla, who is happy in herself, cannot be tragic; in this case tragedy can only be the result of an eventful life. Looking closely at all of Zuckmayer's plays that were directed by Heinz Hilpert, the theater historian William Grange (1991) sees a close relationship between *Der Gesang im Feuerofen* and *Ulla Winblad*. In his opinion, Bellman's songs contain the same humanitarian message Zuckmayer wanted to portray in *Der Gesang im Feuerofen*. On the basis of what he perceives as the play's metaphysical content, he groups *Ulla Winblad* with *Der Gesang im Feuerofen* and *Die Uhr schlägt eins*, ignoring the fact that, as *Bellman*, the drama belongs to a much earlier period. Grange sees the reason for the failure of *Ulla Winblad* in the source of Zuckmayer's music. Whereas Brecht, aided by superb composers such as Kurt Weill, Hanns Eisler, and Paul Dessau, wrote the lyrics for his music specifically for his plays and used it to give his audience a new perspective, Zuckmayer "attempted to shoehorn music written in the late 18th century, in Swedish, into his revised script, in the hope that the songs might capture the essence of a humanitarian alternative to the venality of the court. While the music did provide entertaining, digressive interludes, it was dramaturgically dysfunctional and failed in any effective way to further the playwright's metaphysical purpose" (163). Thus Grange blames the play's failure not on characterization or message but on theatrical weaknesses. Consequently, his verdict is closely related to the early textimmanent interpretations.

Several other interpretations concentrate on parallels between Zuckmayer's work and his life, especially his exile experience. In her "Porträtskizze" of Zuckmayer in the *Festschrift Fülle der Zeit* (1956), Luise Rinser advances the opinion that many of the author's heroes are, to a certain extent, self-portraits — or, more precisely, idealized images of himself. She includes Bellman and Harras, the main character of *Des Teufels General*. The Zuckmayer she knew at the time of her writing was, like Bellman, masculine and sensitive, strong and tender, coarse and sentimental, bursting with energy and sensitive, pleasure-seeking, and melancholic, a he-man and yet gifted with a mysterious knowledge usually present in women. Although she refers to the author's personality and not to events of his life, she thus indirectly views *Ulla Winblad* as a piece of autobiographical writing.

Rudolf Lange (1969) hints that Zuckmayer's painful experiences during the National Socialist era found their way into *Ulla Winblad*, especially in the toasts at the end and the first conversation between poet and king. Mews (1977 and 1981a) takes a cautious stand on relating the author's exile experience to the drama, pointing out that the playwright's choice of historical material cannot be attributed solely to his exile since his preoccupation with Bellman had begun when he was a student in Heidelberg (1919). Moreover, he invented new characters as well as the story itself. Reiterating Rinser's views, Mews believes that, like Harras in *Des Teufels General*, Bellman (as the singer, drinker, and lover) is Zuckmayer's ideal. The play contains allusions to the author's exile, but these are wishful thinking rather than social analysis.

Since she is concerned with the reflection of contemporary history in Zuckmayer's work, Margot Finke (1990) finds more parallels than Mews. She compares the king's attempts to bring freedom and democracy to his people with the Weimar Republic, which failed "because too many people were simply not ready for it . . . . The Weimar Republic was likewise undermined by lack of support from dissenting and fighting parties, and by those who misused the system to gain power" (188). Finke compares Bellman's final arrest to the persecution of many individuals during the Third Reich "because of their race, opinions and political affiliation" (189).

There are several discussions of the presentation of women in the play, although none of them completely embraces contemporary feminist theory. Ausma Balinkin (1976) classifies Ulla Winblad, with Katharina Knie and Barbara Blomberg, among the author's women figures "who initially fail to perceive their guiding voices" (66). Her way to harmony leads through the purifying process of righting an error that is recognized in retrospect. Her capacity for selfless love makes her spiritual survival possible. Balinkin's interpretation is textimmanent; her insights fail to go beyond Ingeborg Engelsing-Malek's (1960) and her *amor fati* model.

By comparison, Gabriele Lindner's (1986) view demonstrates the progress of feminist methodology. For her, Zuckmayer's portrayal of Ulla Winblad shows a male perspective at work. Through similes he describes her physicality in terms normally used for luxury food. Ulla appears as a symbol of womanhood — eternal, natural, and indomitable. In her, woman is mythologized in an archaic manner. She is characterized as a woman who lives for love, as a symbol of femininity, yet without an individual personality. In comparison to the *Bellman* version, in *Ulla Winblad* Zuckmayer characterizes and evaluates his characters to a much lesser degree according to traditional male and female qualities. These changes, however, do not result in a more fully developed female character. He fails to consider the situation of women in the eighteenth century. In comparison to the historical Bellman's "muse," Zuckmayer's Ulla Winblad shows a more moderate idea of femininity; she proves to be faithful and loving, and her sexuality is not an essential character trait. Since Zuckmayer lived as an emigré in Austria during the Third Reich, the fascist mother ideal to which women were reduced by this regime was no influence on his portrayal of women.

In contrast to Lindner, who stresses Ulla's faithfulness, Sonja Czech (1985) deals with Ulla Winblad under the heading "Die Frau als 'Dirne' " (The Woman as a "Whore"). In her view, Ulla is introduced not as an individual but only as a sexual being. She becomes a myth of sensual love; her relationship to the other persons in the play is determined by her function as a "messenger of love" (168). As an incarnation of love, she is equated with nature and is thus an ideal complement to Bellman's view of life. The harmony that dominates the end of the play covers up the realistic implications of her fate as a woman. Being reduced to the idea of love, her character supports the equations of man with reason and woman with sensuality, which was criticized early on by the women's movement.

Barbara Blomberg

Barbara Blomberg, the drama about the young mistress of the sixteenth-century emperor Charles V and mother of Don Juan of Austria, was first performed on 30 April 1949 in Constance under Heinz Hilpert's direction. In chronological order, the critical literature on the play should be addressed following the discussion of *Des Teufels General*. However, not only does *Barbara Blomberg*'s historical subject matter place it with *Der Schelm von Bergen* and *Ulla Winblad*; it is also obvious from Alice Herdan-Zuckmayer's report in *Die Farm in den grünen Bergen* (1949) that Zuckmayer began working on the piece during his early years in Vermont. He thus continued his historical plays, not turning to the Zeitstück until *Des Teufels General*.

Certainly not all scholars have thought of the play as a historical drama. Martin Greiner (1958) takes the year of the play's first performance and publication at face value and jumps to the conclusion that in *Barbara Blomberg* Zuckmayer has returned to the genre of the historical folk play after branching out into the Zeitstück in *Des Teufels Ge-*

neral. Wolfgang Paulsen (1967) also believes that, like *Ulla Winblad* and *Der Hauptmann von Köpenick, Barbara Blomberg* does not fall into the category of historical drama. History is only hinted at by minor characters to provide local color and authenticity. History merely supports the fact that people like Barbara existed.

The textimmanent critics of the late 1950s and 1960s concentrated for the most part on the heroine's personal development. Most of them arrived at negative assessments of the play. Alfred Happ (1956) was puzzled by *Barbara Blomberg.* For him the play has no meaning; its author simply releases a pack of energetic dramatic characters and creates passionate theater with them. In his dissertation of 1958 and his article of 1963, Henry Glade traces Barbara's growth from an embittered, vengeful woman to one who transcends her nature and rises to Zuckmayer's ideal of *Humanität.* Her development occurs in three stages. In the first, the Kegel-Massy-Frayken plot, Barbara's situation can best be characterized as survival of the fittest. During the second stage, Barbara is transformed into an aristocratic being through her involvement with Ratcliff. She achieves ultimate *Humanität* during the third stage, the Barbara-Don Juan plot. Here Barbara represents Zuckmayer's philosophy of wholeness, and Don Juan exemplifies its antithesis. Her ultimate self-sacrifice for love constitutes the high point of *Humanität* in this drama, "consisting of peace of salvation from man's existential individuation through the wholeness of selfhood, coming from the recognition of the essential unity of all existence" (116).

What Glade calls *Humanität,* Ingeborg Engelsing-Malek (1960) calls *amor fati.* In her view, despite the historical material, the final goal of the drama is to show Barbara's development from fatalistic indifference to acceptance of her fate. Engelsing-Malek thus again sees the basic structure of Zuckmayer's plays in terms of *amor fati.* But the various stations in Barbara's life do not communicate a unified picture, in her view; the dialogue remains pale; the stilted sententious style of the drama collides with Zuckmayer's often drastic colloquialisms. The allusions to the present and the jokes are too artificially constructed to be effective. Thus Engelsing-Malek considers the play perhaps Zuckmayer's weakest.

Instead of talking about *Humanität* or *amor fati* as the heroine's goal in life, J. Vandenrath (1960) sees *Barbara Blomberg* as the story of an ordinary person's struggle for a decent life. He concludes that Barbara Blomberg is a character whose dignity has been violated; who begins the struggle for life; and who, in the course of this struggle, becomes entangled in guilt and sorrow. As the emperor's former mistress and mother of his son Don Juan, she experiences an adventurous social climb, leads a life of luxury, and becomes entangled in high politics. Like Engelsing-Malek, however, Vandenrath comes to a negative conclusion regarding the drama's form. In Zuckmayer's development as a dramatist, *Barbara Blomberg* is a step backward to drama because, in contrast to his previous plays, its central character's personal development becomes more important than the exterior action.

The negative judgments of Engelsing-Malek and Vandenrath were echoed by several later critics. Hans Wagener (1983a and c) considers the play weak because of its limited use of historical background as well as its preponderance of long, theoretical discussions. With the drama's symmetrical form and its sententious dialogue, Zuckmayer is clearly working in older forms. Nor does he seem at home in historical drama. Vandenrath's criticism of the play's theatricality was echoed as late as 1991 in the verdict of the theater historian William Grange: "Zuckmayer wanted to write a play true to the sense of history and to its human substance . . . but the play's events seemed to be without consequence; everything that happened to Barbara was accidental, and as a character she remained curiously passive and spoke mostly in solipsistic aphorisms" (209). Since the motivations of the individual characters were not clearly comprehensible to the audience, they failed to create drama.

It is not surprising that the *Carl-Zuckmayer-Gesellschaft* tried to demonstrate that the play *was* dramatically viable and that it could address current issues in historical garb. Published on the occasion of a new production in Mainz, the first issue of the second volume of the *Blätter der Carl-Zuckmayer-Gesellschaft* (1976) is devoted entirely to *Barbara Blomberg*. It includes an excerpt from Happ's 1956 article, a review by Ludwig Emanuel Reindl of the original performance, a selection of the reviews of the new Mainz production compiled by Karl-Norbert Jans and Gerald Martin, and an article by the young director Paul Bäcker (1976). Unfortunately, Bäcker's article is not a scholarly discussion of the play. He summarizes the individual scenes and the historical events behind these scenes. He sees the play on the one hand as a historical tapestry; on the other, he presents Zuckmayer as a great author because he has Barbara initially fail in her seemingly successful fight for social recognition and power, but under the influence of three men, she ultimately finds herself. Barbara rejects the road of violence and aggression, conveying the author's message that the future development and emancipation of man depend on his finding a way that is not shaped, obsessed, and directed by violence. While Bäcker's remarks

are similar to the views of Glade (1958 and 1963), Engelsing-Malek
(1960), and Vandenrath (1960), they are also those of a theater director who interprets the play in terms of what it may teach us about the
present — at the time he was writing, in West Germany leftist terrorism
was using violence as a weapon against society.

Early East German criticism began, like that in West Germany, by
attacking the formal elements of the drama and later condemned its
content and message. Thus in his review of the West Berlin production
of the play in 1949, Fritz Erpenbeck (quoted in Riewoldt 1978), who,
besides Herbert Ihering and Paul Rilla, was the most prominent GDR
critic, calls Zuckmayer one of the strongest living German dramatists in
the creation of powerful, effective theater. But in *Barbara Blomberg* he
sees only remnants of this talent. He complains about the lack of vivid-
ness in Zuckmayer's naturalistic language and a lack of inner strength in
the characters, replaced by too much exterior action, which, after the
climax, falls flat. Erpenbeck blames Zuckmayer's exile in the United
States for this decline.

Wilfried Adling (1959) felt the same way about all of Zuckmayer's
postwar plays. But whereas Erpenbeck directed his criticism primarily at
the technical aspects, Adling applied it to the message as well. He pre-
dictably faults Zuckmayer for evading contemporary problems and mis-
representing historical reality by neglecting to concentrate on the
socially relevant issues. The dramatist fails to depict the fight of the
Netherlands against Spanish suppression or a woman's desire to achieve
justice for wrongs suffered at the hands of the ruling classes. Furthermore, he counterbalances the methods of suppression used by the
Spanish with atrocities committed by the populace of the occupied
countries against Catholic priests. Thus Zuckmayer has painted too
positive a picture of Spanish rule and falsified the just struggle of the
Netherlandic people. Once again Adling judges his idea of what Zuckmayer *should* have written — in this case, a liberation drama of the
Netherlands delivered from the Spanish yoke.

As Riewoldt (1978) points out, Adling applies an interpretive
method that is typical for many Marxist critics. First he presents the underlying historical facts, then their treatment by Zuckmayer. After that
he describes the possibilities of a realistic presentation of the subject
matter, and finally he demonstrates that Zuckmayer does not avail himself of these possibilities, that he is forced to construe arbitrary conflicts,
replacing inner depth with exterior theatrics. Adling interprets Zuckmayer from the viewpoint of his Marxist understanding of history; he is
merely interested in determining how close the dramatist comes to it.

According to Riewoldt, the degree of noncompliance with the Marxist view of history is proportional to the supposed technical inability to come to terms with the subject matter.

Siegfried Mews (1981a) defends the play against Adling (1959) with similar arguments. He points out that Zuckmayer never intended to write it as an ideological thesis. It is "a play of great theatricality and desirable roles for actors; it is not, however, a play from which emerges a clear message or a drama that can be said to have broad social implications" (93). Mews moreover draws attention to the parallels in the inner development of Harras in *Des Teufels General* and that of Barbara Blomberg. "Further, the problem of the individual's relationship to power, the fact that one central character dominates the scene, and the implicit demand that actions in the political realm should be ultimately governed by one's conscience relate *Barbara Blomberg* to *The Devil's General*" (90).

The discussion of the play's women from a nonfeminist and a feminist view is influenced by the textimmanent interpretations of authors such as Engelsing-Malek (1960) and Vandenrath (1960). According to Ausma Balinkin (1976), the feminine trait of intuitiveness has come full circle with *Barbara Blomberg*. The complex Barbara proves to be the opposite of the integrated feminine personalities of Zuckmayer's early period. Until her erroneous ways are pointed out to her in drastic form, she is oblivious to her inner voice, embarking resolutely on a wrong course. Just as in case of the empress in *Der Schelm von Bergen*, her inner conflict involves the transformation of personal attachment into a higher form of love. It is a conflict that is of far greater intensity and depth than that of her predecessors, demanding a complete reversal of attitudes. She must not only renounce immediate personal happiness of her own free will; she must also overcome the debilitating emotion of hate that drives her to seek retribution for past suffering. Thus she ultimately experiences a spiritual rebirth. Balinkin concludes that "Barbara proves to be man's equal in every respect — positive *and* negative" (36).

The question of role-specific behavior is raised more poignantly in Gabriele Lindner's (1986) assessment. She feels that in contrast to Ulla Winblad, whom Zuckmayer characterizes by describing her exterior charm, the description of Barbara stresses her individuality as a human being. Barbara's love for Ratcliff does not take on the same importance as love does for Ulla Winblad, since it is merely one stage in her development. Role-specific attributes become less important as Zuckmayer shows her development into an independent woman who struggles against male domination. Her final inner change is determined by love for humankind and the divine power. Lindner compares Zuckmayer's depiction with those characterizations of Barbara found in historical, biographical accounts that were probably used by Zuckmayer. He points out that her characterization in Paul Herre's biography (1909) is determined by the bourgeois moral ideas of the early twentieth century, which in public matters imposed a lot more restraint upon a woman. Zuckmayer's image of a woman who tries to determine her own life, furthermore, does not correspond to the low esteem in which women were held in sixteenth-century Netherlands; rather, in moral respect and in the consciousness of her behavior, her character is judged more positively by the author. In her case, the learning process that leads to *amor fati* (see Engelsing-Malek 1960) is most clearly expressed when compared with Katharina Knie and Ulla Winblad. In Barbara, Zuckmayer has finally put on stage an autonomous character who does not need antagonists or close friends to find herself. She is proof of the increasing independence of women in Zuckmayer's dramas.

Like Lindner, Sonja Czech (1985) compares Barbara's historical biography with her representation in the drama. In contrast to other plays, Zuckmayer views her character differently in various stages of her development; she is not initially defined as a specific type of woman but rather develops, in a rather unconvincing manner, from a downtrodden soldier's wife to a charming but unscrupulous schemer and finally to a resigned mother. The motivation for her actions becomes clear only when one considers Zuckmayer's underlying image of women. The marriage to Kegel, who views Barbara exclusively as an object of his sexual desires, was the only way for her to escape the fate of being a prostitute. After his death, she uses her position as the mother of Don Juan to take her life into her own hands. During this time, especially in her conversation with the Duke of Alba, she applies internalized male values, a practice that was judged negatively by the women's movement of the past. Zuckmayer's criticism of the manner in which Barbara realizes her personality in the course of her rise to power is, however, not directed against the forceful means she uses but against the role, which is unfitting to her sex. The historic women's movement too judged an orientation in the direction of the male role as a falsification and suppression of women's own character. Having fallen in love with Ratcliff, the ambitious woman turns into an uncompromisingly loving one who voluntarily withdraws from the male world into the role of the lover that has been assigned to her by society. In a final stage, as a caring mother, Barbara now argues against power and force, entirely in tune with the traditional role of women. This elevation of the role of mother with its willingness to make sacrifices reminds one of the role accorded to the female sex in the Third Reich. One might ask oneself whether this is a pointedly feminist conclusion that overshoots the target.

Coming to Terms with the Past

Somewhere in France

Somewhere in France, a drama written jointly by Zuckmayer and Fritz Kortner, deals with the reasons for France's defeat in 1940. It inaugurates the series of Zeitstücke (topical plays), a genre that was going to make up the major part of Zuckmayer's literary output after the Second World War. After its first performance, on 18 April 1941 by the New York Theater Guild in Washington, D.C., the play disappeared.

Mews (1979 and 1981a) is the only one who deals with this play. He points out that the work is an unsuccessful modern adaptation of Anzengruber's *Das vierte Gebot* (The Fourth Commandment, 1878). *Somewhere in France* in some respects continues the milieu and characters of Zuckmayer's adaptation of Maxwell Anderson and Laurence Stalling's *What Price Glory*, titled *Rivalen* (1929), in which Kortner played one of the two main parts. But it does not have a clear message evolving from the dramatic action, a deficiency that was also noticed by the contemporary American reviewers. The two authors did not succeed in profiling the French resistance fighters or producing a dramatically convincing and effective stand against National Socialism. But after the self-imposed political abstinence of his Austrian and Swiss exile, *Somewhere in France* represents Zuckmayer's first attempt to deal with contemporary history in a drama. Its failure meant that the author had not succeeded in establishing himself on the American literary scene.

Des Teufels General

Because he wrote this drama between 1942 and 1944 in Vermont, the dramatist was preoccupied with the political and moral questions surrounding National Socialism in Germany. Since the Allied Powers, however, had misgivings about putting uniformed German officers on the stage, the drama at first could not be performed in Germany, and consequently its premiere took place on 12 December 1946, under Heinz Hilpert's direction, at the Zurich Schauspielhaus. The first German premieres took place simultaneously in Frankfurt and Hamburg during November 1947.

In the play, the exiled Zuckmayer manages to portray the characters and the atmosphere inside Nazi Germany with almost uncanny exactness. Consequently, it became not only the most frequently performed German postwar drama but also Zuckmayer's most hotly debated play, both in public and in Zuckmayer research. Its two most controversial characters were the German General Harras, who because of his passion for flying concluded a pact with the devil (Hitler), and the resistance fighter Oderbruch, who is willing to sacrifice German lives in order to weaken the Nazi cause. Since the author himself was dissatisfied with the Oderbruch character, in 1963 he no longer permitted the performance of his play, and in 1966 he produced a new version in which he had changed the decisive dialogue between Oderbruch and Harras. In this new version Oderbruch's confession of being a resistance fighter does not disconcert Harras anymore, driving him into his death. Rather, he now understands Oderbruch's behavior, gives him positive advice, and goes on his suicidal plane ride to cover Oderbruch. Zuckmayer's attempt thereby to solve some of the play's problems with regard to the resistance question, however, still did not pacify many of his critics.

Like *Der Hauptmann von Köpenick*, *Des Teufels General* raised pedagogical possibilities. Its ability to initiate discussions among students about the Third Reich were recognized, and it was widely read in German secondary schools. As a result, a number of pedagogical articles and commentaries for use by teachers and students appeared over the years. Of these, only those that offer new insights are included here. As the subtitle indicates, Wolf Benicke's 1960 article uses the movie version of the play to make general statements on the use of film versions of literature in secondary education. In his opinion, *Des Teufels General* offers basic values — for example, in the hymn on the beauty of life, the accusation against the madness of war, and in the clear confession of a right to freedom. The more abstract such terms are, however, the less easily they are transformed into this medium. Unfortunately, Benicke does not discuss Zuckmayer's changes in the Oderbruch character, which distinguish movie from drama, as does, for example, Sheila Rooke (1964).

Bernhard Keller (1978) shows how Zuckmayer's *Des Teufels General* and Brecht's *Der aufhaltsame Aufstieg des Arturi Ui* (The Stoppable Rise of Arturi Ui, 1941) can be used in the classroom to illustrate and discuss the very different concepts of fascism that are inherent in both dramas. For Keller, Zuckmayer demonizes the historical events and thus creates the potential for the members of the audience to at least partially excuse their own behaviors. Thus *Des Teufels General* is the attempt to show the existence of the "better Germany"; it is the literary expression of Zuckmayer's stand against the thesis of collective guilt. However, because of his idealistic weltanschauung, Zuckmayer was unable to achieve a critical analysis of fascism. According to his belief in retributive justice, fascism becomes a fatal event that can be overcome only by human renewal and trust. By contrast, Brecht's *Arturi Ui* aims at a dedemonization of the historical events. Where Zuckmayer uses fate to account for the events, Brecht attempts to give rational explanations. Since Zuckmayer's title hero Harras is a positive character, he does not contribute to coming to terms with the past. Zuckmayer's reworking of the play in 1966 did not help in this respect. Even in this new version fascism remained a mythical phenomenon, and Oderbruch failed to embody the antifascist alternative in a convincing manner. Although Keller does not deny Zuckmayer's positive intentions, it is obvious that his interpretation of both plays returns to a view that is ideologically aligned with a Marxist interpretation of history.

It is characteristic of the prevailing intellectual mood in West Germany that the first short article to deal with *Des Teufels General* was from the pen of a Christian conservative critic, Hanns Braun (1948). Braun praises Zuckmayer for having painted, in his robust, theatrically effective, but also humanly likable manner, the fate of the air force general Harras. He praises him for having shown that even under Hitler the human reactions in Germany were much more diverging than propaganda and counterpropaganda would have liked to admit. But in spite of that, he takes issue with the characterization of the idealistic saboteur Oderbruch, who, in order to fight Hitler, accepts that his friend Eilers and ultimately Harras too are sacrificed, all according to the principle "The end justifies the means." Braun emphasizes that the kind of sabotage depicted by Oderbruch did not exist during the Third Reich. He criticizes Zuckmayer for having failed to limit the impact of Oderbruch by introducing a counterpart to him. On the contrary, Zuckmayer has promoted the possibility of misunderstanding this idealist by adorning him with a Christian halo. For Braun, Oderbruch is a strange Christian. He is clearly one who has gone astray, because from a Christian point of view, the question of resistance against a tyrant is clear. Only the tyrant himself — and maybe those who are jointly responsible for abolishing the ethical human order — may be killed, and then only by someone who receives a special call to take such a deed on his conscience. Oderbruch's calculated sacrifice of those who are guilty and those who are not, however, can never be called Christian. Consequently the Lord's Prayer, which Oderbruch recites when Harras goes down with his plane at the end, has a gruesome comic effect. Braun thus applies strict Christian ethical standards to Zuckmayer's play. This attitude is not only the general attitude of the periodical *Hochland*, in which the article appeared and of which the respectable number of 30,000 copies were printed at the time; it also mirrors the mood of the first years after the war, which were characterized by a new reliance on Western Christian ideals.

The first scholarly response to the play in the Anglo-Saxon world appeared in the British journal *German Life and Letters*. Lutz Weltmann (1948–49), who compares the play to Julius Maria Becker's play *Das Mahl des Herrn* (The Last Supper, 1947), does not hesitate to call *Des Teufels General* "Zuckmayer's best play and the most important example of German twentieth century drama since Gerhart Hauptmann" (159). There is a tragic hubris in Harras's honesty, "which is to him, not just the *summum bonum*, but is self-consciousness and trust in his own courage, strength and independence" (160). By calling Harras "a hero in the eternal mystery play of Love and Death" (163), Weltmann is not far from Braun's interpretation.

As Otto F. Riewoldt (1978) reports, in the Soviet Occupational Zone, and later in the GDR, *Des Teufels General* could not be performed. Here Zuckmayer was criticized for unconsciously painting a positive picture of the fascist generals. It was generally conceded that he was honest in his attempt to present the antifascist resistance, but in the end he came close to portraying a rehabilitation and transfiguration of a military daredevil. The evaluative criteria employed by GDR critics corresponded to the prevailing Marxist-Leninist approach. The GDR critics professed to be followers of a "humanist-antifascist" theater, and Zuckmayer's Harras did not fulfill the desired antifascist demand. *Des Teufels General* was considered inopportune, inappropriate, and dangerous.

Employing the above criteria, the most scathing attack during the Cold War came from the pen of the East German critic Paul Rilla (1950). In his brilliantly written satirical essay "Zuckmayer und die Uniform" (Zuckmayer and the Uniform), he finds it criminal that Zuckmayer made a Nazi general into a likable character. He points out the inner contradictions in Harras, who while being anti-Nazi has used the Nazis to further his career in the German air force. He is also enthusiastic about the exact workings of the Nazi war machine (although he refers to the first two years only), and he excuses his successes by stating that he just wanted to please his mother. For Rilla, such contradictions and sentimentalism are the characteristics of bad literature. By praising the masculinity of Harras and providing all the excuses for his joining the Nazis, Zuckmayer makes the same ideological pretexts palatable to today's youth. In Rilla's view, the resistance fighter Oderbruch can be traced back to a Nazi Dolchstoß*legende* (legend of the "stab in the back") to which the poet fell victim. Rilla even criticizes Zuckmayer for accepting criticism of his character Oderbruch during public debates. For Rilla, Zuckmayer is not intentionally attempting to whitewash a Nazi general; rather, he is a talented author who always liked to please his audience and who lacks backbone. *Des Teufels General* is thus a folk play of political *Ungemütlichkeit* (uncomfortableness) with which one can come to terms. Zuckmayer blesses where he should curse, siding with the human dignity of wolves and hyenas. Rilla considers it symptomatic of the state of the theater and theater critique that the play could be so successful in West Germany. In his view, it is tragic that in 1948 two hundred articles on existentialism appeared in West Germany, but only one on Zuckmayer. It is understandable why even this scathing attack on Zuckmayer, coming at the highpoint of the Cold War, had no impact on the West German enthusiasm for *Des Teufels General.*

In 1959 the Marxist critic Wilfried Adling adopted Rilla's view, but, as Riewoldt (1978) points out, he pays closer attention to the extent to which Zuckmayer's dramas are children of their time and therefore considers the ideological and material conditions that brought forth the play. He concedes that there are the beginnings of realistic presentation in the characters of the resistance fighter Oderbruch and the two workers, but after analyzing the character of Harras he concludes that Zuckmayer's emphasis on the difference between fascism and militarism runs the danger of meeting halfway those endeavors that, during the postwar period, branded the aggressive German militarism as antifascism and tried to restore the militarism of the past. He reproaches Zuckmayer for having demonized National Socialism and having obfuscated individual political mistakes by means of mystification. As far as the play's reception in West Germany is concerned, Adling sees a direct connection between it and the cultural politics of the occupying powers. In his view, the drama comes out in favor of a reconciliation with German imperialism and militarism and in favor of U.S. anti-Soviet politics.

As Riewoldt (1978) reports, when the new version of the play came out in 1966, Marxist critics saw in it a conscious confirmation of its alibi effect, which in the original version Zuckmayer had only unconsciously included. Supposedly there was no longer a difference between Oderbruch and Harras; now both appeared as men who tried to revolt against Hitler on 20 July 1944. Consequently, according to the Marxist critics, the new version was nothing but a whitewash of the German generals.

The reception of *Des Teufels General* by critics of the GDR exemplified the principle that, according to Riewoldt (1978), was going to underlie the reception of all future Zuckmayer plays. From the supposedly deficient message of these plays it was concluded that the formal aspects of Zuckmayer's dramas were also characterized by stagnation or even regression. In the eyes of the Marxist critics, a positive development would have been possible only as the result of a change of perspective, namely by approaching "democratic-socialist" opinions.

In 1987 the East German Werner Lüder wrote a dissertation on the reception of *Des Teufels General* both in East and West Germany, with an emphasis on West Germany. In his view, Oderbruch's actions were necessary to save Germany. For Lüder, Oderbruch is the yardstick for responsible antifascist resistance. He explains the negative reactions to this character in West Germany as a result of the fact that Russia continued to be viewed as the enemy. Because of preconceived opinions, the majority of readers and theatergoers were unable to accept the drama's strategy. The play could have provided the impetus for a productive discussion of the past, but that would have entailed a discussion of the roots of fascism and the background of the imperialistic world war. A firmly preconceived picture of the German army in the Second World War prevented the West German audience from seeing the strategy of the play and from critically viewing the character of Harras. Lüder describes Zuckmayer's changing view of Oderbruch and Harras as expressed in interviews and public discussions, a view that no longer corresponded to the text of the drama. The author thus contributed to his play's failure to provide a productive impetus for a critical *Vergangenheitsbewältigung* (coming to terms with the past). In the final analysis, the West German news media represented the political goals of the government and interpreted the play as a warning of the totalitarianism of the communist systems. As is obvious, Lüder tries to demonstrate Zuckmayer's supposed lack of character in not sticking to the original concept of the play, which was determined by the rigid attitude of Oderbruch, and to show that subsequently the West used it as a propaganda tool in the Cold War. A detailed discussion of the changes in the new version of 1966 and of the movie version is used to prove these points. Lüder's final conclusion is that the drama does not supply us with the subject matter to discuss recent history.

A number of Western critics, of course, took issue with the East Germans', especially Rilla's, views. Siegfried Sudhof (1973) countered their arguments by saying that such interpretations miss Zuckmayer's intentions entirely. The dramatist wanted to show the tragic character of a person who was bound to the military by an oath that was not valid but from which he could not free himself. In Sudhof's view, *Brecht's Furcht und Elend des Dritten Reiches* (*The Private Life of the Master Race*, 1945) is not the opposite of this drama but its complement. As late as 1981 Siegfried Mews (1981a) reproached Rilla for having almost totally ignored Harras's moral purification. Admitting the problematic character of the play in its "sympathetic portrayal of the fellow traveler Harras" (89), Mews carefully defends the work by pointing out its important role in Germany's coming to terms with its past.

But Rilla's and Adling's ideas were also taken up by a number of liberal and leftist Western critics. In this context the pedagogical article by Bernhard Keller (1978) has already been mentioned. Coming perhaps closest to Rilla's damning arguments, although not from a Marxist point of view, Marianne Kesting (1969) finds it a paradox that in *Des Teufels General* the emigré Zuckmayer has created the legend of great times including real men and soldiers who unfortunately were gathered under the wrong flag and were prevented by the Nazi Party from using their talents for a noble cause. In her view, Zuckmayer had failed to view Harras's heroism critically but stylized it instead. Because of his enthusiasm for flying, he did not see early enough what this war was actually about. The realism of the play says little about the true social context. In *Des Teufels General*, as in Zuckmayer's following *Zeitstücke*, the dramatic tension rests on the subject matter alone. Therefore, the number of exciting scenes must be increased in order to maintain the excitement. This procedure brings Zuckmayer close to the magazine novel and to the majority of German postwar movies.

Kesting's words are more polemic criticism than scholarly investigation, and they have also evoked opposition. In Heinz Geiger's view (1973), the criticism of Harras advanced by Kesting would imply a satirical or parodistic alternative. Zuckmayer could not possibly have used such an approach since he intended to write a drama in which Harras is tried for his collaboration with the Nazis. In order to pass sentence on Harras, Zuckmayer first had to detail his behavior. In response to

Kesting's criticism, it must furthermore be asked whether Zuckmayer did not paint a more convincing picture of the schizophrenic situation under a totalitarian regime by showing Harras's behavior without commentary.

In his Zuckmayer biography of 1977, Thomas Ayck tries to be fair to the author, but in the final analysis he is unable to conceal his leftist point of view. He admits that Zuckmayer had provoked one of the first public discussions of the recent German past to come from the stage, a discussion on the possibilities of active resistance and passive toleration. His description of the Third Reich milieu is accurate, but not his fairy-tale characterization of good and evil. Ayck feels that, after all, it was not the devil who lost the Second World War, and it was not the principle of retributive justice that was victorious but the Allied Forces with their military planning and material superiority.

Like Rilla and Kesting, Jennifer Taylor (1981), in the British journal *New German Studies*, considers the "dilemma of patriotism" in Zuckmayer's play, Paul Zech's *Die drei Gerechten* (The Three Just Ones, written in 1945, not published), and Johannes R. Becher's *Schlacht um Moskau (Winterschlacht)* (The Battle for Moskau [Battle in Winter], 1953). In her view, Zuckmayer has placed the moral bankruptcy of his hero, Harras, into the center of his play, acted out against the backdrop of the threat of Germany's defeat. Although the high moral tone of the original version is somewhat modified by the political considerations of the 1966 version, the alterations do nothing to change the course of the play. Taylor sees Harras in negative terms only. In her opinion, Zuckmayer's drama lacks any positive characters since Harras's death is the result of his own moral failure. In accordance with the great weight placed on the demonic, Zuckmayer subscribes to a school of thought popular at the time — expressed, for example, in Thomas Mann's *Doktor Faustus* (1947) — that regards National Socialism as a political expression of the diabolical. In identifying Hitler with the devil, the author "comes near to exonerating his protagonist from personal responsibility" (188). What distinguishes Zuckmayer's play from the others considered by Taylor is above all the fact that he nowhere presents any message of hope or refers to national values, such as culture, that will survive Harras's death. Although it was seductive to conceive of Hitler and National Socialism in terms of the demonic at the time, annihilation "was perhaps not the best basis for a plea of German integrity and with which to begin the work of reconstruction" (190).

Andreas Huyssen (1976) also sees the drama as part of the metaphysical theories of explaining the origination of fascism. He points out that one of Zuckmayer's main themes is the question of collective guilt, and he refers to striking parallels between his drama and Karl Jaspers's position in his influential treatise *Die Schuldfrage* (*The Question of German Guilt,* 1946). Huyssen sees the beginning of the Cold War and the preparation for a Western military alliance as the reason for the success of Zuckmayer's play in Germany. By comparing *Des Teufels General* with Weisenborn's *Die Illegalen,* he also comes to the conclusion that from 1947–48 on, a noticeable phase of demonization and suppression of the past followed earlier attempts to come to terms with the question of resistance. By setting *Des Teufels General* against *Die Illegalen* and placing it in the context of bourgeois humanist culture, Huyssen is arguing from the standpoint of the leftist student revolt of 1968, which found fault with all West German attempts to come to terms with the Third Reich past, even that of documentary drama, or (Huyssen is teaching in the United States) as a representative of the leftist studies of German literature that were dominating a number of German departments in the 1970s and 1980s.

But the most characteristic feature of the West German interpretations of the 1950s and 1960s was again the textimmanent approach with its primary concern for form. Completely in tune with this method, Wolfgang Teelen (1952) deals with the dramatic form of the play and not with its message. Applying Staiger's terminology, he comes to the conclusion that, as far as the structure of the play is concerned, the term *drama* is justified, although he feels that the various actions are not connected in a dramatic sense; rather, they result from the momentary conditions of General Harras or other persons. In the final analysis, the individual acts are not chapters in the development of action but partial pictures of a general state of change. Since the author asks the audience for sympathy, not merely understanding, for Oderbruch, Teelen shows that Zuckmayer has not conceived this character exclusively in dramatic terms. The lack of sympathy engendered by a character shows most clearly the "undramatic." In contrast to Harras, Zuckmayer does not succeed in securing enough sympathy for Oderbruch. Oderbruch is thus epically devised. His character shows most clearly where Zuckmayer has failed. It is interesting to see that as a result of his concern about form and his strict adherence to Staiger's system of genre affiliation, Teelen is able to ignore the powerful and highly debatable message of the drama. His interpretation thus shows the limitations of the textimmanent approach. Later Paul Meinherz (1960) agreed with Teelen. Harras's conflicts are there not to be solved but to add visibility to his character. Consequently, the play can be only reservedly called a drama. The *character* of Harras is more important than his *actions*, it is responsible for the conflict.

Alfred Happ (1956) finds strong elements of his concept of "poetic theater" even in *Des Teufels General*: poetic theater, in his view, recreates historic times, connecting actual events with possible ones, taking real people and connecting them with invented persons, combining reality and invention according to poetic necessity. Zuckmayer succeeded in recreating the situation of the Third Reich in historical and interhuman respects. As dramatically most interesting, Happ sees the twofold death sentence pronounced on Harras by the resistance fighters and by the Nazi Party. Both powers converge upon him and crush him.

Henry Glade (1958) feels that "the drama is so weighted down with the theatrical figure of Harras that the essential facets of life and thought in Nazi Germany become blurred and what there is of the visible remains of the culture tends to be caricatured and overdrawn as especially in the delineation of Dr. Schmidt-Lausitz and Oderbruch" (87). The figures are types rather than flesh and blood.

Two years later, J. Vandenrath (1960) sees similar weaknesses in *Des Teufels General*. For him the drama presents the same basic dramatic situation as *Schinderhannes* and *Der Hauptmann von Köpenick*: a man against the order of society. The action again consists of the development of this conflict. Zuckmayer's ability to create a milieu reaches a high point in *Des Teufels General*. The liveliness and exactness of the depiction of the milieu were responsible for the play's success. Merely on the basis of the conflict situation, *Des Teufels General* is more of a drama than Zuckmayer's previous plays. Zuckmayer elevates the conflicts to the highest ethical level by characterizing National Socialism as inherently evil and Hitler as the devil. Nevertheless, the play betrays weaknesses in its tendency to make caricatures of the wicked (Schmidt-Lausitz), weaknesses in sentimentality, love, and sexual brutality. Vandenrath expresses doubts that the play will be of lasting impact after its topicality has been exhausted.

At the same time, other textimmanent interpreters concentrated on the ethical values advocated by Zuckmayer and on the methods he employed for their advancement. For Murray B. Peppard (1952), *Des Teufels General* initiates the postwar period of Zuckmayer's creativity, in which he places much greater stress on the ethical, humane, and moral considerations than he did in his earlier works. Peppard realizes early that *Des Teufels General* is essentially a drama of inner human conflict, portraying an eternal human situation that transcends its specific German setting. The inner action of the play consists of Harras's gradual inner awakening, which takes place in four stages: 1. "After learning that Bergmann, a Jew, whom he had tried to save, has committed suicide, he gives up his self-deception" (351); 2. Harras's "interview with Hartmann. In the face of the young man's sincerity and need for guidance, Harras finds it difficult to comfort him with phrases" (351); 3. his "interview with Eilers's widow. Not until now does Harras come to realize his full responsibility" (351); 4. his conversation with Oderbruch, who reveals to Harras that he is a leader of the resistance to Hitler.

Just as Andreas Huyssen (1976) did subsequently, Henry Glade (1958) uses Karl Jaspers's influential book *Die Schuldfrage* (1946) as a point of departure. Glade states that Harras walks the road to moral and spiritual regeneration through a number of important encounters. Thus Glade takes up Peppard's (1952) idea of Harras's development in four stages without Glade giving Peppard due credit, and he adds new interpretations to these stages. The story of the Jew Bergmann's suicide makes Harras realize his criminal complicity by default since he did nothing for the thousands of other Jews. The encounter with Hartmann makes him recognize his religious guilt, arousing his sense of responsibility. The encounter with Anne Eilers leads him to recognize his moral guilt; now he accepts the ultimate responsibility for her husband's death. The final encounter with Oderbruch brings about his recognition of eternal justice. Although Peppard's and Glade's model makes eminent sense for *Schinderhannes* and particularly for *Der Schelm von Bergen*, one must ask the question here, how else but through encounters and his consideration of them is a dramatic hero supposed to change?

According to Glade, in the final moments of the play Harras "bows to the verdict of eternal justice and seeks freedom through death in the full acknowledgement of his guilt and his willingness to atone for it" because "no amount of exuberant temperament and obsessive concern with flying can exonerate the selling of one's soul to an antihumanitarian cause" (98). Harras's hybrid nature reflects a change in Zuckmayer's own personal and literary development in that the superb *theater* of the first half of the play is sacrificed to the demands of the tendentious *Humanität*. Although the drama deals with a contemporaneous sociopolitical matter, its actual theme is man's eternal need to measure up to the commonly accepted standards of *Humanität*. In his article of 1963, Glade confirms these views and emphasizes that in or around 1940, Zuckmayer enters a new creative phase of his work, the

most significant change being his primary interest in the subject matter
of present-day import.

Ingeborg Engelsing-Malek (1960) criticizes Peppard's (1952) four
stages of Harras's development by pointing out that the conversations
with Mohrungen, the first conversation with Hartmann, the conversation with Buddy Lawrence and with Pützchen are also important stages
in this development. For Engelsing-Malek the conflict of *Des Teufels
General* arises from Harras's personality versus his position. As in *Der
fröhliche Weinberg*, the hero slowly recognizes his own nature, his own
fate and its relationship to life and death. In the case of Harras, it is
much more consciously connected with his recognition of God. He ultimately finds himself by subjecting himself to divine judgment. Consequently his death is not only to be considered a suicide but also a
justifiable sacrifice for a good cause. Engelsing-Malek joins those who
criticize Oderbruch. In her view, his sabotage does not go with his pi-
ousness and human reliability. He appears cold because he subjects his
fate to the law and the means to the end to such an extent that he for-
gets himself. Harras, on the other hand, brings his life-affirming nature
into harmony with the "eternal law." His death remains faithful to his
destiny; he dies in the consciousness of serving life even beyond death.

Wolfgang Paulsen (1967) agrees with the above interpretations in
that *Des Teufels General* marks Zuckmayer's return to morality. This
also was a return to the type of play that had dominated the nineteenth
century up to naturalism. It includes *Der Gesang im Feuerofen*, *Das
kalte Licht*, and *Die Uhr schlägt eins*. However, *Das Leben des Horace A.
W. Tabor* is again biographically structured world theater. *Des Teufels
General* combines the genre of biographical epic drama, drama around
a central character, with that of problem drama. Only because the human being and not the action is of primary importance in this play are
we able to forgive Harras, who has been driven into a corner, for a behavior that otherwise would be unforgivable. Paulsen admits that the
ending is problematic, but at the same time he asks himself what other
kind of ending there could have been for a vitalistically drawn character.

The characters' transformation is also the main concern of Helen
Swediuk-Cheyne (1980). She sees the leitmotif of "starting all over
again" realized in the character of Hartmann. For Harras, no new beginning is possible any longer, but he is able to reconcile himself with
the universe because he pays with his life, unwilling to serve evil anymore.

But not all critics are convinced of Harras's fundamental change. In
an article in the British journal *Modern Languages*, Alan Robertshaw

(1985) outlines "the changes in the critical reception of the play and reexamines the text in the light of the controversy that it has aroused" (242). In contrast to the above interpretations, Robertshaw does not believe that there are enough unequivocal indications that Harras undergoes a change of outlook. He rather speculates that Zuckmayer evidently realized that a change of heart in Harras would be unconvincing, and Robertshaw therefore views Harras's final exit as the expression of considerable dramatic skill. By submitting himself to a trial by ordeal, he is true to himself to the end. When Zuckmayer changed and added to the text in order to tone down Oderbruch's single-mindedness, he misjudged the political climate of 1966. But time had caught up with Harras too. In 1966 Zuckmayer's audience was no longer the same group that had lived through the Nazi period and that could and wanted to identify with someone like Harras. It was a new generation that judged him harshly. Robertshaw criticizes the fact that the play focuses on Harras's personal tragedy which is only tenuously linked with the political backdrop. He criticizes Harras for committing suicide, because this ignores the needs of the people around him. With the change of the political climate in Germany, "time has exposed flaws in the way the play was conceived and constructed" (246).

The reference to religious elements contained in Glade's (1958) and Engelsing-Malek's (1960) remarks about the play was by no means new. Murray B. Peppard (1952) had already voiced the opinion that in Harras's conversation with Oderbruch, with its references to a so-called eternal law, it is evident that the play is ultimately of a religious nature. Indeed, the interpretation of *Des Teufels General* as a drama about a religious quest was taken up by a whole series of other critics. For example, in his dissertation of 1955, Arnold John Jacobius also sees the drama as an expression of views that go beyond topical concerns. For him it is not Harras, the Nazi pilot, who is in the center of the tragedy, but Harras, the twentieth-century man who at the moment of his deepest humiliation cries out to God. J. Vandenrath (1960) had pointed out that the drama is not an allegory but that it tries to answer the question how it was possible that Germany fell into the hands of the devil. All characters, not just Harras, give a different answer to their fate within the Nazi system. Since the Hitler regime is seen as evil incarnate, the play finally leads to the metaphysical question about the existence of evil in the world. Thus the problems discussed here are much more serious than those in *Katharina Knie* or *Der Schelm von Bergen*. Raymond Erford Barrick (1964) finally presents an outright religious interpretation. For him, Harras, like Wolters in *Das kalte Licht* later on, is obstinate in his refusal to recognize the presence of the eternal spirit behind life. But, unlike Creveaux in *Der Gesang im Feuerofen*, Harras and Wolters "are allowed by the author to repent for their Promethean defiance of the divine will and to accept total judgment" (131). Seeing Harras in these mystical terms does help to clarify some of his statements that are more spiritual in nature than one would consider appropriate for the character of a Nazi general.

Later, Hans Wagener (1983a and c) agreed with a religious interpretation, but he also took a critical position toward such an exclusive and narrow view. In his opinion, Zuckmayer's theory of fascism simplifies the historical facts and returns to literary tendencies of mythologizing reality that were already popular in the Weimar Republic. But during the late 1940s, he was in total conformity with the spirit of the time, which suspected that the struggle of spiritual and moral principles lay behind historical processes. By placing Harras's inner change into the center of the drama, Zuckmayer personalizes the events of the Third Reich, and the play becomes a religious drama. Harras should have refused to go along with Nazism and rather suffered in imitation of Christ than act against his convictions. In the final analysis, his guilt is rooted in his distance from God, in his pact with the devil. Thus Zuckmayer has written a drama based on a dualistic, Christian worldview, a drama about the religious road a guilty man takes to find himself, about his insight into and acceptance of his guilt. Zuckmayer's positive view of reconciliation and his concentration on the private, individual aspects allowed the Germans an opportunity for catharsis and a new beginning.

In a Finnish contribution, Keijo Holsti (1984), too, sees Zuckmayer's drama, like Thomas Mann's *Doktor Faustus*, as part of a trend that views the Third Reich as Germany's pact with the devil. Holsti concentrates on the comical aspects of the play and finds them inadequate in trying to expose the devil and his regime. He then tries to point out the differences between Zuckmayer's play and the Faust tradition. Harras serves the devil in this life and not in the next one; hell has come to the earth. Moreover, the service the devil renders in return proves unsatisfactory in every way. Harras and the people in his circle are no free parties to the contract, as Faust was. Thus the new aspect in Zuckmayer's version is that one can be pressed into the devil's service. The play thus adds new features to the traditional motif of the devil's pact. Like Roy C. Cowen (1976), Holsti sees the play in the German literary tradition and tries to point out its novel aspects.

The theater historian William Grange (1991) discusses *Des Teufel's General* as part of his study of the collaboration between Zuckmayer and Heinz Hilpert. Commenting on the construction of the play, he observes that it is not episodic like *Der Hauptmann von Köpenick*. Unlike Gunderloch in *Der fröhliche Weinberg*, its central character, Harras, carries the entire dramatic weight of the play. In addition to such remarks about form, Grange refers to the religious elements of the drama, demonstrating that this interpretation has remained viable until recently: "The most interesting difference between this and the other plays of the trilogy however was the playwright's use of thought; the play's casual plot and documentary atmosphere were subjected to the playwright's metaphysical purpose" (118). Not surprisingly, leftist critics such as Andreas Huyssen (1976) and Jennifer Taylor (1981) had already taken issue with Zuckmayer's metaphysical interpretation of National Socialism and its followers.

As mentioned with regard to *Bellman*, Luise Rinser in *Fülle der Zeit* (1956) sees in Harras an ideal picture of Zuckmayer himself. Although Zuckmayer had become a writer, his ideal, his childhood image of himself, had always been the man of action. From this premise, Rinser concludes that the reason that Harras is a great fellow in the first act and then becomes increasingly weaker in the second and third acts is not for artistic reasons but because the depiction of his character is affected by Zuckmayer's doubt in the moral justification of the original conception of his hero.

In contrast to his studies of 1958 and 1963, Henry Glade, in his article of 1966, continues Rinser's thoughts by interpreting *Des Teufels General* as a disguised autobiography. He believes that Zuckmayer has recreated the possibility he briefly considered for himself, namely not to go into exile but to stay in Germany and go along with the government in power. Glade observes that the quality of the drama weakens in the course of the action. After the superb theater of the first half of the drama, contrived, self-conscious moral concerns take over around the middle of the second act, foreshadowing Zuckmayer's future problem dramas. As Peppard had already pointed out in 1952, Harras undergoes "a spiritual regeneration through a step-by-step process in which a series of encounters leads towards a recognition of his guilt" (58). For Glade, the unresolved duality of the ending — Harras's suicide, on the one hand as the final consequence of his daredevil life, on the other hand as expiation for his sins — mirrors Zuckmayer's own position at this time; in Glade's view, Harras *is* Zuckmayer, and not Udet. These autobiographical components in the play also explain the fanaticism of

Oderbruch and the uprightness of young Hartmann, the representative of the "other Germany"; both embody Zuckmayer's views at this time. For Glade, the strength of the play then lies in its superb autobiographical character study, particularly in the first half; its historical accuracy is only one aspect of this. The autobiographical elements are responsible for the drama's ambiguities and thus for its dramatic weaknesses.

Examining *Des Teufels General* within the context of exile drama, Volker Wehdeking (1973) in many respects reiterates Glade's ideas. For him the play is a strange mixture of topical subject selection and a very distanced perspective, with anachronistic form and ahistoric problems filling the second half. In the course of the drama, Harras undergoes a moral education from human encounters — as earlier described by Peppard (1952) and Glade (1958) — which leads him to understand that it is important to subject oneself to an "eternal law." After Zuckmayer's neorealistic phase, which lasted from *Der fröhliche Weinberg* to *Der Hauptmann von Köpenick*, and the apolitical works of the exile period (from *Der Schelm von Bergen* to *Der Seelenbräu*), *Des Teufels General* marks a clear turning point in Zuckmayer's work, resulting in more problem dramas during the following decades, as Paulsen (1967) had already emphasized. Whereas the first act succeeds best with its naturalistic dialogue and its characterization of Harras, the second act uses expressionistic techniques, and the characters are painted with a demonizing foil. The third act is close to Schiller's dramas in its use of religious and expressionistic symbolism. Thus the form, particularly of the second half of the drama, is epigonic. The topicality of the subject matter, the break in style after the first act, the problem of the Harras and Oderbruch characters, and a conversation about the Faustian nature of the German national character are the outgrowth of the author's exile. Wehdeking thinks that Zuckmayer realized in Harras the possibility of playing out his own theoretical alternatives to emigration. He thus consoled himself by proving that it would have been impossible to fight actively against National Socialism. Wehdeking also sees the weaknesses of the Oderbruch character as connected with the author's decision to drop the idea of fighting against Hitler within Germany. Harras's conversation with the American Lawrence marks a decisive turning point in Zuckmayer's work by casting doubt upon the vitalistic image of man, which he had accepted without questioning in his dramas written before the Second World War. Wehdeking praises Zuckmayer's withdrawal of the play in 1963 since it had been misunderstood by the Germans.

But not all critics agreed with Rinser's, Glade's, and Wehdeking's autobiographical approach. Siegfried Mews (1981a) explicitly argues against Harras as a purely wishful self-image: "Harras' increasing moral stature and ultimate atonement reveal the playwright's dissociation from his youthful dreams about an active life unencumbered by introspection and awareness of moral categories" (88).

The majority of the scholarly articles that appeared during the 1960s and beyond are devoted to the theme of *Vergangenheitsbewältigung*, one of the major topics of German literature after 1945. The question of resistance against Hitler ranks foremost in this research, in most cases stimulated by the discussion surrounding the controversial character of Oderbruch. In an article on the resistance movement in recent German dramas, which appeared in the American periodical *German Quarterly*, Ian C. Loram (1960) deals with a total of eight contemporary dramas, including *Des Teufels General* and *Der Gesang im Feuerofen*. In his interpretation, Oderbruch comes away as much more human than in most other considerations of *Des Teufels General*. He "is not a cold fanatic. His convictions are of an almost religious nature" (7). Loram interprets Harras's death as a form of resistance. It is the only form in which he can resist, confirming the suspicions of the Nazi Party. All of Harras's personal remarks about Nazism are seen by Loram as part of a *personal* attempt at resistance, though halfhearted. "Despite all his shortcomings, Harras does illustrate, although he may not realize it, the surest resistance to all brutality: a belief, however well camouflaged, in the essential decency of humanity" (8). This is not only diametrically opposed to the Marxist and other leftist interpretations; it is also trying hard to make the drama fit the theme of the essay.

Sheila Rooke's 1964 article in a British publication still reflects the general enthusiasm about the drama at the time of her writing. She reports that *Des Teufels General* "is generally acknowledged to be Zuckmayer's greatest work. It will almost certainly go down in history as the most powerful play about the Nazi régime to be written by a German so soon after the end of the war" (216). With regard to Oderbruch she concludes that "there seems little doubt that it was not Zuckmayer's intention to give him any more significance other than that of a last link in the chain of the events leading up to Harras' suicide" (218). The interesting aspect of Rooke's essay is that she compares the treatment of Oderbruch in the drama with that in the 1954 film version, which she does in a much more scholarly manner than the pedagogical article by Benicke (1960). Tacitly assuming that the changes in the film version go back to Zuckmayer, which was not the case, she feels the film's al-

terations in the character of Oderbruch "mark the beginning of a new
and cautious Zuckmayer, imbued with a feeling of social responsibility.
From Oderbruch onwards this earnest school of heroes follow their im-
pulses initially as much as Bückler and Harras, but come to the ultimate
realization that this is a selfish and sinful path" (221). It is interesting
that Rooke does not come to this conclusion with respect to Zuckmayer's earlier dramas, although she lists Ingeborg Engelsing-Malek's
(1960) study in her bibliography.

The German scholars of this time for the most part share the opinion of their Anglo-Saxon colleagues. Like Loram and Rooke, Rudolf
Lange (1969) sees *Des Teufels General* primarily as a drama about German resistance against Hitler, as a drama in which Zuckmayer tries to
vindicate the other, better Germany. In his view the play's success is
based on the fact that it deals with problems that occupied people in
Germany after the collapse of the Third Reich. Tracing these problems
back to their timeless roots is a typically Zuckmayerian procedure.

Henning Rischbieter (1965) sees a lot of weaknesses in the drama,
but he ultimately also feels that it contributed to *Vergangenheitsbewältigung*. He calls Zuckmayer's play a "naturalistic problem drama"
(45). In his view, however, the author's dramatic calculation is proven
wrong. In the first act, Harras feels too good about himself; the second
act contains too many sensational elements; and the third act presents,
much too late, Harras's decisive moral change. *Des Teufel's General*
certainly contributed to the inner German process of clarification, to
the official, decisive distancing from National Socialism, and also to the
official praise of the resistance movement. The vital figure of Harras
may have contributed to sweetening the bitter pill of coming to terms
with the past for many. Rischbieter points out a number of parallels
between Zuckmayer's play and Hochhuth's later documentary drama
Der Stellvertreter (*The Deputy*, 1963).

Arnold Bauer (1970) also attributes the success of the drama to the
fact that with the character of Harras and with many of the minor characters, Zuckmayer had recognized the image the majority of Germans
had of themselves who, because of their patriotic traditions, had half-
heartedly welcomed the successes of National Socialism. Heinz Geiger
(1973) also discusses the drama clearly in terms of *Vergangenheitsbewältigung* on the stage. He praises Zuckmayer's superior exposition
of all important characters — with the exception of Oderbruch. In
contrast to Rilla (1950), for example, Geiger interprets Harras's remarks about his relation to National Socialism as evidence of his understanding the contradiction between his personal anti-Nazi

convictions and his actions, thus as indirect self-criticism. In the course of the drama, Harras then becomes increasingly aware of his guilt, for which he atones by flying to his own death. In Harras and Oderbruch two basic modes of behavior clash: exterior support, together with inner rejection, on the one hand and absolute resistance on the other. Zuckmayer does not, however, succeed in making Oderbruch into a likable character. He is too cold and ethically rigorous, whereas Harras's warmth of character seems to excuse his actions. Geiger points out that in the 1966 version Oderbruch's radical rationale is decisively mitigated because he no longer consciously includes the death of innocent people in his calculations. But in the end, Oderbruch's radical theses remain, and Zuckmayer fails to make his attitude plausible. His character is still pale and without contour.

In Blake Lee Spahr's (1992) view, "the play is condemnation not of the Nazis — they are satirized with gallows humor — but of the 'good German' who protested that he had never been a Nazi and had disapproved of Hitler, and refused to accept guilt by association" (465).

Several other critics tried to place the drama into a literary tradition. Martin Greiner (1958) is primarily concerned with Zuckmayer as an author of folk plays, but he ends up discussing *Des Teufels General* as a drama about coming to terms with the past. Since he refers to the author's historical dramas as historical folk plays, in his opinion *Des Teufels General* marks a turning point in Zuckmayer's creativity. The folk play is now replaced by dramas dealing with freely roaming spirit and political ideology. Yet Zuckmayer depicts the air force general Harras as a folk hero, as the unadulterated, natural human being who is entangled with the devil, a fate he does not recognize until it is too late. Ultimately Harras does not sacrifice himself, because it is too late for that; he just ends it all. The play is ideologically unclear. It glorifies a man who in all his glory turns out to be helplessly weak, involved in error and guilt. He is not a "positive hero"; he is not transformed into a resistance fighter, and he is not ready to be one. Thus Zuckmayer consciously renounces the political thesis play. In Greiner's view the ending is a personal, private one, but, in contrast to East German critics, he calls it decent because someone faces the consequences of his mistakes instead of covering them up. With all its human warmth and closeness to life, the play is in artistic respects a last and extreme possibility of a folk play: the emotional identification of the poet with his hero, of the creator with his creature. With this drama the *Volksdichter* (popular poet) Zuckmayer has reached his limit. The folk play fails when the

subject matter requires artistic distance. Now Zuckmayer had either to
turn back or to change his genre.

The American scholar Roy C. Cowen (1976) too considers the literary traditions of *Des Teufels General.* He credits the drama's success to
its naturalistic representation of Nazi Germany of 1941 and its depiction of factually accurate charactertypes. Almost every geographic area
of Germany is represented among the characters, as are, in vertical
terms, the various social classes and age groups. Among the younger
and the older generation, all possible motives for their participation in
the Nazi state are systematically explored. What all the types have in
common is that they reveal the impact of social change on man's behavior. There are no demonic or Satanic overtones, not even in the ardent
Nazis. In Cowen's view, Zuckmayer's use of geographical and social
types is almost too "slick." His "quantitatively complete presentation of
all conceivable reactions — economic, artistic, moral and otherwise —
to Nazi rule and war" runs the risk "that each character personifies attributes so thoroughly, so purely, that he comes close to becoming a
mere abstraction of historical forces" (86–87). By the "coincidental"
appearance of all the main types of the Third Reich at the same time in
the same place, however, Zuckmayer tests our credulity. In contrast to
these types, Harras, with his single-minded indifference to political and
social changes, borders dangerously on a Hollywood-type hero, a hero
who, as Cowen points out and as Jacobius (1955) had already hinted
at, bears many similarities to Georg Büchner's Danton (1835). Cowen
thus sees many of the play's weaknesses, but he still believes that Zuckmayer has accomplished a lot by portraying the burning questions of his
time; as a dramatist, he is not obligated also to solve them.

Finally, several critics compare *Des Teufels General* with other contemporary works dealing with the period of the Third Reich. In a short
article that goes back to a presentation he made as part of a summer
course at the University of Mainz, Erwin Rotermund (1976) looks at
Zuckmayer's *Des Teufels General* in comparison with Wolfgang Borchert's *Draußen vor der Tür* (*The Man Outside,* 1945) and Max Frisch's
Nun singen sie wieder (*Now They Sing Again,* 1946). He uses the theses
of Alexander and Margarete Mitscherlich's book *Die Unfähigkeit zu
trauern* (*The Inability to Mourn,* 1967) as criteria for evaluation and
asks himself to what extent the works in question have a part in the attempt to introduce "collective mourning" (77). He agrees with
Wehdeking (1973) that Zuckmayer seems to share the demonological
perception of National Socialism that was held during the Third Reich
by many representatives of the so-called "inner emigration" and that

was used time and again after 1945 as a means of coming to terms with the past. On the other hand, he points out the many concrete, rational insights contained in the author's drama. In spite of the superimposed mythical-demonic elements, Zuckmayer was the most successful one of the three dramatists in this respect. Rotermund concludes that, although the subject of guilt has been clearly exposed by Zuckmayer, the drama offered certain groups of the postwar audience the possibility of exoneration and denial. Thus *Des Teufels General* could be one-sidedly understood "by means of fragmentary identification" (84), just as the Mitscherlichs theorized twenty years after the play was written.

Like Rotermund, Herbert Lederer (1980) compared *Des Teufels General* to other works of literature, taking a close look at the treatment of the German aviator Ernst Udet. In addition to Zuckmayer's play, he looked at a novel by an American, Martha Dodd, *Sowing the Wind* (1945), and, based on that novel, a play by an East German, Hedda Zinner, titled *General Landt* (written in 1950–51). As the comparison of the two plays demonstrates, Zuckmayer concentrates on the individual conflict of conscience within his protagonist, who is basically a decent human being, whereas Zinner uses a more doctrinaire approach, developing the villainy of the collaborator more prominently. Lederer compares Udet to Harras and points out all the traits Zuckmayer has borrowed from his old friend from the First World War. He recognizes Harras as "a tragic figure, although not a heroic one. In spite of the personal courage he often demonstrates, it is his essential weakness, his self-indulgence, which constitutes the tragic flaw of his character and is the cause of his destruction" (178). Harras is in the middle between the Nazi Schmidt-Lausitz and the resistance fighter Oderbruch, caught in an insoluble ethical dilemma. Whereas Martha Dodd's novel is an unsuccessful prose melodrama, Lederer points out that Hedda Zinner's play constitutes a political response to Zuckmayer's drama. In contrast to Zuckmayer's Oderbruch and his associates, who resist out of personal conviction, Zinner's heroes are communists who subject themselves to strict party discipline. Seen against the backdrop of her black-and-white propaganda play, Zuckmayer's drama fares much better in Lederer's estimation because it provides "insights into the infinite variety of human individuality" (183).

Finally, Reinhold Grimm (1981), in an interesting note on the reception of the play, reports about a production that premiered on 23 January 1979 in Dallas, Texas, under the direction of Harry Buckwitz, originally from Frankfurt, who directed the first Munich production. As a result of a drastic shortening of the first act, the drama gained momentum in this production, and Oderbruch was successfully turned into a humanly convincing, moving character. The short article is not only a testimony to the international viability of the play; it seems to repeat a view often voiced in the *Blätter der Carl-Zuckmayer-Gesellschaft*: that the audience appreciation of the play was greater than that of the arrogant critics who were only looking for excitement and entertainment.

Since the drama does not contain major women figures, a feminist interpretation is missing. The lack of attention the play received during the past decade is probably responsible for the fact that other modern critical approaches have not been applied either.

Der Gesang im Feuerofen

Der Gesang im Feuerofen, the drama about French resistance and treason, German complacency and cruelty, and love on both sides, premiered under Heinz Hilpert's direction on 3 November 1950 in Göttingen. Ten days later a new version that the author had approved was performed, under the direction of Heinrich Koch, at the Schauspielhaus in Hamburg. Koch had shortened the play considerably; cut out the allegorical characters of Father Wind, Mother Frost, and Brother Fog; and divided the court action of the prologue into a prologue and an epilogue, for which Zuckmayer wrote a "dance of death" as a conclusion. With 415 performances at thirty-two theaters, the play became the hit of the 1950–51 German theater season. But the reviews were mixed. Audience and critics did not accept Zuckmayer's leap into the mythical-allegorical sphere. This criticism is also reflected in the scholarly response to the drama.

As usual, the early textimmanent interpretations concentrated on the formal aspects. In his 1952 dissertation, Wolfgang Teelen presents a grouping of the characters into good and bad, loving and hating, even providing a table to illustrate his point. According to him, there is a balance of the personality types, making the whole drama appear calculated. The play is a total view of the possibilities of human existence.

In judging the form of the drama, Teelen again applies Staiger's terminology, showing that Zuckmayer has eliminated the possibility of a dramatic development. The characters do not change; the drama is not concerned with the purification of the characters through the action but with demonstrating the dangerous condition of man in general. Zuckmayer presents situations instead of dramatic discussions. He is successful to the extent that he succeeds in producing irritation and excitement on the part of the spectator by the use of visual effects and situations. But when the spectator is forced to absorb maxims directly that are intended symbolically or poetically, the play looses in comparison to other, similar ones. It confirms what has become obvious in Zuckmayer's other dramas too, namely that he prefers a kind of stage presentation intent on producing effects that differ from the classical drama of conflict. Teelen thus reaches his conclusions from a purely formal point of view. One might add that he could have arrived at similar conclusions by exclusively focusing on content and message.

In contrast to Teelen, J. Vandenrath (1960) believes the play is richer in "drama" than any previous Zuckmayer play. The ending marks a high point of dramatic theater in Zuckmayer's work.

Formal concerns are also the focus for Arnold John Jacobius (1955). He sees *Der Gesang im Feuerofen* as documentation of Zuckmayer's increasing turn away from naive realism. The representation of symbolic characters and the addition of an extra dimension through the introduction of divine and elementary powers are innovations. In its vertical division of the stage into three parts, the drama reminds us of the mystery plays of the Middle Ages. But a number of the stylistic elements may rather be called expressionistic — for example, the symbolic function of characters, the transformation of characters into several others, the use of masks, the symmetrical arrangement of several groups with similar names, the playing of several roles by the same actor, and the stylization of stage and costumes. But *Der Gesang im Feuerofen* does not represent a return to the techniques of *Kreuzweg*; rather it is the end of a cyclical development. The problem of fate is the only one that both plays have in common.

Alfred Happ (1956) too is concerned with the play's turn away from realism, and he ultimately arrives at a negative conclusion regarding the realistic and mythic levels of the play. In his opinion, the angels in the play pronounce the human insight that we all bear responsibility for what happens around us and that we all must change for the better. Zuckmayer has thus withdrawn to a position of tragic wisdom, granting good and evil a place on the stage of life and lighting a small flame of hope that human beings can effect change in each another. The alternation of realistic events and lyrical intermezzi leads to a vacillation between abhorrence and calming with an effect that is at the same time stirring and cathartic.

For Martin Greiner (1958) the nature-myth frame, the tragedy of jealousy, the heroic love, the massacre on Christmas Eve, and the chorale of the dying in the burning house are all the strong elements of the folk play; but in this case Zuckmayer tries to elevate them into the sphere of the symbolic and meaningful, the gruesome and topical, and thus into timelessness. Zuckmayer wants to conjure up a phenomenon of political demonic nature, an hour of judgment and tragedy for our world.

The fact that the drama contains several levels and that their characters are often symbolical representations of abstract ideas has concerned a number of other critics, too. J. Vandenrath (1960) feels that the allegorical aspects are not very convincing because of the weaknesses in the theological and philosophical ideas expressed by them. The doubling of the allegorical framework weakens the force of expression. Sheila Rooke (1964) is also very critical of the fact that the play is enacted on two levels: "It is not that the blending of the cosmic and the earthly is not a valid device, but a certain lip service to an out-of-date Expressionism is noticeable in the introduction of the figures Vater Wind, Mutter Frost and Bruder Nebel" (222). She criticizes the "confused biblical references" (222) and the character of the traitor Creveaux, who "fails to convince as a symbol of international hatred, for he is so uncompromisingly evil and sub-human that he lacks credibility" (222). Rooke feels that *Hochland* must have been placated at least to some degree by this play — a reference to Hanns Braun's (1948) Christian conservative essay on *Des Teufels General* — since the priest Francis is a most acceptable replacement for Oderbruch.

For Rudolf Lange (1969) the fusion of the two levels of action, the realistic and the mythic, is not compelling since reality and mythical reality do not penetrate one another. Arnold Bauer (1970) criticizes, above all, the character of Creveaux as overdrawn; he is too similar to his biblical model, Judas. The relation between the characters and the natural elements is too direct and artificial. Zuckmayer's intention of contributing to a Franco-German reconciliation fails insofar as he has disparaged those French who accepted German domination after France's military collapse. Thus Creveaux might be taken as representative for the Pétain French. Thomas Ayck (1977), for whom good literature should be rational and sociocritical, judges that instead of *persons* there is obtrusive *symbolism*. Melodrama, vulgar philosophy, a drive to preach, and pathetic aphorisms displace the drama's realistic elements.

Most other critics have looked at the drama in terms of its humanitarian and moral message, and they defend it, particularly the fact that it takes place on different planes, because in their opinion this division of the action serves its intended mission. It is interesting to note that the voices that are closest in time to the drama's writing, particularly the American critics, take a more positive view than the later, mostly German ones. Murray B. Peppard (1952) points out that Zuckmayer's postwar plays show "an even greater emphasis on humanity than that which distinguishes his earlier work" (349) and that they all, including *Der Gesang im Feuerofen*, focus on moral problems. G. Guder (1953–54) sees the drama in connection with Zuckmayer's other dramas in which an inner voice speaks the truth to man, enabling him "to remain true to the divine voice in death and destruction as well as in life" (55). Seeing it in the tradition of the ancient Greek dramas, Guder views it as "the new German drama in which thought, expression, language and scenery, the poet's vision and its artistic treatment form together one perfect unity" (56).

Henry Glade (1958) states that in *Der Gesang im Feuerofen* Zuckmayer's "concern for the moral welfare of men reaches its most self-consciously moralistic and willfully antidramatic stage of development" (117). This comes out in the "symbolical-theological level" (118) of the drama, which presents its message in realistic, allegorical (the powers of nature), and surrealistic (the two angels) levels of dramatization. The character of the mother appears on all three levels, on the realistic one as Soularde, on the allegorical as Mother Frost, and on the surrealistic one as the archetype of the mother. On the realistic level, *Humanität* is embodied in the protagonists as bearers of principles. On the allegorical and surrealistic levels, the ethical credo evolved on the realistic level is seen in its transcendental implications. *Humanität* in this drama is focused on in the concepts of freedom, justice, and love. On the realistic level, there are forgiveness and love without any recourse to juridical justice; on the allegorical level, there are unconcern and revenge; and "on the surrealistic level, . . . there is wrath and the verdict of forfeit of grace." (132) Glade's sensitive interpretation is entirely in accordance with the spirituality of Zuckmayer's drama. He follows the trend of the 1950s in interpreting the crimes of the recent past in metaphysical terms, going even further than in his treatment of *Des Teufels General.*

In the only article that has so far been devoted exclusively to *Der Gesang im Feuerofen*, Glade (1974) repeats some of his above theses. He sees the drama as part of Zuckmayer's attempt to create a new moral climate in Germany after the war; as a new realization of Zuckmayer's *Humanität* concept in all its ethical and metaphysical respects — that is, in terms of "restoring the natural relationship of man to organic life" (163). At the heart of this endeavor is the author's faith in the essential goodness and sacredness of life. Wholeness, freedom, justice, and love, the components of Zuckmayer's worldview, are personified in the various characters of the play. Glade thus elaborates on the philosophical tenets underlying Zuckmayer's drama, pointing out that it contains the quintessence of his reflective *Humanität*. His distinction of the three levels, however, which he repeats in this essay, has evoked criticism. In Siegfried Mews's view (1981a), for example, Glade "perhaps unnecessarily complicates matters by speaking of three . . . levels" (155).

Ingeborg Engelsing-Malek (1960) investigates *Der Gesang im Feuerofen* with regard to the realization of her study's theme of *amor fati*, which in this case is presented not on an individual level but on a higher one. The play discusses the question why some people succeed in achieving agreement with their fate whereas others incur more and more guilt and are not able to free themselves from this entanglement. There is no longer an individual hero, only the forces of good and evil, love and hatred. The groups of persons represent mankind as such. Love is ultimately victorious. Paul Meinherz (1960) comes to the same conclusions with regard to form and message. He calls the drama Zuckmayer's most modern and at the same time his most somber play. It lacks a central character who could hold together the individual scenes; his place is taken up by the overcoming of hatred. But in its perfection, this love, which is close to Christian love, endangers the drama just as much as a perfect hero or a saint would.

J. Vandenrath (1960) uses the same Christian terminology when he states that it is the evil in the world itself that occupies Zuckmayer in this drama. Even more than in *Des Teufels General*, he sees it as a religious rather than a political phenomenon. What is new is that at no point in the drama does Zuckmayer hint at the possibility of a positive, happy solution; thus he creates the impression of an inescapable course of destiny. For Vandenrath, Sprenger is the only absolutely evil character in the play; he is the devil himself. By comparison, in the character of Creveaux, Zuckmayer develops evil psychologically as the result of a hurt ego. In the general fight of good against evil, the good ultimately remains victorious and the good characters forgive their enemies. Since, in contrast to *Des Teufels General*, *Der Gesang im Feuerofen* demonstrates that not only Germans fell victim to the evil during the last war, Zuckmayer again comes out against the notion of German collective guilt. The play is directed not only against National Socialism but also against communism. As in *Der Hauptmann von Köpenick*, Zuckmayer demands respect for the life of the individual, which he places above the claims of ideologically determined forms of society.

The Christian ideological framework also determines Ausma Balinkin's interpretation (1976). For her, *Der Gesang im Feuerofen* has the predominantly religious theme of "redemption through love": "In that play the purification process involves literally going through the cleansing fire — 'Fegefeuer' — towards attaining inner peace and harmony" (86). Using similar terms, William Grange (1991) summarizes the play's message even more succinctly, stating that "the play was essentially a portrayal of evil's effect upon the world and a preachment for the need of love which transcended evil's power . . . . Given mankind's exposed situation, the play advocated man's embrace of a universal, all-encompassing love to achieve the sublime, inner freedom" (138).

But not all critics have emphasized the timeless, metaphysical themes of the drama. In accordance with the theme of his article, Ian C. Loram (1960) regards it from a political point of view, as a resistance drama. He sees similarities between Sylvester and Harras with respect to an affinity in their love for what is beautiful and elemental in life. The communist Marcel, on the other hand, shows his immaturity in the political motivation of his resistance, until at the end he understands that love is of overruling importance. In referring to Peppard (1952), Loram rightfully points out the moral aspect of the decision to resist.

Heinz Geiger (1973) too deals with resistance and joint guilt in *Der Gesang im Feuerofen*. Since, given his topic, he was forced to take into consideration the unrealistic elements of the drama, he had to regard the play negatively as a resistance drama. In Geiger's opinion, the situation in this drama is more pointed than that in *Des Teufels General*. No individual character is at the center of attention, but rather a "case." And whereas General Harras was only indirectly responsible for the crimes of the Nazi regime, the military figures in *Der Gesang im Feuerofen* must decide between absolute obedience and refusal to carry out orders. Zuckmayer produces this conflict in several versions on both the German and the French sides, placing its representatives into similar situations and allowing them to act in similar ways. The resistance in *Der Gesang im Feuerofen* is more determined by Harras's absolute love than by Oderbruch's rigorous contempt for life. In stressing the polarity of good and evil, the play becomes a secularized mystery play, a spiritual concept, a fact that is confirmed by the tendency to raise events onto a symbolic plane. Geiger considers this symbolic plane, though reduced and simplified in Zuckmayer's new version, to be questionable. The lyrical and reflective passages, in which the author ponders guilt and sorrow, good and evil in man, demonstrate once more that his strength lies in the presentation of lifelike characters and scenes filled with atmosphere, and not in the presentation of philosophical and ethical ideas. The discrepancy between the realistic and surrealistic planes of action is maintained to the end with the play's final turn toward the mythical expiation and redemption of the traitor and his acceptance by a half real, half symbolic mother figure. This mixture of a realistic topic and a mystery play renders Zuckmayer's play unsuccessful, in Geiger's view.

The problem of reconciling the two possible interpretations, namely as a drama about metaphysical or moral issues and as a resistance drama, has troubled several critics. Siegfried Mews (1981a) simply declares that "it is evident that Zuckmayer was not primarily interested in exploring the political aspects of the resistance movement but rather in probing metaphysical problems — problems that transcend the specific historical situation in the Savoy mountains of Southeastern France in 1943 and 1944" (93–94). Following this line of argumentation, Hans Wagener (1983c) points out that the reception of Zuckmayer's topical problem dramas was based on a permanent misunderstanding on the part of his audience and the professional critics because Zuckmayer was only secondarily concerned about his own time; his primary interest was the development of his hero or heroine toward *Humanität*, the realization of the divine on earth. Thus *Der Gesang im Feuerofen* was not intended as a realistic resistance drama but as a metaphysical one. The play is a drama in which the author professes his belief in the necessity of the renewal of man by reminding us of his position within divine creation. Echoing Geiger's (1973) judgment, but without using the realistic resistance drama as a yardstick, Wagener concludes that with its religious content, the drama is in the tradition of one large strand of world literature. It was not successful because of its experimental form, its court scenes in heaven, and its nature-myth personifications.

As in the case of *Des Teufels General*, the misunderstanding of the play was a factor in its East German reception. The GDR reviews of the West Berlin production followed Otto F. Riewoldt's (1978) premise that GDR criticism would view the appearance of angels and all mystical elements of the drama negatively. Herbert Ihering, as quoted by Riewoldt, considered the transposition of the drama onto the mystical plane escapist. From his Marxist vantage point, Wilfried Adling (1959) called the play a "falsification of reality" (240). Since in his view reality is the only basis for a drama, he must judge negatively all religious and symbolic aspects. As in the case of *Des Teufels General*, he sees a correlation between the message of the play and contemporary U.S. politics. The play pronounces a reconciliation between the French and German fascists and thus supports the expansive cosmopolitanism of the United States. It does, however, present itself as antifascist in that it contains the beginnings of criticism of the barbarity of fascism. As a result of this unintended effect, the play had become the most frequently performed drama in the Federal Republic during 1950–51. Siegfried Mews (1981a) later countered, with specific reference to Adling, that "there is an inherent element of unfairness in the attempt to cast Zuckmayer in a political mold. After all, the playwright was quite explicit in emphasizing that his concerns were not primarily political" (97).

The East German Werner Lüder (1987) finally sees in the play a mystification of individual responsibility. It can be understood as Zuckmayer's reaction to the reproaches that were directed against *Des Teufels General*. Consequently, he now moves further away from his image of the resistance as he had presented it before in Oderbruch. Lüder feels that the extrarational elements lead away from the core of the subject matter. In spite of grave concerns, *Der Gesang im Feuerofen* was performed in Rostock in 1957, after most of the mythical passages had been eliminated.

Reworking of Hauptmann's *Herbert Engelmann*

Zuckmayer's admiration for Hauptmann and his work is evident by the fact that Hauptmann's widow asked Zuckmayer to rework the drama *Herbert Engelmann*, which Hauptmann had essentially completed in the early 1920s. The drama is about a man who returns from the First World War and robs a *Geldbriefträger* (postman delivering money), accidentally killing him as a consequence. Zuckmayer's version premiered in Vienna's Burgtheater on 10 March 1952. Barbara Glauert's (1977) anthology of reviews strangely contains none on *Herbert Engelmann*, but a number of scholarly articles that come to opposing conclusions are devoted to Zuckmayer's reworked version.

In a review of the first book edition of 1952 containing both versions of the drama, C. F. W. Behl (1952) describes the stages of Hauptmann's writing and reworking of the original manuscript. He criticizes the publication of elements of Hauptmann's later abandoned version and Zuckmayer's turning Herbert Engelmann from an aspiring young writer into a nuclear physicist. He considers Zuckmayer's first act an improvement over Hauptmann's version because of its added color. Zuckmayer's reworking loosened up the dialogues, tightened some scenes, effected a more immediate stage impression, and worked out the contours of individual characters. Behl's final judgment is extremely positive. He feels that Zuckmayer's reworking was done with all the sensitivity due an idol.

Helmut Boeninger's 1952 article deals in much more detail with the changes that Zuckmayer made in the original version. He claims that Zuckmayer brought the language up to date by introducing a more modern and more appropriate idiom and cleaned it up in its purely grammatical aspects. There are also more precise stage directions. But Zuckmayer also changed the attitude and the interpretation (or the philosophy) of the play. Thus he shaped the tragedy by toning down and partly omitting the frequent references to the formative influences on Herbert's life. He "intends to focus the argument upon absolutes, upon permanent values, away from the relativistic *tout comprendre — tout pardonner*" (348). Boeninger concludes with the positive evaluation that "the younger dramatist has brought to life the timebound, temporal drama of his senior" (348). Like Behl's, Boeninger's attitude toward Zuckmayer's version is thus extremely favorable. Although he provides good examples of the stylistic changes, his documentation for the changes in attitude and interpretation is incomplete.

Blake Lee Spahr (1954) continues this line of positive assessment, which he repeats in his encyclopedia article of 1992. He intends to provide a more complete delineation of the complex psychological motivations of the hero to complement Boeninger's article. According to him, Zuckmayer made changes that Spahr summarizes under the heading of "dramatic economy" (339), particularly expository improvements — for example, building up suspicion in the audience regarding Engelmann's crime. The dialogues and actions of the characters are far more in keeping with their personalities, and they are more directed toward furthering the plot than forming background atmosphere. Additions provide further motivation for the characters' actions, particularly for Herbert Engelmann himself, whom Zuckmayer has provided with a motivation for his suicide. He has made *Herbert Engelmann* into a "succinct and intricately drawn psychological study" (345).

Ingeborg Engelsing-Malek (1960) too comes to a positive assessment. She tries to show that the *amor fati* structure, which she has proclaimed for all of Zuckmayer's plays, also applies to the reworking of Hauptmann's drama. Thus she feels that Zuckmayer has freed Hauptmann's hero from his passiveness and his contempt for life. Through his love for Christa, Engelmann is purified and regains his belief in life, against which he has sinned. This inner purification is due to Zuckmayer, whose adherence to the idea of *amor fati* is skillfully developed out of Hauptmann's love for another human being.

Later critics disagreed with a number of these contentions and overall positive assessments. Siegfried Muller (1962), for example, takes issue with Boeninger's claim that Zuckmayer's changes are necessary improvements. He furthermore argues that some of Hauptmann's grammatical errors may have been intentional, introduced as a naturalistic feature to reflect the fact that ordinary people do not always use grammatically correct language. He also notes some additions by Zuckmayer that allow pinpointing the exact time of each act and several historical inaccuracies. J. Vandenrath (1960 and 1961) too criticized his predecessors for their favorable attitude toward Zuckmayer's version by objecting strongly to his weakening of the antiwar message. In Vandenrath's opinion, his predecessors Boeninger and Spahr made the mistake of assuming that Zuckmayer's reworking constituted an improvement vis-à-vis the original. Furthermore, they adhere too closely to what Zuckmayer himself stated in his afterword without testing whether it actually reflects the two texts. Vandenrath interprets Hauptmann's work as an antiwar drama that turns the best, noblest people into persons like Herbert Engelmann. Zuckmayer, however, has turned the hero into a special psychological case and has thus changed and possibly falsified the antiwar character of the play. In Hauptmann's drama, Engelmann's crime is the result of the condition into which the war has put him. He takes his own life, which has become unbearable for him. In Zuckmayer's drama, a man who has returned from the war has knowingly and consciously committed a murder. Thus he is guilty, is unable to come to terms with his guilt, and atones for it with his voluntary death. Zuckmayer has changed the atmosphere of seriousness and gruesomeness by adding comical aspects, and — on this point Vandenrath picks up one of Behl's (1952) objections — he has added a cheap topicality by turning Engelmann from a writer into a nuclear scientist. On the whole, Vandenrath asks himself how Zuckmayer came to believe that Hauptmann's play needed to be reworked at all. His version cannot be viewed as an improvement; it is less unified, less tragic, and weaker in its message.

Marvin Robert Maddox (1975) agrees with Vandenrath that the antiwar message is weakened by the change in the motivation for Herbert's crime that places the responsibility solely upon Herbert himself. But he objects to Vandenrath's overall negative evaluation: "Zuckmayer's version is not, however, rendered 'weniger einheitlich' [less unified] nor 'weniger tragisch' [less tragic] by his alterations" (178). Maddox uses the two versions of the drama to discuss the differences in the worldviews of Hauptmann and Zuckmayer. According to him, it is in their view of man himself that the two dramatists differ the most. Hauptmann's Herbert lacks free will and is the product of heredity and environment; Zuckmayer's Herbert, however, has free will and must accept full responsibility for his criminal act. Throughout the play, Zuckmayer's Herbert shows an increasing awareness of his complete responsibility for the murder. Whereas Zuckmayer condemns Herbert for his crime against humanity, Hauptmann makes society responsible for having made his life unbearable. According to Hauptmann, Herbert has incurred guilt against his will. Zuckmayer retains the influence of metaphysical forces, but they are not strong enough to prevent Herbert from acting against them. "Hauptmann's *Herbert Engelmann* contains an affirmation of the value of each human life and, primarily, a condemnation of society which denies this value by resorting to warfare. Zuckmayer's *Herbert Engelmann* also contains an affirmation of the value of each human life; rather than focusing upon a condemnation of society, however, it primarily condemns the individual who denies this value by murdering one of his fellow human beings" (177). Consequently, the suicide of Zuckmayer's Herbert is to be viewed as the execution of a death sentence imposed on him by a metaphysical court, as in the case of Harras. In Maddox's view, Zuckmayer's alterations indicate Zuckmayer's increased concern for ethical and moral problems following the Second World War. In contrast to Muller (1962), he speculates that it is likely that Hauptmann would have approved of Zuckmayer's stylistic changes since they give the language of the play a more naturalistic flavor.

In a balanced assessment, Siegfried Mews (1981a) for the most part echoes the opinion of Maddox, who had written his dissertation under Mews's guidance. He states that Zuckmayer essentially adheres to Hauptmann's drama in structure and plot, but he did change the dialogue and Hauptmann's concept of the main character. By adding a passage in which Engelmann proclaims the sanctity of each individual life and declares any offender against it sentenced or condemned, "it appears that Zuckmayer's Engelmann carries out a self-imposed sentence and commits suicide as a final act of atonement, almost in the fashion of General Harras in *The Devil's General*" (109). Zuckmayer's Engelmann thus incurs guilt by a moral transgression, becomes fully aware of his guilt, acknowledges it, and ultimately atones for his crime. Narrowing down Engelsing-Malek's (1960) view but adhering to it in principle, Mews feels that Zuckmayer thus employed the structural pattern of *Des Teufels General* and, though it was written later, *Das kalte Licht*. He changed the thrust of the play in making Engelmann an autonomous individual who is fully responsible for his deed. The adaptation demonstrates that Zuckmayer is not a mere imitator of Hauptmann but a playwright in his own right.

Zeitstücke about the Present

Das kalte Licht

Zuckmayer's atomic espionage drama *Das kalte Licht* premiered under Gustav Gründgens's direction on 3 September 1955 in Hamburg. The first essayistic articles that appeared in literary magazines were critical of the play for a number of reasons. In his review in *Der Monat*, Hellmut Jaesrich (1955) talks about one of the main questions posed by later scholarly criticism: the relation of Zuckmayer's hero Kristof Wolters to the historical atomic spy Klaus Fuchs. He stresses that both have a number of exterior features in common but that their character is entirely different. Whereas it is possible for us to understand Klaus Fuchs's actions, although we must judge them negatively, the opposite is the case with Kristof Wolters. We do not understand his actions because Zuckmayer has failed to make them plausible. In addition, Jaesrich criticizes the love action, which has qualities of operetta-like confusion. In a similar article in *Deutsche Rundschau*, Moritz Lederer (1955) sees the action of the play as a bad parody of a detective story. By defending the American position of 1945 — that the atomic bomb might best be controlled if only one nation knows its secret — Zuckmayer does not, in his opinion, dramatize the general opinion of 1955 — that the bomb in the hands of only one state is a deadly danger and that only resolute revelation of its scientific basis will make it a security guarantee for all. Zuckmayer thus ignores the ethical mission of the theater. Without stating it, Lederer thus turns Wolters's/Fuchs's betrayal into a moral act that the old-fashioned dramatist failed to see. In *Frankfurter Hefte*, Joachim Kaiser (1955) calls the dramatic framework meager. Zuckmayer's motivation for Wolters's betrayal is insufficient; it does not gain dramatic power. There is no struggle between persons and worldviews; a young man is overcoming his personal inhibitions and becomes a traitor for almost private reasons. Apart from a couple of discussions, the characters only voice opinions, and these fail to advance the action. Zuckmayer only touches upon problems without following up on the questions posed by Marxists regarding the dangers arising from great inventions or Western individualism. He has taken countless facts from Alan Moorehead's Klaus Fuchs biography, which stresses that Fuchs was a fanatical traitor who followed his conscience only. Zuckmayer, on the other hand, was too conciliatory, too humane, to portray a tough traitor who nevertheless is not a scoundrel. All the negative arguments presented in these essays were going to be taken up again in the scholarly discourse of the following decades.

The only unequivocally positive review among the early ones is by Alfred Happ (1956), which is very general and does not address the problems presented in the drama. Happ praises the play for its imposing density of invention and the physiognomic diversity of its characters on the realistic level, for the uncanny exactness of the human environment and the sometimes ghostly contrasts the characters are exposed to as a result of the events of the drama. Happ's textimmanent positive interpretation was to remain an exception.

In his dissertation of 1958 Henry Glade at first counters contemporary criticism by reiterating Zuckmayer's own justification for the drama: "The main purpose of the play is not the delineation of a contemporary problem which in any case would soon be a matter of history . . ., but rather an attempt to resolve the moral, social and transcendental problems under a perspective of eternity" (135). But in contrast to *Des Teufels General,* Glade considers *Das kalte Licht* chaotic because the moral, transcendental, and theatrical strands of the play never blend. The major characters are cardboard figures; "only the two Jewish figures (Friedländer and Löwenschild) have any degree of warm humanity. The dialogue is characterized by insensitivity and a facile and flippant superficiality" (136). As he did in the case of *Der Gesang im Feuerofen,* Glade analyzes Zuckmayer's realization of the concept of *Humanität* in terms of freedom, justice, and love. The international subject matter of the play reveals Zuckmayer's expanding range of contemporaneous interest. Since its main theme is the force of conscience, the drama's *Humanität* content is pitched to a high level. But conscience does not lend itself to a moral dissection. Wolters is simply miscast in his role; the outcome of the play is not even tragic. The concepts of freedom and justice show no noticeable progress since *Der Gesang im Feuerofen;* "they are merely given a more realistic and scientific coloring. Love likewise is less spiritualized in its equation with confidence and decency" (153). Although Glade places the play in Zuckmayer's development as an artist, his main criticisms are textimmanent, referring to lack of characterization and other formal weaknesses.

In accordance with Zuckmayer's own remarks about the play, a number of scholars interpret the play, like most of Zuckmayer's other dramas, as dealing with the personal development of its hero from his realization of error to atonement. Thus Murray B. Peppard (1957) sees a parallel to *Des Teufels General* in that the heroes of both plays lose their way in life, assume guilt by selling their souls to the devil, and ultimately atone for their actions. But in contrast to the betrayal in *Des Teufels General*, the betrayal here results from personal confusion and not from dedication to an ideal. While initially Wolters does not seem to have a problem of conscience or of an ethical nature, the play's meat consists in his realization that he has one. In Peppard's opinion, this process of gradual awakening constitutes the play's inner action, which takes place in Wolters's soul. Rather than reporting events of political importance, Zuckmayer focuses on the dilemma of the conscience of modern man. Thus Wolters's only criterion of judgment is the nature of his relation to those who are bound to him in trust. As in all of Zuckmayer's plays, trust in the goodness of man is the highest criterion of action. Restoring Wolters to the community of trust is the meaning of Hjördis's final words spoken to Northon, leading to Wolters's confession. Thus interpreting the subject of the play as the crisis of trust, Peppard probably comes close to the author's intentions. What makes his article interesting is his comparison of the inner structure of the play to other Zuckmayer dramas — not just to *Des Teufels General* but also to *Herbert Engelmann* and *Der Gesang im Feuerofen*.

Ingeborg Engelsing-Malek (1960) in many ways echoes Peppard's ideas but applies a somewhat different terminology. According to her, the basic theme of the play is the relationship of faithfulness to treason. The main concern is again the hero's own decision, his surrendering to his own fate. Like Gunderloch thirty years earlier, Wolters deceives himself when he believes that he can govern the world through reason alone. Through love he finds his real personality and gives up his original life plan. He is thus on the road to *amor fati*. Unfortunately, in Engelsing-Malek's view, the extended debates of the play fail to have the desired impact upon the audience and on Wolters.

J. Vandenrath (1960) also echoes Peppard's (1952) view that *Das kalte Licht* is concerned with the mental and spiritual development of its hero. Zuckmayer thus continues the theme of treason from *Des Teufels General*. The "drama" of Wolters's inner development is combined with the "theater" of a detective story. The hero's treason lies in his idealistic conviction that he has a responsibility toward all of mankind but not toward an individual nation. In the second act the political aspects of guilt are shifted toward personal, human relationships of trust. This, however, constitutes a logical mistake. Since Wolters has arrived at his deed from political considerations, the question of guilt has to be seen in conjunction with the political circumstances. Vandenrath sees *Das kalte Licht* repeatedly as an answer to the problematic character of Oderbruch in *Des Teufels General.* In *Das kalte Licht* Zuckmayer has come to different results. Vandenrath concludes that Zuckmayer did not succeed in adequately presenting the problems he had tackled; indeed, maybe they could not be solved in a *Zeitstück.* The inner dramatic elements of *Das kalte Licht* are stronger than those in other Zuckmayer dramas: the play consists almost entirely of dialogue, and in this respect, it constitutes a new stage in Zuckmayer's development. On the other hand, the play is poorer in theatrical elements than any previous one and is thus far removed from the colorfulness of his early ones.

Finally, in his article on the motif of encounter, Glade (1963) is mainly concerned with Wolters's personal development. Interestingly, he does not pass such harsh judgment upon the play as he had done in his dissertation of 1958. He points out the importance of Wolters's encounter with Löwenschild and Northon, which demonstrates "a shift from encounter leading to a recognition of an ultimate reality in the pan-erotic and mystical sense to recognition of love in an ethical sense" (188).

Another fairly uncritical article is the pedagogical one by Uwe Maßberg (1965). In quoting Zuckmayer, Maßberg, like Peppard (1957), Glade (1958), and Engelsing-Malek (1960), interprets *Das kalte Licht* as a drama of trust and stresses the return to the old Western ideas of justice and honor in the end. Thus the drama does not provide a solution to the conflict of today's physicists beyond the realm of the personal. As far as the form is concerned, Maßberg feels that *Das kalte Licht* corresponds very much to traditional ideas about the structure of a play. Zuckmayer's means are the conventional elements of the mystery story and the love story, which, however, impair the effectiveness of the portrayal of the inner split of man. Maßberg asks himself whether the form of a scenic reportage à la Kipphardt would not have been more appropriate to the fate of a Klaus Fuchs, lending the play greater topical importance.

The drama's subject matter made it particularly suitable for comparison with other dramas about the crisis of conscience of modern scientists: Bertolt Brecht's *Leben des Galilei* (*The Life of Galileo,* 1943), Friedrich Dürrenmatt's *Die Physiker* (*The Physicists,* 1962), and Heinar Kipphardt's *In der Sache J. Robert Oppenheimer* (*In the Matter of J. Robert Oppenheimer,* 1964). Maßberg's article is a good example of this, since he reports on a discussion, held in a German Gymnasium, in which *Das kalte Licht* is compared to the above dramas about scientists.

In accordance with the goal of the periodical, *Der Deutschunterricht*, in which the article appeared, he wants to provide other teachers with ideas on how to achieve lively instruction. The dramas are compared not only with regard to the basic conflict the modern scientist faces — the demands of science on the one hand and the demands of the powers providing the funds for research on the other; Maßberg also uses them to demonstrate the various possibilities of writing drama today.

Karl S. Weimar (1966) takes a similar approach, dealing with Brecht's *Galilei*, Dürrenmatt's *Physiker*, and Zuckmayer's *Das kalte Licht*. Repeating Zuckmayer's own interpretation that his drama is about the intellectual and ethical confusion of modern man, he does not view the play critically. According to him, Wolters's case is more complex than that of Klaus Fuchs who was a devoted communist. In Zuckmayer's drama, which he quotes, we are dealing with "misguided conviction," "a short circuit of conscience, a fission of the personal feeling of right and honor" (437). Zuckmayer's Wolters is unable to communicate as a human being. He passes on information because it does not really matter. The author ultimately leads his hero out of the impersonal world of science to a committed sense of responsibility, above all to himself. His drama is a Christian melodrama inasmuch as Wolters is snatched from certain damnation, the religious undertones being as strong as the purely psychological ones. In the inner development of Wolters and his relationship with Northon, Weimar sees the peculiarly German traditional attachment to the idea of development and guidance. As is obvious from Weimar's and earlier from Peppard's (1957) study, interpreters were able to come to a positive evaluation of *Das kalte Licht* only if they accepted Zuckmayer's own interpretation of the drama as one about a crisis of trust, relegating concrete political implications to the background.

The following interpretations from the late 1950s and beyond are all negative. The reasons for this are similar; they have to do with form, deficiencies in the characterization of Wolters and his motives for his betrayal, melodramatic elements (particularly at the end of the drama), and the incompatibility of the private motivation with the political potential of the drama.

For Martin Greiner (1958), Zuckmayer has lost his way from his predestined and appropriate road. In his view, the intellectual Kristof Wolters does not fit into the company of Zuckmayer's folk heroes. In the playwright's hands Wolters suddenly changes into a sentimental hero. Laboring under confused political circumstances, Zuckmayer turned against his own nature by writing a play on subject matter that would have been better suited for Brecht.

Sheila Rooke's (1964) general article on Zuckmayer contains most of these critical elements. According to her, it was obviously Zuckmayer's intention to write a continuation of the "Oderbruch-Marcel 'Problematik' " (225). (A few years later Wolfgang Paulsen [1967] agreed.) In comparing Fuchs and Wolters, Rooke concludes that whereas Fuchs is a man of definite views and his crime is one of ideological betrayal — just like Oderbruch's — Wolters is a confused, immature case for psychiatrists. His motives are particularly unconvincing since his superior, a man of outstanding wickedness, is beyond credibility. Further, "when a love affair between the superior's wife and Wolters develops, the bounds of the ludicrous have been not only reached but overstepped" (225). A conversion in such a confused personality as Wolters, moreover, is worthless. One gets the feeling that Northon is introduced not to lift the weight of guilt from Wolters's shoulders but to serve as a mouthpiece for Zuckmayer's own theories. The main defect in Zuckmayer's major postwar works "is the tendency to force a character to fit into a fixed compartment which meets the author's approval — in this case, the subordination of the individual and his ego to the requirements of society" (225).

Rudolf Lange (1969) criticizes the play's lack of a tight dramatic structure and the fact that the military and scientific events are not well connected to the private and inner happenings. Individual scenes are executed awkwardly. Some dialogues are too philosophical or theoretical; the language is bookish. Remy Charbon (1974) goes even further in his negative evaluation. For him Zuckmayer's drama looks like a mediocre colportage. In his view, it is worth looking at only because of the way it failed. After reporting the case of Klaus Fuchs and stating the problems of a modern scientist in detail, Charbon concludes that Zuckmayer did not succeed in dealing with his topic. Zuckmayer closely follows the events surrounding Klaus Fuchs and uses his character traits, but he simplifies the inner events and reinterprets them in an irresponsible manner, drawing the psychogram of an introverted social outsider who takes revenge on a society that constantly discriminates against him. In this respect Charbon confirms Rooke's (1964) assessment. At the root of Wolters's betrayal is his playful relationship to power. In Charbon's view, Zuckmayer did not succeed in making this a classical tragedy as he claimed in his afterword because Wolters did not fall victim either to an enormous guilt or to an unchangeable fate. He just did not have the ability to overcome the actual and imagined human distance to the people in his immediate environment. His actions appear as mere rationalizations of an inferiority complex, and the consequences of them concern only his own soul. After his voluntary confession, the drama slips into melodrama. In making the question of trust his main theme, Zuckmayer neglected important questions such as that of the responsibility for scientific problems, the problems of an enormous increase in power, the perspective of a global dictatorship based on science, and the consequent ability to annihilate humanity. Zuckmayer's belief in the unbroken order of the world, in models and norms of behavior, and that simple human decency can solve this world's conflicts prevent such important questions from being raised at all. Thus he fail to present adequately either the psychological aspects of the Fuchs case or the crisis of trust. At the end Wolters merely undergoes a sentimental conversion. Charbon's essay is less a scholarly examination of the drama than a biting critique. His voice is part of the chorus of those critics who consider Zuckmayer's late work as not responding to modern social and political problems.

Jim Elliott, Bruce Little, and Carol Poore (1976) also return to the question of features taken over from the historical Fuchs case. They believe that Zuckmayer has taken only personal traits of Fuchs and facts that have very little to do with the historical importance of the case. In their view, Zuckmayer minimizes the ethical considerations that led to Fuchs's betrayal, and he makes light of the entire historical context. Zuckmayer remained a petit bourgeois for whom his private life is more important than anything else, and conversely, for him political engagement can originate only from banal personal motivations. The turbulence of events at the end cannot cover up the decisive lack of realism. Hans Wagener (1983a) summarizes such arguments. He criticizes Zuckmayer for not dealing with the problems of the scientist in the modern world. The danger of such avoidance is that he seems to suggest that all problems of the world could be healed by interpersonal trust. Such an attitude seems somewhat naive in view of the international problems that lie behind the treason of a nuclear scientist. The endless debates, sensational action, and melodramatic ending lead Wagener to conclude that Zuckmayer went off the subject. In a public discussion on the topic "Zuckmayer's Werk zwischen Volkstümlichkeit und Realismus" (Zuckmayer's Work between Popularity and Realism, [Anonymous] 1986) Dieter Kafitz returned to the question of adequacy of form and subject matter by evaluating the form of *Das kalte Licht* in terms of the author's own intentions. He expressed the opinion that *Das kalte Licht* has innumerable artistic flaws. To be sure, Zuckmayer did not evade the issue by writing a parable or by exemplifying the problems of the modern scientist in a character like Galilei, but he used the traditional form of drama, incorporating only slightly modified contemporary figures. The form he chose, however, was entirely unsuitable to express what *he* wanted. In Kafitz's opinion, the political element of the play contains very reasonable views. Blake Lee Spahr (1992) agrees with the play's critics. For him its flaws are tedious argumentation and a lack of convincing characters. Furthermore, he notes, "Zuckmayer tries to combine the problem of responsibility of the nuclear physicist with the problem of love and trust on the personal level, and on neither level is he persuasive" (466).

Ausma Balinkin (1976) merely discusses the women characters in *Das kalte Licht* and thus bypasses all the important problems presented in the drama. In her view, the drama initiates a new period of Zuckmayer's central women characters that also includes characters in *Die Uhr schlägt eins, Kranichtanz, Das Leben des Horace A. W. Tabor*, and *Der Rattenfänger*. It is characterized by the fact that intuition is now completely absent from the women figures, whose insight comes too late. Their resilience and sustaining inner strength are severely reduced, leaving them as vulnerable as the men who depend on them. In Balinkin's view, *Das kalte Licht* brings a further convergence of the sexes toward a composite image of mankind: "Zuckmayer places the leading feminine figure in the same professional setting with the two central male figures — all three are physicists" (39). It seems odd to see the conservative Zuckmayer thus characterized as an advocate of women's lib.

Otto F. Riewoldt (1978) points out that, for GDR critics, *Das kalte Licht* was unacceptable and unperformable. As he reports, Lily Leder, in a GDR review of the Hamburg production of 1955, criticizes a lapse into purely private conflicts. Besides, there is a subliminal linkage between fascism and communism; the Soviet Union is attacked as being at least equal to fascism, maybe even more unscrupulous in its struggle for the possession of the atomic bomb. In an article in the East German periodical *Theater der Zeit*, Fritz Erpenbeck (1955) went one step further. For him Zuckmayer's drama could have been directly ordered by Mr. Dulles — the American Secretary of State at the height of the Cold War. Just as Paul Rilla (1950) had pointed out with respect to *Des Teufels General*, Zuckmayer uses the popularity of the *Zeitstück* without solving the dramatic conflict he postulates and without taking a clear political position. It goes without saying that, for the East German critic, Zuckmayer should have been in favor of passing along the atomic secrets since, in his view, only this would assure the peaceful use of atomic power. Zuckmayer should have said that his hero was right even if he perishes tragically. Wolters's final decency in Zuckmayer's play is then simply lack of character; his admission of guilt means denying and betraying the desire for a peaceful coexistence of peoples, giving up one's humanity, and being an accessory of the atomic strategists in the Cold War and actual ones.

Such views are echoed by the Marxist Wilfried Adling (1959), who calls *Das kalte Licht* the low point in Zuckmayer's development since here the dramatist has become a colportage dramatist of anti-Soviet agitation. As in the case of *Barbara Blomberg*, Adling discusses the dramatic possibilities of the subject matter, here the exposing of the intrigues of the Cold War and the function of the nuclear espionage trials in England and the United States. Zuckmayer sees these inherent possibilities but does not make use of them. Consequently, he must distort reality in such a way that his position is justified. Such an obvious falsification of reality can be achieved only with the help of blunt colportage. Thus again Adling judges Zuckmayer by what he thinks the playwright should have written, ignoring the fact that Zuckmayer was neither a Marxist nor a materialist. Like Adling, the East German critic Werner Mittenzwei (1961), as quoted by Riewoldt (1978), places the drama in the historical situation at the time it was written: on the one hand, the antinuclear movement that was supported by the Soviet Union and the other socialist countries; on the other hand, the investigation against J. R. Oppenheimer in the United States in 1954. In the dispute between these two poles, Zuckmayer clearly took the reactionary side. This resulted in a qualitative decline in his work. In Mittenzwei's opinion, *Das kalte Licht* is therefore proof of the thesis that today it is impossible for reactionary forces to produce great literature; humanistically intended great art is possible only on the side of the masses. History has refuted this view many times over. The more recent comments by Werner Lüder (1987) follow Adling's line when he argues for a drama he believes Zuckmayer *should* have written: Wolters's motivation for his espionage should have resulted from his attraction to communism. Zuckmayer serves the viewpoint of reactionary circles in the Federal Republic. The drama demonstrates rigidified political and philosophical views that were present in an embryonic stage in Zuckmayer's concessions in the postwar discussions surrounding *Des Teufels General*. Thus Lüder's comments testify to the fact that in 1987 the Cold War was not over yet.

Die Uhr schlägt eins

Die Uhr schlägt eins, Zuckmayer's drama about the Third Reich set in the context of the Federal Republic, premiered under Heinz Hilpert's direction at Vienna's Burgtheater on 14 October 1961. Under the heading "Schlägt dreizehn" (Strikes thirteen, a pun meaning "That's the limit"), the news magazine *Der Spiegel* published an anonymous review (1961) of the first performance that, without explicitly expressing an opinion, was devastating just by quoting negative reviews from daily newspapers. When the article finally quotes Zuckmayer, who supposedly stated that he intended to write at least twelve more plays, the implication is: let's hope that he doesn't. It is interesting that, by comparison, the review of the book edition of the drama by Helen Hodgson (1962) that appeared in the British journal *German Life and Letters* does not make any value judgment. It simply points out that Zuckmayer's solution for the problems of our times is that a change should take place in the life of the individual. Thus it is an expression of the respect the author enjoyed in Anglo-Saxon countries and the traditional hesitance of their reviewers to pass harsh judgment.

German scholars were not that bashful. They all felt that, like *Das kalte Licht,* the play is overburdened with clichés and sensational events. Wolfgang Paulsen (1967) feels that Zuckmayer has overdone it in terms of action. The whole fable seems too much like literature. Rudolf Lange (1969) concurs that so much action and so many problems have been stuffed into the play that the important questions are merely touched upon and the general impression remains superficial. The events correspond to the overused clichés of a magazine novel.

In their more recent evaluations, two German Zuckmayer scholars working in the United States agree with their colleagues, though they add a couple of special considerations. Siegfried Mews (1981a) feels that the thrilling events of the play tend to obscure the inner action, and he asks himself "whether a drama that is ostensibly concerned with coming to terms with the political past should entirely dispense with the ideological dimension" (123). Even a rudimentary degree of political awareness would have added to the depth of the main characters. For Hans Wagener (1983a) too the play is overburdened with clichés and sensational qualities. Zuckmayer does not succeed in creating a believable atmosphere, not even in the scenes that play in Germany. Gerhard is a typical Zuckmayer hero who finally takes responsibility for his life and accepts it. He professes his belief in man and in love as the remedy for the conflicts of the present and the past. Thus the work ends as a religious drama that wants to heal the present on the basis of Christian theology, beginning with the individual — not on the basis of historical and social analysis and not by means of a program based on reason. In Wagener's opinion, the play was unsuccessful because in 1960 Zuckmayer was alone in still believing that man is able to determine his own fate; he was out of touch with the reality of theater at the time. Lee Spahr (1992) continues Wagener's line of argumentation, calling the play "a lurid and unconvincing attempt to combine the theme of the prodigal son with a critique of postwar Germany's 'economic miracle' " (467). It is probably the worst of Zuckmayer's plays. "It is full of trashy clichés, and Zuckmayer's former strong points — the creation of atmosphere and the depiction of convincing and appealing characters — are lacking" (467).

Since Ausma Balinkin (1976) discusses only the women figures in Zuckmayer's dramas, she gains a limited perspective. For her, Gudula recognizes and acknowledges her part in a collective guilt. She is not resilient and cannot generate a new will to live; she is unable to adjust to her familial role or to banish the shadows of her past. In choosing security for the sake of her child, she had sacrificed not only herself but the memory of her dead husband as well. Unlike Barbara Blomberg, she does not experience an inner transformation, and she does not transcend the emotional sterility that follows dehumanization. Like Harras in *Des Teufels General*, "she expiates in death — a fate never before associated with a woman figure." (41). She thus shows that for Zuckmayer "men and women are equally helpless and vulnerable in a world where the deeper moral values are obscured by social, economic, and technological preoccupations" (41–42).

The New World Revisited

Kranichtanz

There are no investigations exclusively devoted to the one-act play *Kranichtanz*, which takes place within one family in a farmhouse in New England. It was written in 1961 and first performed under the direction of Leopold Lindtberg at the Zurich Schauspielhaus on 10 January 1967 as part of a celebration of Zuckmayer's seventieth birthday. Gerald P. Martin's 1977 article merely publishes a letter from Günther Fleckenstein, who was planning the play's first German performance in Göttingen, and a number of what Martin calls representative reviews of this production. The reviewers show a certain uneasiness in relation to the play. On the one hand, they praise the fact that Zuckmayer has pinpointed the consciousness of the young generation, which wants to live only in the present. On the other hand, they are mostly critical of the fact that Zuckmayer has his characters talk too much, the result of the fact that most events took place before the beginning of the action. For a one-act play, the story contains too many problems. The play's lack of success on the stage seems to prove the reviewers right. Hans Wagener (1983c) feels that a drama that tries to imitate Greek tragedy was no longer in demand on the German stage of the 1960s. Blake Lee Spahr (1992) criticizes the play for a lack of realistic accuracy when he states, "to an American it is completely artificial. The theme of the prodigal son is tritely presented" (467).   The only detailed assessment of the play is included in Ausma Balinkin's (1976) discussion of the women figures in Zuckmayer's dramas. For Balinkin, insight rather than instinct characterizes Rhoda, the central figure of *Kranichtanz*. Although she is realistically drawn, the more important dimensions of her role, like those of the other characters of the play, are mythical. "In keeping with her characteristics as a mortal, as priestess and a goddess, she displays an insight which borders on clairvoyance" (69). But unlike Katharina Knie and Barbara Blomberg, Rhoda does not attain self-fulfillment and inner harmony through an act of unselfish love. When she kills her husband at the end, she sacrifices not only him but also herself "by isolating herself from active life through the act of murder" (93). In contrast to all the other women figures in Zuckmayer's drama, she is not only man's equal; she is his master, not only dominating but disposing of his life. She is clearly a mythical figure. Balinkin's narrow focus does not provide a valid general interpretation of the drama, and she uncritically accepts some reviewers' claim that Zuckmayer had indeed written a Greek drama in modern garb.

Das Leben des Horace A. W. Tabor

Das Leben des Horace A. W. Tabor is about the rags-to-riches-to-rags life of a nineteenth-century Colorado silver king. With this play Zuckmayer returned to the scenery of his early play *Pankraz erwacht*. The premiere performance of this play too took place under the direction of Werner Düggelin, with Gustav Knuth and Marianne Hoppe playing the lead parts, on 18 November 1964 at the Zurich Schauspielhaus. The reviews of the Swiss and the following first German performances, some of which have been reprinted by Glauert (1977), were devastating. For example, the anonymous review of the world premiere of *Das Leben des*

Horace A. W. Tabor in the news magazine *Der Spiegel* (1964) had only sarcasm for Zuckmayer's new play. Though admitting that it contains a number of theatrically effective scenes and parts, it criticizes the author's love for tough men on the stage. In the reviewer's opinion, the action and psychology of the play are as unsophisticated as those of a fairy tale. The article concludes that the play might be suitable for the children's hour in radio programs.

The scholarly response was not much different. Several scholars feel that Zuckmayer had returned to older forms of drama, thus implying the play's outdatedness. For example, in Wolfgang Paulsen's opinion (1967), *Das Leben des Horace A. W. Tabor* is a biographical drama whose structure is marked by a circular movement. In her polemical article of 1969, Marianne Kesting posits that Zuckmayer had returned to a kind of folk play and thus to a subject matter appropriate to his mentality and his dramatic technique. The subject matter, however, presented the opportunity for a political or social analysis, which Zuckmayer does not undertake. The whole social action is only background for a simple, robust type, the hero Tabor. Thus Zuckmayer is following the tradition of the naturalistic and late realistic social drama about the greatness and dignity of the simple man who was able to advance socially. Kesting feels that if he had wanted to make his subject matter relevant for the stage today, it would have required a more precise or psychological analysis; levels other than the "purely human ones" would have had to be made visible. Instead, Zuckmayer presented a milieu description and a detailed biographical study. Such a value judgment makes Kesting's article more of a newspaper review than a scholarly investigation, but it is typical of the kind of criticism advanced against Zuckmayer from the mid-1950s on.

Like the anonymous 1964 *Spiegel* reviewer, Rudolf Lange (1969) views Tabor rather as a fairy-tale figure, a kind of Unlucky Jack from Colorado; but there is no distance from reality; so the play does not gain the convincing character of a parable. Because of its thematic distance from the 1960s, it appears as if it had been completed decades earlier. Thus Lange also judges the form of the drama as outdated.

The American Germanist Siegfried Mews (1973b and 1976) has devoted two studies to Zuckmayer's view of America in general and *Das Leben des Horace A. W. Tabor* in particular. He points out that, in contrast to the unbridled exoticism of *Pankraz erwacht*, Zuckmayer now describes conditions in the early American West carefully, avoiding to romanticize it. He tries to depict the Colorado milieu of the 1870s and 1880s realistically. At the same time, however, "as the title indicates, it is the atmosphere of the fairy tale in which riches and power are magically bestowed upon the pure in heart that pervades the drama" (Mews 1973b; reprint 1977: 492). Mews places the drama in the tradition of Ferdinand Raimund's *Das Mädchen aus der Feenwelt oder Der Bauer als Millionär* (The Girl from the Fairy World or The Farmer as Millionaire, 1826).

Quoting Marianne Kesting (1969), Mews admits that the author failed to come to grips with the social dimension of the characters. In contrast to *Pankraz erwacht*, however, the play contains more manifestations of the industrial world and its concomitant social problems than Zuckmayer's plays usually do. The time of the old West is gone; the real conflicts arise between entrepreneurs and workers. Mews admits, however, that Zuckmayer's attempts to replace Karl May with Karl Marx "are often inadequate and unintentionally comical" (Mews 1973b; reprint 1977: 493). He has thus given away the chance to present political, social, and psychological analysis, restricting himself to depicting a noble-minded, rough, and earthy character. For Zuckmayer the social reality is of secondary importance only; the drama focuses on the human aspects of Tabor, the man. Although he presents a much more balanced view of the play than most of the reviews he quotes, Mews thus agrees in principle with Zuckmayer's contemporary critics who demand more of him than the presentation of individual psychological problems.

Hans Wagener's (1983c) assessment also confirms the judgment of most of Zuckmayer's critics. He agrees with them that in 1964 Zuckmayer's realism was an anachronism. Zuckmayer's underlying structural model for the development of Tabor presupposed the belief in an intact world and the potential for man's renewal from insight into his nature and from love. Blake Lee Spahr (1992) judges the play from the point of view of an American. In his opinion, "Zuckmayer's most resounding failure contains all the clichés about America that are rife in the popular European imagination. The locales are those of the cheap Western film; the language is an unauthentic attempt to portray that of the gold-rush days; and the characters . . . do not rise above the level of Hollywood stereotypes" (467).

Since the drama contains two important women figures, Augusta Tabor and Tabor's second wife, Baby Doe, Ausma Balinkin (1976) and Sonja Czech (1985) have analyzed their roles. In her textimmanent study, Balinkin takes a very critical attitude toward Tabor's first wife, Augusta, who, in her view, shows a rigidity that mirrors the worst shortcomings of the protagonist, although her intuitive perceptiveness

parallels that of Zuckmayer's early women figures Annemarie and Julchen. Neither Tabor nor Augusta is willing or able to adjust to the
other: "While she [Augusta] recognizes a problematic situation, she
cannot cope with the problem after she has diagnosed it. Thus she
knows that her marriage is threatened by the changed life style of the
Tabors, but, like the real Augusta, she fails to grasp the source of the
trouble — her own inflexibility" (64). On the other hand, the real and
fictional Baby Doe is a good judge of character and clever in attaining
her goals.

Sonja Czech (1985) considers Zuckmayer's women under the categories of lover, comrade, mother, and whore. She comes to a similar
conclusion as Balinkin on the basis of the qualities Zuckmayer assigns to
the role of women in their relation to men — without, however, implying a negative value judgment. In Czech's opinion, the character of
Augusta Tabor finally avouches a traditional image of woman. Geared
toward the needs of her husband, she distinguishes herself as a house-
wife and a kind of spiritual mother. Resignation also characterizes Tabor's second wife, Baby Doe, who, despite being accustomed to wealth
and luxury, chooses the uncomfortable life in the mountains out of love
for Tabor, thus filling the role of a female comrade, like Augusta. According to Czech, the motivation for such behavior comes from a
Catholic stress on devotion. It goes back to the traditionally perceived
difference between the male, who wrestles with fate, and the role of
women, which was perceived in terms of motherliness and "life-giving
self-sacrifice" (140). In *Das Leben des Horace A. W. Tabor*, Zuckmayer
demonstrates that when the woman lacks one of the qualities requisite
for her role, there are serious consequences for interpersonal relations.
Thus, whereas in the first act there is a mutual recognition of role distribution between Tabor and Augusta, the sudden wealth leads to an
increasing estrangement between husband and wife. According to
Zuckmayer, the conflict between them results from the difference between the sexes, although he does not realize that the actual reason is
the difference between the roles of the sexes. In the course of the
drama, Tabor criticizes Augusta for her lack of sympathy. His standpoint reflects a view of women that judges them strictly in terms of
partner-oriented qualities. Like Julchen in *Schinderhannes*, the role of
the woman here is not based on her individual personality but on devotion. The end of the play displays, with a specifically male view, the
death of a pleasure-loving man who owes his luck in adversity solely to
two unselfish women. Although Czech's evaluation is not determined
by a feminist viewpoint, which in her opinion would not do justice to

Zuckmayer's works, she successfully applies contemporary views of women's role expectations to the interpretation of the drama.

Der Rattenfänger

Zuckmayer's last play, *Der Rattenfänger*, which is loosely based on the legend about the Pied Piper of Hamelin, premiered on 22 February 1975, under the direction of Leopold Lindtberg, at the Zurich Schauspielhaus.

Because of the publication of Zuckmayer's correspondence with the Hamelin city councilor Günther Niemeyer, edited by Gerald P. Martin (1982a), we are fairly well informed about how the writing of the play came about. Unfortunately, the publication contains only Zuckmayer's own letters — those by Niemeyer are only summarized by the editor. The correspondence provides an excellent picture of the evolution of the drama. It demonstrates that, as the author wrote the play, his ideas underwent a considerable transformation, and thus it provides a unique insight into the poetic process. It shows Zuckmayer's concern regarding the adverse tendencies of both contemporary theater and the critics and shows his hopes that within a few years the theater will once again change in his direction. Martin's comments between the letters are an essayistic defense against the reviewers' criticisms of the play, written from the viewpoint of a Zuckmayer admirer. As the editor states at the end, a critical, scholarly appreciation of the correspondence is not the intention of its publication.

Respect for Zuckmayer dominates the editing, by Gerald P. Martin (1982c), of some reviews of the Zurich premiere performance in the same issue of the *Blätter der Carl-Zuckmayer-Gesellschaft*. Georg Hensel's review in the *Frankfurter Allgemeine Zeitung* compares and contrasts the drama with Brecht's sociocritical dramas. A certain I. V. points out in the *Neue Zürcher Zeitung* that Zuckmayer has presented the sum total of his dramatic possibilities. For Günter Zehm in *Die Welt*, Zuckmayer presents his message in unrealistic naiveté with scenes of great embarrassment. Martin counters this attack by quoting an article by Alice Schwarz in the *Israel-Nachrichten* in which she takes issue with the many negative reviews although she has not seen a performance of the play. The individual reviews — others follow — are also less interesting than are the interjections of the editor, who, out of his love for Zuckmayer, presumes that a reviewer like Zehm must have deepseated antipathies — perhaps against today's youth, perhaps against the author himself, whom he purposely misunderstands. This kind of polemic against anyone who does not praise Zuckmayer unfortunately characterized the tenor of the *Blätter der Carl-Zuckmayer-Gesellschaft* at that time.

Walter Heist's 1975 remarks about *Der Rattenfänger*, written following its premiere in Zurich, are also determined by his admiration for Zuckmayer. He finds the play imposing because of its balladesque triviality, its overaccentuated language, its confused action. In his accusation of social injustice, he sees Zuckmayer as having come closer to Brecht in this play than anywhere else. Taking the part of the *Rattenfänger*, whom he sees in Camus's terms as an "homme révolte" (18), he interprets the play as revolutionary world theater. In another early reaction, Anton Krättli (1975–76) recognizes that Zuckmayer has interpreted the old legend about the *Rattenfänger* from the perspective of the social conditions of the present. For him it is a utopia of liberation that, however, may be too vague and have traits that are too edifying. Filled with a romantic feeling, Zuckmayer's play has atmosphere, offers great parts to the actors, and provides the audience with insights. The play of the eighty-year-old dramatist is filled with the same enthusiasm and impetus as those of the young Zuckmayer; the author here demonstrates that he has remained faithful to himself. In formal respects the drama is antiquated, however. The skepticism toward language, which characterizes contemporary literature, is foreign to its author, who revels in poetic imagery, strong verbal expressions, and expressions of feeling. Yet through all its alienating, partly naive and antiquated traits shimmers a possibility of man that should not remain unconsidered. In contrast to many critics, Krättli thus recognizes the validity of Zuckmayer's humanism in today's world. As is obvious from both early reactions to the play, they are determined by respect for the grand old man of German theater and the attempt to find positive features in spite of perceived weaknesses.

The only scholarly publications that exclusively praise the drama are by Helen Swediuk-Cheyne (1979 and 1980). In her 1979 article she arrives at the opinion that *Der Rattenfänger* is in some respect Zuckmayer's most mature play as it is the most successful realization of metaphysical theater. Its dimensions go beyond social conditions, and at its center stands man as an organic human being with a spark of immortality. By taking Zuckmayer's concept of metaphysical theater as her point of departure, Swediuk-Cheyne can only arrive at positive comments and conclusions about the drama. She sees the concept of metaphysical theater realized in Bunting, the play's hero, whose qualities become obvious when recognized as an intensification of those of Schinderhannes. Like Schinderhannes, Bunting fights for freedom;

neither can resist the temptation to exercise power over others, and both misuse this talent and become conscious of their offense. But whereas Schinderhannes dies for his hubris, Bunting stays alive and becomes the leader of the young generation on its road to a new life. Swediuk-Cheyne reemphasizes this motif of "starting all over again" in her article of 1980: Zuckmayer trusts in those of the young generation who have the strength to start all over again. Thus his last play is an appeal to life in the belief that any difficult situation can be overcome if man taps the power of his soul and starts over again. In the final analysis, such resistance against annihilation is also an overcoming of death. With her uncritical acceptance of Zuckmayer's views and her interpretation of the drama in developmental terms, Swediuk-Cheyne follows the tradition of textimmanent interpretations like Glade's (1958) and Engelsing-Malek's (1960).

The German-born American Germanists Siegfried Mews and Hans Wagener use the social demands placed on literature during the 1960s and 1970s as the yardstick for their evaluations. Mews (1981a) takes a comparative approach to point out a number of similarities between Brecht's plays and *Der Rattenfänger*: the existence of a narrator and of songs; the rigid division of the characters into rulers and ruled, exploiters and exploited; the absence of a middle class; and the use of the profit motif, resulting in a scathing indictment of an unjust social order. But he also points out the difference: Zuckmayer's play "does not end with a clearly stated moral or with an appeal to the spectators to change that which is rotten in Hamelin and, by inference, elsewhere; rather, the promised land to which Bunting leads the children appears dimly on the horizon. It is a hope-inspiring vision, not a concrete goal that can be reached by means of concerted action" (132). Implicitly, Mews states that Zuckmayer has not fulfilled the sociocritical demands made upon literature as Brecht had done. Mews thus takes a much more critical attitude toward the author, approaching him from a view of literature that had evolved during the 1960s and 1970s. The same applies to Wagener (1983a), who first characterizes Bunting's development in terms of the developmental structure identified by Engelsing-Malek (1960) and then applies the same criticism as Mews: Zuckmayer has made Bunting into a hero who is typical, someone who becomes guilty of the sin of hubris, pays for it, and then gets the chance for a socially useful life. With its vague social criticism and fuzzy utopian contours, however, the play lacks the wit and humor of Zuckmayer's early dramas as well as their pointed sociocritical jabs. The play demonstrates that Zuckmayer has lost his dramatic power. In an article published the same year, Wagener (1983c) criticizes the playwright's lack of concentration on a few important motifs that could decisively advance the action; he criticizes the lack of rational cohesiveness and the vagueness of the utopia at the end. He attributes the drama's failure to a vagueness in the characterization and analysis of social problems. The American Blake Lee Spahr (1992) calls the play "an incredible display, the more astonishing as the product of an aged author" (468).

4: Poetry, Prose, and Films

Poetry

ZUCKMAYER WROTE LYRIC poetry throughout his career, but in comparison to his dramatic output, the volume of poetry in his collected works, *Werkausgabe in zehn Bänden, 1920–1975* (1976), is small. Nevertheless, Zuckmayer's lyric productivity was not tied to a particular period of his life; rather, it was present throughout his career. A number of poems that were written during the First World War appeared in Franz Pfemfert's periodical *Die Aktion*. Many of them became part of Zuckmayer's early anthology *Der Baum* (1926), in which he also included lyric passages from his first drama, *Kreuzweg* (1921). In 1948 a second, more comprehensive collection appeared under the title *Gedichte: 1916–1948*. A third, expanded collection was entitled *Gedichte* (1960). The poetry volume of the *Werkausgabe* differs slightly from this collection as several poems have been taken out or exchanged. A new collection, also entitled *Gedichte* (1977), included for the first time poems from the First World War as well as poems from Zuckmayer's literary bequest.

The most typical poems are contained in the first collection, *Der Baum*, which also drew most of the critical attention. It was, after the drama *Kreuzweg*, Zuckmayer's second published book. Literary critics have said little about his later poetry.

During the Weimar Republic there was no critical response to Zuckmayer's poetry except for several reviews of *Der Baum*, which were by first-rate critics and will be included here since they are often mentioned in the scholarly discourse. For Ernst Lissauer (1926–27) the poems do not contain enough natural energy; they lack concentration, although, in contrast to much abstract contemporary poetry, Zuckmayer's poems are abundant in nature and concrete subject matter. Only the spiritual and contemplative poems of the second and third parts of the collection are weak. Lissauer praises the optimism inherent in this book and hopes that Zuckmayer will achieve the goal of combining the depiction of nature, true spirituality, and tragic optimism. Zuckmayer's fellow writer, the lyricist Oskar Loerke (1926), who also wrote nature poetry, praised the poems of *Der Baum* for their immediate relationship to this world, although, because they lack social critique, he doubts that they will gain much popularity. In Loerke's view, Zuckmayer does not try to change the world but instead points out what the world has to offer him, the pleasure he derives from everything alive, and how beautiful life is. Loerke thus recognizes essential features of the poet's lyrics as summarized and symbolized in the collection's first and last poems. As a matter of coincidence, Julius Bab (1927) compares and contrasts Loerke's and Zuckmayer's poetry. In his opinion, the two authors demonstrate how large the scope of lyric poetry is in general. Whereas Loerke is a magician for whom reality is merely a cipher behind which he senses metaphysical connections, Zuckmayer does not look for anything behind nature, behind the objects he describes. The simple sensual appearances themselves are wondrous for him. Only when he transcends the description of nature with spiritual symbols do he and Loerke touch each other.

After the Second World War, Luise Rinser, another fellow writer, was the first to draw attention to Zuckmayer's poetry. In her "Porträtskizze" of 1956 she states that Zuckmayer's lyrics follow the tradition of the folk song. She sees lyrical strength in his musicality: his poems are singable and extremely musical, the result of his ability to play the guitar and to sing along like a "troubadour" (25).

The scholarly work on Zuckmayer's poetry did not begin until 1976, with two articles in *Blätter der Carl-Zuckmayer-Gesellschaft*. The first one, by Alexander Hildebrand (1976), is hymnic in tone and tries to demonstrate in flowery language that Zuckmayer's lyric poetry has been underestimated. In Hildebrand's view, the poems of *Der Baum* are progressive and avant-garde because, after the period of expressionism, they again celebrate nature and naturalness. He quotes the three above reviews in detail but adds little of his own to the evaluation of *Der Baum*. Apart from that, he praises the poetic images contained in the newer poems of the collection *Gedichte: 1916–1948*. In his view, these newer poems display an increased turn toward the reader, with whom they seem to engage in a dialogue.

Hildebrand's article is determined by a preconceived hymnic defense of Zuckmayer and based on a strong reliance on the opinion of the initial reviewers. By contrast, the Norwegian scholar Knut Brynhildsvoll (1976), in a first truly scholarly article, tries to categorize Zuckmayer's early lyric production and to highlight certain core areas of his thinking and views of life by carefully analyzing his poetry. He establishes that Zuckmayer's thinking is rooted in the Romantic, vitalistic tradition, which was extremely popular in Germany during the first decades of the century, and he stresses the erotic element in his view of nature and his desire to regress to life's beginnings and to its creatures, particularly reptiles and amphibians. Not only in nature but also with regard to human beings Zuckmayer concentrates on procreation, birth, and origin, origin in a geographic sense being the region into which man is born, which determines his fate and from which he derives his creative powers. His ties to his region of birth prevent man from going astray in life. The preservation of one's human identity is possible only in close contact with one's native region. Life is an eternal cycle of origination and decay; the individual living being is part of the infinite chain of being, thus suspending the opposites of life and death. In his poems, Zuckmayer transfers the idea of a life cycle to the whole universe. God is venerated in His works, but at the same time He affects happenings on earth from the outside. He is the goal and end of all earthly development; the entire creation is striving back toward Him, to its origin. Although the experience of the First World War made Zuckmayer insecure in his faith in Divine Providence, on the whole the moments of hope and trust in God predominate. According to Brynhildsvoll, Zuckmayer's ideas extend from orthodox Christian ones to a vitalistic, pantheistic concept of the world and the universe. The poet wants to become one with life again, to suspend the separation of subject and object. He wants to return to the undivided, happy existence of a natural state. Brynhildsvoll also makes clear that during the time he was working for *Die Aktion* and during the following years, Zuckmayer was sympathizing with communist ideas and goals, but at heart he still adhered to Christian ideas, not Marxist ones. By pointing out all these concepts and quoting corresponding poems, Brynhildsvoll succeeds in describing the entire worldview of the young Zuckmayer. His article on the author's poetry is thus not only the first and only scholarly exploration of Zuckmayer's poetry but at the same time a characterization of the basic ideas that underlie all his works. Brynhildsvoll is less concerned with form than with content and message. His method is therefore very much akin to that of the American dissertations by Glade (1958), Lehrer (1962), and Barrick (1964).

By comparison, Günther Fleckenstein's (1979) article on the macabre in Zuckmayer's poems is not scholarly. Nevertheless, it succeeds in isolating an important aspect of the author's poetry. Fleckenstein notes that an important part of Zuckmayer's character was his enjoyment of the macabre, which, particularly in his poetry, he uses as a counterpoint against the danger of sliding into sentimentality. He employs the macabre to place the evil, terrifying elements of reality in the universal.

In addition to these interpretive essays, there is one short article on the reception of Zuckmayer's poetry abroad. In 1985 the *Blätter der Carl-Zuckmayer-Gesellschaft* published a note by Bruno Hain on the reception of Zuckmayer's lyric poetry in England, pointing out that four of the author's poems are contained in a British anthology of German poetry of 1941, edited by Jethro Bithell, including a first printing of the poem "Fülle der Zeit" that slightly deviates from later, better-known versions. Hain also quotes the editor's laudatory remarks about Zuckmayer's poetry.

Prose and Films

Apart from reviews and a limited number of articles, Zuckmayer's prose has so far not become the object of scholarly investigation. Admittedly, most of the prose cannot compete in quality with the best dramas, particularly since several pieces were written with possible movies in mind; but a number of novellas, such as *Ein Bauer aus dem Taunus, Eine Liebesgeschichte, Der Seelenbräu,* and *Die Fastnachtsbeichte,* as well as the autobiography *Als wär's ein Stück von mir,* are of high literary quality and demand attention for that reason alone, while others contain many parallels to Zuckmayer's lyric and dramatic work. Consequently, a closer look at them might well help to elucidate Zuckmayer's oeuvre.

This applies in particular to Zuckmayer's first book of prose, the collection of stories *Ein Bauer aus dem Taunus und andere Geschichten* (1927), which, like his first collection of poetry, *Der Baum* (1926), mirrors his experiences of nature, of the First World War, and on a trip to Norway that he undertook in summer 1922. The collection received relatively few reviews, which were mixed.

In Erich Franzen's (1927) view, Zuckmayer's stories are reductionist. Talking about "Die Geschichte vom Tümpel," he contends that we are not familiar enough with the secret excitement between procreation and death, the bustling activity in the ponds and in the air, to be moved by it. Zuckmayer condenses his subject matter. As a result, the extraordinary events make the characters appear sketchy, their vitality pathetic and blurred. For Erik-Ernst Schwabach (1927) the stories are rather heterogeneous but connected by their earthiness and their closeness to nature.

Since right after the Second World War the scholarly interest in Zuckmayer was exclusively focused on his dramas, the scholarly discourse on any of his prose did not begin until 1964. In his dissertation on Zuckmayer's mystical philosophy, Raymond Erford Barrick (1964) gave a detailed interpretation of the title story, *Ein Bauer aus dem Taunus*. For him the author's primary goal is to reveal that the protagonist, Schorsch Philipp Seuffert, is totally driven by an overpowering invisible force. He "is confronted with obstacles so formidable as to preclude any possibility of success except to a divinely guided entity" (92). In the character of his wife, Anna Barbara, Zuckmayer makes clear that Seuffert's adventure is preordained. The power that guides and protects Seuffert also permits his wife the foreknowledge that he will return home safely. Seuffert becomes an instrument of divine revelation; he was "chosen by the divine intelligence to serve as a symbol of love in the midst of all the unbridled wrath and hate raging about him at the time" (104). Zuckmayer's story demonstrates divine intervention into human affairs and the supreme power of love. Barrick thus interprets the story in terms of his view of Zuckmayer as a mystic who wants to bring the individual into accordance with the divine and vice versa. By contrast, Arnold Bauer (1970) considers the metaphysical implications of the story less than its topical content. Nevertheless, for him it is not so much an indictment of war but rather a documentation of the peaceful mentality and the unadulterated feeling of pristine people who unwaveringly walk straight ahead through the confusions of dark times.

The similarity of motives in many Zuckmayer stories prompted Hans Wagener (1984) to trace the motif of birth from Zuckmayer's lyric poetry through his prose, particularly of the 1920s and 1930s, beginning with several stories from *Ein Bauer aus dem Taunus*, such as the title story, "Die Geschichte vom Tümpel", and "Geschichte von einer Geburt," to "Eine Weihnachtsgeschichte" and *Herr über Leben und Tod* (1938). He shows that the stories of *Ein Bauer aus dem Taunus* are rooted in Nietzsche's and Driesch's ideas of neovitalism. Zuckmayer focuses on animalistic and unthinking nature, equating nature and goodness. In the stories of the 1930s such description of physical and animalistic aspects gives way to Christian symbolism and questions of moral decision in the big-city environment. Decisions in favor of *Humanität* are no longer made instinctively but as a conscious recognition of the goodness of all creation. The history of the motif of birth thus reveals Zuckmayer's development from enthusiasm for nature to critique of socially perverted morality, thus paralleling the author's development as a dramatist.

The novella *Eine Liebesgeschichte* (1934), set in Prussia a few years after the Seven Years' War (1756–63), appeared in Germany in spite of Hitler's seizure of power (30 January 1933). It came out in 1933 in the February and March issues of the *Berliner Illustrierte Zeitung* and then during 1934 in book form, published by S. Fischer in Berlin. Probably written during 1932, it cannot be considered exile literature; not only does its publication in Nazi Germany speak against it, but its content does too. The inherent glorification of Prussian ideals, possibly stimulated by Zuckmayer's work as an extra in the Fridericus Rex films starring Otto Gebühr, would hardly have been written by a victim of these perverted ideals. Since at the time of its first publication in book form the author was already in disfavor with the Nazi authorities — from 1933 until the end of the Second World War his plays could not be performed in Germany — it is not surprising that no reviews appeared in German publications at that time. It was not until 1952, when the novella was republished in Germany, and in 1954, when the movie version was released, that it was reviewed by newspaper and magazine critics. At that time it also received scholarly attention, first in the United States. In his dissertation of 1955, Arnold John Jacobius states that in *Eine Liebesgeschichte* the problematic nature of Prussianism (*Preußentum*) appears in a tragic light; it is perhaps the only truly tragic work Zuckmayer ever created. Two completely irreconcilable worlds clash in this novella: the world of the Potsdam officers, based on duty, obedience, soldierly honor, loyalty to the king, cold reason, and strictest convention; and the world of the actress Lili Schalweis, dominated by the inner imperative of feeling, drive, and passion — the world of art. The Prussian cavalry captain, Jost Fredersdorff, who falls in love with her, is broken by the attempt to bridge the gap. Jacobius sees the novella, like *Der Schelm von Bergen*, as Zuckmayer's answer to the misled nationalism of the Third Reich, as Zuckmayer's personal declaration of loyalty to Germanness (*Deutschtum*). In contrast, Raymond Erford Barrick (1964) concentrates on the mystical, supernatural elements of the story and states that in it "the element of compulsive direction in love is given its most pronounced expression" (107). The divine intelligence has brought the lovers together through deep spiritual affinity. It is understandable that in Barrick's ideohistorical interpretation the social dimension is far less important than is a higher reality.

By contrast, Gisela Pankow's article of 1962 is a motif study. She uses the mirror motif to demonstrate the division of two worlds in the novella: the world of love and the outside world of social order; the hero Fredersdorff's conflict between his private world of love and the historical part of his existence as an officer in the Prussian army. When the outside world makes its demands, he kills himself. Although psychological aspects are alluded to, the interpretation follows entirely the textimmanent method that was so popular during the early 1960s. The same applies to Johannes Pfeiffer's (1965) interpretation, which is a typical example of this school of literary criticism. Pfeiffer emphasizes that the story takes place at a specific point and place in history. This is important for the convincing depiction of the social conflict, the increasing transfiguration of the events in the direction of the essence of things, and the creation of a background atmosphere. He points out that Zuckmayer has masterfully hinted at the unavoidability of the final catastrophe, but he sees a weakness in a certain expressionistic exaggeration. Quoting the then popular existential philosopher Karl Jaspers, he makes clear the tragic situation of Zuckmayer's hero Fredersdorff, whose forced choice between absolute love and the social world necessitates betrayal and guilt no matter what path is chosen.

Hans Wagener (1983a) praises the story for its tight structure. For him it does not question the value of the absolute feeling of love, but it clearly states that this is only one part of human life. In addition, human life is also determined by social forces and experiences. Thus Fredersdorff finds out that his existence is inseparably connected with his past and with his social rank.

It is not surprising that for a Marxist critic such as Wilfried Adling (1959), the story's meaning lies in its relation to contemporary politics. He sees it as related to the historical drama *Der Schelm von Bergen* (1934) because both deal with a flight from responsibility and with man's relation to his homeland. Applying these themes to the contemporary political situation, Adling sees Fredersdorff, who takes himself seriously, as the counterimage to the emptiness of the fascist system. His death stands as a warning about the difficulty of deciding between a human relationship on the one hand and life in the service of an inhuman state on the other. Since the story was written before the Nazi takeover, Adling has obviously fallen victim to the distorted view through red-tinted glasses. Moreover, such an interpretation is tainted by his presupposition of the negative qualities of Frederick the Great's state, which are nowhere evident in the novella itself. He gets around this problem by criticizing Zuckmayer's too affectionate depiction of Fredersdorff's love for his rank as an officer. In his view, such a depiction meets the fascists' Prussia myth halfway.

It is also questionable whether the novel *Salwàre oder Die Magdalena von Bozen* (1934) may rightfully be called a work of exile literature. Its introductory chapter appeared during November 1935 in the German periodical *Neue Rundschau*. Its first book edition was confiscated in 1935 in the bookbindery of the Bibliographisches Institut in Leipzig. It was, therefore, republished in 1936 by Bermann-Fischer in

Vienna. In 1937 translations appeared in in fascist Italy and in Budapest. English editions came out during the same year in London as well as in New York.

Most critics are fairly puzzled by the novel's lack of action and its precise message. They try to get around this problem by praising its beautiful descriptions of nature and its mood or by trying to distil the meaning of its extensive discussions. In her review of 1950, Zuckmayer's colleague Luise Rinser gave a psychoanalytical interpretation. In the first scholarly article, Ian C. Loram (1954) set the tone by interpreting it as Zuckmayer's version of the problem of the artist. His hero, Thomas Stolperer, searches for perfection and does not find it. "He thinks he has found it at one time or another in each of three women, one who lives almost entirely in an intellectual world, one who exists solely for her family, and one who lives in a world of physical love and passion. Each of them seems at first to be the embodiment of his ideal, but each turns out eventually to be a disappointment" (147). At the end, Stolperer succeeds in finding himself. Loram thus tries to see the novel in the context of Thomas Mann's early works, superimposing on Zuckmayer the problems Mann deals with in them.

For Henry Glade (1958) the novel is "partially autobiographical and partially philosophical-critical" (41). Glade's approach, which he also applies in his discussion of Zuckmayer's dramas, demonstrates that he is almost exclusively concerned with the ideas inherent in Zuckmayer's works and not with their aesthetic form. Consequently, he is the only one who gives a detailed discussion of the ideas contained in the novel. In many respects he elaborates on Loram's (1954) ideas because, according to him, the novel's philosophical debates raise the question of the rationale of life with special reference to the task of the artist as it was perceived prior to the Second World War. Zuckmayer thus deals with the sociopolitical problems of his time and gives a view of the European society in which he lives. As an answer to the questions raised, the figure of Firmin incorporates the concept of wholeness of selfhood as an artistic ideal. By insisting on the principle of form and a belief in a metaphysical determinism and setting it within the contemporary sociopolitical situation, he provides the artist with a set of values opposite to those of the fascists as represented by Mario. Exemplifying the principle of love of destiny, Stolperer and Menega, on the other hand, provide the practical application of the wisdom contained in the humanitarian debates. By being rooted in eros and imagination, Stolperer is a somewhat autobiographical figure. "Through his encounter with Menega, in whom Zuckmayer embodies his idea of womanhood at this time, and its tragic consequences, Stolperer awakens to an ethical perception of the responsibilities and obligations of life" (55).

Wolfgang Paulsen (1967) was the first to provide circumstantial evidence for an autobiographical interpretation. In his opinion, Zuckmayer intended to show the ambiguity of the feminine in two characters, who, not accidentally, both bear the same name; one is ruled by the sun, the other one by the moon. The man in his confrontation with them takes and loses again, without tragic consequences. There is no either/or, but an as-well-as. Paulsen also shows that the protagonist's experience is based on Zuckmayer's own, which he reports in *Pro domo*. While vacationing with his parents in Belgium shortly before the First World War, he was in love not only with a girl from a respected burgher family but also with a Dutch maid. Later on, Mews (1983) took up the autobiographical ideas and demonstrated that the main character, Thomas Stolperer, bears a number of features that are borrowed from Zuckmayer himself, including his vitalistic, affirmative attitude toward life.

Sheila Rooke's (1964) approach seems influenced by contemporary textimmanent methods. She is not interested in the novel's discussions about art or fascism but rather in the character constellations. She praises the novel, which, as Adling (1959) had pointed out earlier, is reminiscent of Thomas Mann's *Magic Mountain* (1924) in many ways — Hans Wagener (1983a) adds Hermann Broch's *Der Versucher* (The Tempter, 1953) — as the culmination of Zuckmayer's sexual and social protests. She sees Thomas Stolperer's love affair with Mena, the waitress, as a short-lived, bittersweet experience that neither regrets. In its passionate enrichment, this relationship stands in sharp contrast to the barrenness of the aristocratic brother and sister, Firmin and Magdalena, who are both incapable of happy sexual relations. She sees the problem of the artist represented by Firmin. His emotional barrenness is also reflected in his inability as a poet to complete a single work of art. His tragedy "is that his intellect has forced his *eros*, his natural, warm productive self, into submission" (215). Firmin fails because he isolates himself from society.

Even more restricted to aesthetic aspects are the remarks of Arnold Bauer (1970) and Siegfried Sudhof (1973). Bauer calls the main characters somewhat romantically overdrawn. The tragic pathos of their behavior goes to the limit of probability. By comparison, the minor characters are drawn more realistically. Bauer praises the landscape descriptions of the Southern Tyrol. Sudhof feels that the highpoints of the novel sometimes coincide with the best parts — for example, the description of nature, especially the nightly landscape. But Zuckmayer does not succeed in keeping up this stylistic standard throughout the novel. In the parts where demonic or metaphysical relations are suggested, the author runs the danger of losing his credibility; the end of the story is least convincing. Hans Wagener (1983a) interprets the novel in Zuckmayer's own terms. He feels that the main thrust of the long discussions is to present Zuckmayer's idea of the restoration of the original connections, which have been lost — the message that underlies most of Zuckmayer's works.

It is interesting that when one looks at the novel from contemporary political conditions, it is possible to see it in a totally different light. The Marxist Wilfried Adling (1959) is again not interested in the aesthetic or metaphysical aspects of the discussions but in the political power play of the time when the novel was written. Therefore he feels that the entire discussion about fascism is conducted not on the basis of reality but in abstract terms and ultimately for the conciliatory purpose of making fascism acceptable. For him the novel thus corresponds to the contemporary politics of the Allied Powers, who were trying to come to a reconciliation with fascism by making renewed concessions.

Siegfried Mews (1983), by contrast, is interested in Zuckmayer's personal situation at the time of his writing and its influence on the novel. He lays stress on the fact that the novel is the work of an exile. Written during 1934–35 in Henndorf, it reflects the fact that its author was living in exile even though it seems to have no connection with the contemporary political situation since all comments on conditions in Germany are carefully avoided. Mews picks up any traces of time-bound reflections. These include a discussion about the position of the artist in society; the ideas about America as the last refuge of creative people; and the beginnings of an analysis of fascism, which, however, takes place in totally abstract terms only. Political events are considered unimportant in relation to timeless cosmic processes. A consideration of the reception of the novel in America and England, where it was published in 1937, and, after the war, in Germany shows that it was not received as an exile novel. Mews's article thus not only gives an interpretation of the novel's time-bound aspects; it also evaluates its reception on both sides of the Atlantic. Immediately after Mews's article, Gerald P. Martin (1983) published reviews of the Vienna edition (1936), the British and American editions (1937), and the German edition (1950).

A more modern approach, in comparison to previous research, is taken by Dieter Kafitz (1983). He justifies his focus on the women in

Salwàre by pointing out that women and nature are largely identical for Zuckmayer. Because of their holistic way of feeling, they are exempt from the reality of specialization and mechanization. Kafitz points out that the initially perceived spatial contrast between castle and inn is suspended by the fact that each of these spheres is characterized by the ambiguity of opposing forces. In discussing the various women of the novel, Kafitz stresses the natural, irrational femininity of Firmin's wife and the decadent, demonic elements and provoking self-willedness of his sister Magdalena. In her character, traits of the *femme fatale* and the *femme fragile* are fused. To be sure, she is determined by nature, but in a way that reveals the dangerous, unrestrained aspects of natural being. On the other hand, she is at the stage of decadent sublimation that barely allows for natural life. The waitress Menega is not to be seen in contrast to the women in the castle but as their dialectic synthesis. Stolperer's love affair with Menega remains entirely irrational, without any consideration of the realistic implications. In the epilogue it becomes obvious that Zuckmayer is basing the roles of the sexes in this novel on traditional ideas about man and woman. Kafitz then demonstrates the influence of vitalistic philosophy on Zuckmayer's image of women and points out that, in contrast to Ausma Balinkin's opinion in her 1976 dissertation, women and men are equal only in a biological sense, not in legal or sociological respects. Since Zuckmayer does not present his figures within their realistic social context, it is easy to come to this false conclusion. Women *and* men in Zuckmayer's works act on the basis of natural drives. In accordance with the vitalistic philosophy of the time, Zuckmayer's women are closer to nature; they are an expression of the immediacy of life. The value of Kafitz's interpretation, in comparison to much of previous Zuckmayer research, is that he evaluates the novel in terms of Zuckmayer's vitalistic thinking and that he considers the role of women and men dispassionately.

The reason for taking up Zuckmayer's work for the movie industry as part of this chapter on prose is that, with the notable exception of *Rembrandt* (1980), most of his extensive work for the film industry, which was done between 1933 and 1938 during his stay in Austria, resulted in published prose. Thus *Eine Liebesgeschichte* (1934), *Ein Sommer in Österreich* (1937), *Herr über Leben und Tod* (1938), and *Rembrandt*, all published independently, were originally or specifically written with film versions in mind. In contrast to the novel *Salwàre*, these prose works are clearly the work of an exile, undertaken for film studios and directors, mostly for Alexander Korda, in London, Paris, and Amsterdam. Since it was impossible for Zuckmayer to publish in

Germany or have his plays performed there, the market for a German-language author was greatly reduced. In order to make a living, he resorted to the type of work that has as its unifying feature, as Siegfried Mews (1977) rightfully points out, its highly apolitical nature.

Arnold John Jacobius's bibliography (1971: 333–35) identifies a number of movies from 1925 to 1955 for which Zuckmayer had either written the script in toto or to which he had made decisive contributions. Considering the number of entries, too little scholarly work has been done so far on Zuckmayer and his work for the movie industry in general. In the revised 1989 version of his "biographical essay," Jochen Becker (1984) reports on Zuckmayer's collaboration with the film director Kurt Bernhardt for the script writing and direction of the silent movies *Qualen der Nacht* (Agony of the Night, 1926) and *Schinderhannes: Der Rebell vom Rhein* (Schinderhannes: The Rebel from the Rhine, 1928). Produced for the leftist Prometheus Film, the latter movie was innovative for Germany at this time with regard to both its subject matter and its political message. It was not a glorification of Prussia; rather the protagonist was an underdog and robber at the time of the French, left-Rhenish occupation during the Napoleonic wars. According to Becker, this collaboration with the movie industry sheds light on Zuckmayer's political attitude during the time of the Weimar Republic.

Jacobius also lists a number of film treatments that were never realized as films. These include *Stroller[']s Fate* (1935) and *I Claudius the God* (1936–37) as well as the unpublished film novellas *Die letzte Fahrt der Madagaskar* (The Last Trip of the Madagaskar), *Das Kind der Legion* (The Child of the Legion), and *Pocahontas* (all three around 1938–39). On the other hand, in 1936, the film script *Rembrandt*, written solely by Zuckmayer, was turned into a movie under the direction of Alexander Korda in England. Zuckmayer wrote the scripts for *Escape Me Never* (1935) and *De Mayerling à Sarajewo* (1940; directed by Max Ophüls) as well as the German versions of the script for *Entscheidung vor Morgengrauen* (*Decision Before Dawn*, 1950; directed by Anatole Litvak), *Die Jungfrau auf dem Dach* (*The Moon is Blue*, 1952; directed by Otto Preminger), and *Der Mann mit dem goldenen Arm* (*The Man with the Golden Arm*, 1955; directed by Otto Preminger). In 1958 the novel *Ein Sommer in Österreich* became a movie titled *Frauensee* (Women's Lake; directed by Rudolf Jugert), and the novels *Eine Liebesgeschichte* and *Herr über Leben und Tod* were ultimately turned into movies (also directed by Rudolf Jugert) in 1953 and 1955 respectively.

Heinz Grothe (1977) is the only one who deals specifically with Zuckmayer's relationship to and work for the film industry. Originally written for a film magazine, his short article does not pretend to be scholarly, but it goes beyond Jacobius's bibliography in that it also lists film versions of Zuckmayer's literary works. Jochen Becker (1986b) has published a number of contemporary reviews of *Frauensee*. Since these are for the most part taken from magazines serving the film industry, their purpose is for advertisement. For that reason they rightfully received no comment. Becker merely states that the film was one of the many German *Heimatfilme* (sentimental films with regional background) of the 1950s and that it did not do justice to the narrative *Ein Sommer in Österreich*.

Apart from that, the various novellas and the script for *Rembrandt* have been dealt with purely as literature. So far, Hans Wagener (1986) is the only one who has taken a scholarly interest in the script *Rembrandt: Ein Film*, which, written as early as 1936, was not published until 1980. By comparing historical facts with Zuckmayer's version of Rembrandt's life, Wagener demonstrates that Zuckmayer has selected and interpreted the facts and added invented scenes and characters to make the film into a typical Zuckmayer drama. As in many of his dramas, the outward decline of his hero's fate from fame to poverty and loneliness is contrasted with his inner development. He proves himself in the face of the vicissitudes of life and learns to accept his own character and fate. Wagener thus applies the paradigm of Zuckmayer dramas developed by Engelsing-Malek (1960), the concept of *amor fati*. He furthermore shows that Zuckmayer has used traditional elements of the classical drama as well as film techniques. He furthermore has made it possible for the reader and viewer to associate various scenes with well-known Rembrandt paintings. Future research will thus have to consider *Rembrandt* side by side with Zuckmayer's stage dramas.

Wolfgang Paulsen (1967) looks at *Ein Sommer in Österreich* and *Herr über Leben und Tod* as literature, but he stresses the fact that they are epically executed film ideas. In his opinion, this intended purpose has had negative effects. In comparison with Zuckmayer's other prose works they are disappointing because they lack a specific Zuckmayer atmosphere. There is so much action that there is no time to pause, none of the quiet introspection that are the high points of Zuckmayer's work. For him the filmic is the antithesis to the lyric. Wagener (1995) has taken an even more critical view of *Ein Sommer in Österreich*. After reporting how its writing came about, he points out the comic features of the novel and some close structural parallels to *Der fröhliche Wein-*

berg, demonstrating that here too Zuckmayer's heroes undergo a transformation on the road to their true character. Yet in Wagener's opinion, *Ein Sommer in Österreich* has all the qualities of a trivial novel — to be more precise, of a *Heimat-* and *Bergroman* (regional and mountain novel). The home region represents the highest value. True values are at home in the tradition-oriented countryside in contrast to the decadent city and modern industrial society. In *Ein Sommer in Österreich* Zuckmayer has thus created a utopia of the past by describing a society with a patriarchal unity of nobility and simple folk whose life is based on the beauty and simplicity of the country — the way he experienced it in Henndorf. His characters are not individuals but types drawn in black and white. All conflicts and contrasts are resolved in the end when several couples are united. Typical of Zuckmayer, the novel ignores political and social reality. The style is characterized by the frequent inclusion of obvious, general truths, sentimental or pathetic clichés, and pseudoreligious innuendoes. The author has not escaped the danger of falling victim to banalities. These deficiencies are most likely the reason, Wagener argues, that the novel was not included in the collections of 1960 and 1976.

The novella *Herr über Leben und Tod* (1938) received somewhat more critical attention. In his 1958 dissertation Henry Glade provides a detailed discussion with respect to Zuckmayer's developing concept of *Humanität.* He sees this concept embodied in the three figures of Lucile, Raymond, and Norbert, while Lady Stanhope presents the polar opposite. According to Glade, the play discusses: "1) the question of the rationale of life with particular reference to the physician's ethos; and 2) the travails of spirit and soul of Norbert on his road to self-fulfillment" (76). The ethical "ideal is expressed in the concept of self-realization through the Thou in conjunction with an ethos of goodness, brotherhood and love" (77). Glade concedes that Norbert's *Humanität* is achieved in a rather unconvincing and contrived fashion as a result of the chastening encounter with Lucile; this is one of the few value judgments contained in his study.

In contrast to Paulsen (1967), Siegfried Mews (1981a) sees *Herr über Leben und Tod* as an example for the fact that "movie work" (73) could yield artistically satisfying results, but he criticizes the many unlikely coincidences of the action that might destroy the reader's suspense of disbelief. Hans Wagener (1983a) echoes the negative aspects of Paulsen's and Mews's assessments. He points out that the exiled Zuckmayer deals with the theme of euthanasia, which was to become in distorted form a macabre reality during the following years in Nazi

Germany. Since the author clearly sides with the representatives of life, the story is a demonstration of the extent to which his life-affirming views are contrary to those of the Nazis. In Wagener's view, neither the exaggerated emotional style and pathos nor the deus ex machina solution of the train accident at the end is convincing, however. The author is not excused by the fact that the story was written with a future film in mind.

Zuckmayer's last piece of prose from his exile period, the novella *Der Seelenbräu* (1945), was published by the exile publishing house of Bermann-Fischer in Stockholm. It is in many respects a reflection of Zuckmayer's exile. With it Zuckmayer had written a prose idyll, creating an idealized picture of his new *Heimat*, the Salzburg region. This peaceful setting was diametrically opposed to the political reality of his time of exile in the United States. The novella elicited a number of studies soon after its first appearance. For Hilde Cohn (1946) the indeterminacy of the time of the action lends a touch of the fairy tale to the story, as does its optimism, the basic faith in life that permeates this prose idyll. For her Franz Haindl is a fairy-tale hero who passes all the tests to which he is subjected. Ursula Seyffarth's (1947) review places it in the same group and on the same level as the narratives of Gottfried Keller and Theodor Fontane or Kurt Kluge, and she praises its charm and liveliness.

Whereas the above two titles are nonscholarly reviews, Johannes Pfeiffer's (1953) essay, like his later remarks on *Eine Liebesgeschichte* (Pfeiffer 1965), is a purely textimmanent interpretation. For Pfeiffer the focus of the story is on the characters rather than on the action. He first analyzes the structure of the narrative, paraphrasing its events to demonstrate the artistry of the construction. He points out the means Zuckmayer employs to make the characters come to life and, above all, his humor. In his colorful sensuality Zuckmayer is consciously striving to get close to nature, but his human and artistic power is great enough to make up for this literary consciousness in a kind of higher naïveté.

Although Josef Moser's (1962) report on reading *Der Seelenbräu* in the German Gymnasium is primarily didactic and thus directed at teachers, it does contain a number of interpretative remarks based on close reading. In particular, Moser points out the various kinds of humor contained in the novella. In his view, humor is the key to understanding the characters of the novella and their world; it brings about the reconciliation at the end. The coexistence of humor and benevolence lends a special kind of worldly wisdom and joy of life to the story. Moser considers the ready acceptance of the world and its human beings — ultimately a Christian attitude — as the basis for Zuckmayer's humor and the overriding spirit of benevolence displayed in the novella. It is not surprising that no scholarly essays exclusively devoted to *Der Seelenbräu* have appeared since Moser's study. Around 1960 in Germany, one of the most important demands made upon literature was that it be sociocritical and political. Obviously Zuckmayer's idyllic novella did not meet this requirement. This becomes clear from Thomas Ayck's (1977) verdict that a cultural break is visible in Zuckmayer's attitude as displayed in *Der Seelenbräu*. During the 1920's he had still been able to combine criticism of contemporary issues and the "folk sound" (107). Siegfried Mews (1981a) merely confirms that the idyll Zuckmayer depicted here belongs to the past, and he interprets it as a piece of escapist literature: "The paradise Zuckmayer evoked had been permanently lost and could not be regained. Thus the story could afford his German readers of 1945, when the story was first published, escape from the cataclysm of World War II" (113). Hans Wagener (1983a) agrees: whereas other exile authors used the historical novel to escape from contemporary problems, Zuckmayer used the idyll, establishing a harmonic world with attributes of literary *Biedermeier* and fairy tales. In the final analysis all conflicts are overcome here by the goodness of the main characters. Zuckmayer's life-affirming attitude and his ability to harmonize and to be conciliatory are present in all the main characters. It is obvious that the new demands made upon literature — to provide a discussion of the timely problems and to take a critical stance toward society — have led to a more negative attitude toward *Der Seelenbräu* after the waning of the apolitical, escapist spirit immediately following the Second World War.

Henry Glade (1958) is so far the only one who has dealt in detail with "Die wandernden Hütten" (written in 1948), a fairy tale closely linked to the essay *Die Brüder Grimm* (1948). Although the characters are drawn as types, Zuckmayer's ultimate ideal is perhaps given its most perfect embodiment in the heroine, Petra Maria. Through her magic powers, which are derived from her attunement to the macrocosmic realm of God, wholeness of selfhood is raised to transcendental proportions. Petra Maria "exemplifies the great and necessary quest of man in the naive eros-drive of the male and the male's explorations reaching into the normally unattainable. Lucas, on the other hand, is the individual self-contained and devoid of all love of destiny, and here little more than a convenient foil for the two phases in the longing for the transcendent" (105–6.).

Although it ultimately received mostly praise, Zuckmayer's last novella, *Die Fastnachtsbeichte* (1959), did not evoke any immediate scholarly response. Therefore two reviews that came out soon after its first publication are introduced first. In the opinion of Friedrich Sieburg (1959), at that time the star critic of the *Frankfurter Allgemeine Zeitung*, the reader is dealing here not with a detective story, despite a murder at the beginning, but with a true narration (*Erzählung*), in which people commit sins and are in need of mercy. For Sieburg the fascination of the story is brought about not by the events but by their connections, their ambiguity, their seeming coincidences, confusions, and repetitions. He praises Zuckmayer's relation to reality as completely healthy, unspoiled, innocent, and praises also his confidence in the inexhaustibility of the human heart, which he has been able to preserve through the years. In his review, which appeared a few months later, the Austrian writer Alexander Lernet-Holenia (1960) shows that Zuckmayer's language, which is influenced by his native Rhine-Hessian dialect, places the novella between lyricism and mystery story. Particularly in the character of Lolfo — who bears the features of a dog — the human, the animalistic, and the demonic merge.

After these initial reviews, the novella was rarely commented upon in scholarly publications. Siegfried Sudhof (1973) points to Heinrich von Kleist as the model for the structure of the story but not for the language. Siegfried Mews (1981a) agrees. He also points out that "Zuckmayer's emphasis is on the confrontation of the various characters with the guilt they have incurred rather than on the resolution of the crime by a sleuth" (116). Hans Wagener (1983a) calls the story a classical novella, written in its characteristically tight style and with a clarity of structure evident nowhere else in Zuckmayer's works. The stiletto with which Ferdinand is stabbed to death could be seen as the *Dingsymbol* (object symbol), the confession of the older Panezza as the *Wendepunkt* (turning point) which are characteristic features of a novella. The story is almost overly constructed. In spite of all advance indications, the revelation of the secrets at the end seems too artificial. Again there are Zuckmayer's old readiness for reconciliation and his Christian ethics, for which, in spite of guilt, the human life is a task that God has assigned to man.

In the only separate study dealing with the novella, Michaela Frankmölle (1993) describes the guilt that the major characters incur. In spite of her attempt to place the narrative in the period shortly before the First World War and to relate it to Zuckmayer's view of religion, her sensitive descriptions of the main characters remain textimmanent. Since, however, human guilt and love are the themes of the novella, in this case such an approach may well be the most adequate one.

Clearly there is a lot of scholarly work to be done on Zuckmayer's prose fiction, which seems to have been forgotten in favor of the author's more public image as a dramatist.

Zuckmayer's work on his autobiography goes back to his exile period. It was a time of self-reflection for him, of coming to terms with his position in relation to Germany and later on to America. He did that in two books that are precursors of his later autobiography *Als wär's ein Stück von mir* (1966). The first is the autobiographical essay *Pro domo*, which was published in 1938 in Stockholm by Bermann-Fischer. In a 1939 review, Alfred Polgar had praised *Pro domo* not only for its brilliant style but also for Zuckmayer's position vis-à-vis his Jewishness, though Polgar uses irony when he talks about the author's belief in Germanness (*Deutschtum*). Such irony is not present in Margot Finke's (1990) verdict. She sees *Pro domo* as the author's "declaration of loyalty to true Germanness," (190) with the great German minds being the representatives of justice, freedom, and *Geist* (spirit).

In 1940 Zuckmayer's first autobiography, *Second Wind*, came out in New York. After *Salwàre*, this was Zuckmayer's only major publication in English published during his exile in the United States, unfortunately with modest success. It did not succeed in establishing the author as a writer in this country. Since it was in English, the book was practically forgotten by German critics until recently. It is amazing, however, that *Als wär's ein Stück von mir*, rightfully highly praised by German newspaper critics, has not received much scholarly attention either.

A contemporary of Zuckmayer's, Friedrich Michael (1966), reviews this final autobiography with the sensitivity of a like mind. He praises the poetic character of the book, the convincing way in which Zuckmayer has described his transformation from patriotic enthusiasm at the beginning of the First World War to pacifism, and the portraits of Zuckmayer's and his own friends. As in many other reviews of the book, there is no attempt to subject it to any kind of real criticism. Thus it must be classified with all the other encomiastic secondary literature written by the author's friends. Arnold Bauer (1970) points out that Zuckmayer has presented his memoirs, even though he does not expressly say so, through Goethe's concept of art. His animated declaration of faith in his life restricts the book's value as a source, at least to a certain extent. It is thus a confession rather than a documentary retrospective. It is above all a human document, not a documentary contribution to contemporary history. Zuckmayer's humanity, his belief in man and in the goodness of creation, leads him to see harmony in a world dominated by dissonance. This careful criticism was later taken up and sharpened by Jörg von Uthmann (1983). In his afterword to the separate edition of the chapter "Austreibung: 1934–1939" (Expulsion: 1934–1939) in the popular series Reclams Universal-Bibliothek, he takes issue with Zuckmayer's claim that some kind of expulsion was taking place in every person's existence and he interprets it as a typical case of "Sinngebung des Sinnlosen" (lending sense to something senseless [Theodor Lessing], 128), of a striving for prestabilized harmony with which Voltaire's Maître Pangloss in *Candide* also attributes even the greatest monstrosities to the wise plan of creation. Whether or not one wants to fault Zuckmayer for his conciliatory attitude obviously depends on one's own philosophy. Thus Siegfried Sudhof (1973) is able to explain Zuckmayer's attitude, although he also sees the dangers inherent in his conciliatory posture. He points out that nowhere else does the difference between the generations become as clear as in this book. Zuckmayer's own generation was able to recognize itself here. The author reports his encounters with many important people. All this he tells in a very sympathetic manner, always playing down the difficulties, with the sure knowledge of the positive outcome. Without saying it, he thus mitigates the horrors of the Nazi era. Zuckmayer was exclusively concerned about reconciliation; he wanted to help bury the hatred.

Other scholars have taken a closer look at the emergence of this final autobiography by comparing it with its antecedents. Thus in his English-language book on Zuckmayer, Siegfried Mews (1981a) points out that, unlike *Pro domo*, *Second Wind* concentrates on occurrences and people rather than presenting an essayistic philosophy of life. In many respects, for instance in its subdivision into chapters, it anticipates *Als wär's ein Stück von mir*. In his essay of 1983, Hans Wagener (1983b) conducts a more detailed comparison of the three books to demonstrate the evolution of the final autobiography and to demonstrate Zuckmayer's change of consciousness depending on his personal situation and the political circumstances at the time of writing. As Wagener points out, *Pro domo* was intended not as an autobiography but, as Zuckmayer stated himself, as a "determination of one's standpoint" (78) in the face of world events. Wagener feels that Zuckmayer has nevertheless unintentionally written a kind of autobiography; social and historical influences play an even larger part in it than in the autobiography of 1966. As Wagener shows, the various chapters correspond on the one hand to essayistic contexts and on the other hand to chapters in Zuckmayer's own life. The perspective of *Pro domo* is clearly that of 1937–38; all events are related to this time, to the author's exile, and to the Third Reich, and they gain their importance or unimportance from that vantage point. At the end, Zuckmayer postulates the "other Germany" in contrast to that represented by the leaders of the Third Reich.

Second Wind, which is clearly directed at an Anglo-Saxon audience, cuts short all references to German culture and its representatives during the Weimar Republic and stresses information about the rise of National Socialism in Germany and Austria. In its celebration of the adaptability of man and his will to survive, Zuckmayer targets a specifically American spirit. His own odyssey and exile thus become an American challenge, a destiny that is supposed to be embraced as a second chance in life. At the root of this view of life is Nietzsche's concept of *amor fati*, the transference of Zuckmayer's vitalistic optimism to American society. Whereas in *Second Wind* Zuckmayer dreams of reestablishing the creative connection of all life in the future, in *Als wär's ein Stück von mir* he looks back elegiacally and sees this connection in his *Heimat* and in his friends, whom he now, addressing a German audience, all calls by their names. *Als wär's ein Stück von mir* integrates a look back at his life, his friends, and the changes he has undergone as a writer. Wagener criticizes Zuckmayer's use of numinous elements and the enumeration of encounters with friends. In tracing the genesis of this work, he accounts for the structure of *Als wär's ein Stück von mir* and demonstrates the basic unity of Zuckmayer's work through the decades. The study is thus part of the "motif studies" that attempt to document unifying and developing ideas in Zuckmayer's work. Making a final judgment in his German-language monograph on Zuckmayer, Wagener (1983a) calls *Als wär's ein Stück von mir* Zuckmayer's best prose work. In spite of its weaknesses — for example, the irrational, superstitious elements — it is probably so successful because it grew over several decades, being the end product of several autobiographical writings.

5: Conclusion

The basis for literary research is the availability of good critical editions. In Zuckmayer's case the *Gesammelte Werke* of 1960 and the *Werkausgabe in zehn Bänden, 1920–1975* (1976) together provide such a foundation, although both are essentially reproductions of previously published texts without critical apparatus. Textual variants, particularly original versions in cases such as *Ulla Winblad (Bellman)* or *Des Teufels General*, where several versions exist, are missing. Moreover, neither one of the two editions is complete. For example, whereas the *Gesammelte Werke* contain the fragmentary "Indian novel" *Sitting Bull*, the *Werkausgabe* does not, but it does make available again some early stories, such as "Die Geschichte vom Lappenvogt Bal." Neither edition includes the novel *Ein Sommer in Österreich*, the early drama *Prometheus*, or several early poems that were published in Pfemfert's *Aktion*. A great number of the author's essay's were collected for the first time under the title *Aufruf zum Leben* in 1976. The early drama *Pankraz erwacht* was first published in the yearbook *Carl Zuckmayer '78*. Zuckmayer's film scripts, including the one for *Der blaue Engel*, are not available in any edition. Also, the adaptations of Hemingway's *A Farewell to Arms* under the title *Kat* and Maxwell Anderson and Laurence Stalling's *What Price Glory* under the title *Rivalen* have never been published. The same applies to a manuscript for a novel, "Vermonter Roman," which is still awaiting publication in the Zuckmayer collection of the Deutsches Literaturarchiv Marbach. But, as Mews (**Bibliographies**, 1977) points out, "Although Zuckmayer disclaimed any involvement in its planning, the *Werkausgabe [in zehn Bänden, 1920–1975]* constitutes, for all practical purposes, an 'Ausgabe letzter Hand.' For in the 'Nachwort' the author bestowed his public blessing on the edition and the occasional notes were penned by Zuckmayer himself. At any rate, despite its tendency to canonize a major part of Zuckmayer's work, the present edition will provide the basis for further research" (299). This is true, of course, for the time being, because a complete critical edition, including letters, is still a desideratum for Zuckmayer research roughly twenty years after the *Werkausgabe*.

The second prerequisite for Zuckmayer research is good bibliographies. Fortunately, Arnold John Jacobius (**Bibliographies**, 1971) collected literature by and about Zuckmayer, altogether over two thousand items, as part of his 1955 dissertation, written at New York University. In 1971 Harro Kieser, librarian at the Frankfurt Deutsche Bibliothek, brought it up to date and published it. The bibliography contains not only scholarly publications but also the most obscure articles about Zuckmayer's books and the performances of his plays from German newspapers. Many items, such as the ones about the award of prizes and honorary citizenships, are, of course, worthless for research on his works. It is indeed sometimes difficult to separate the chaff from the wheat. Kieser continued the primary bibliography in publications of 1976, 1985, and 1993. Barbara Glauert provides an even more comprehensive primary bibliography for the years 1971–77 in *Carl Zuckmayer '78: Ein Jahrbuch* (1978), continuing the efforts by Jacobius and Kieser. The secondary literature was first critically reviewed by J. Vandenrath (**Bibliographies**, 1961), who in particular characterizes the early dissertations, and then by Siegfried Mews in 1972, 1977, and 1978 (all listed under **Bibliographies**). Mews's critical *Forschungsbericht* of 1978, an expanded version of his report of 1977, is exemplary in its completeness and balanced judgments. What is missing to date is a primary bibliography from 1985 and beyond. Also, since the *Forschungsberichte* by Vandenrath and Mews noted above are by their very nature selective, a more complete secondary bibliography is needed for 1972 on.

Other useful research tools are Barbara Glauert's (1977) edition of reviews of Zuckmayer performances as well as her catalogue for the exhibition "Carl Zuckmayer auf der Bühne" (Glauert 1976a), which was shown in Mainz from December 1976 through February 1977. It lists materials relevant to the staging of Zuckmayer's plays such as programs, reviews, promptbooks, and photographs. As Mews points out in his "Special Report" (**Bibliographies**, 1977), "With its listing of the precise locations of more than 600 items, many of which were on public display for the first time, the catalogue is a valuable supplement to the Zuckmayer bibliography" (305–6).

As has become obvious in the evaluation of the individual items, there simply is no Zuckmayer research dating back to the Weimar Republic except for reviews of first publications and performances. Because of the Third Reich and the author's inability to publish in Germany, the same applies to the period 1933–45, except that the reviews are restricted to the few publications in translation outside of Germany, particularly in the United States. In short, Zuckmayer research did not begin until after the war.

German Germanists have always been suspicious of popular authors; their works are suspected of a lack of philosophical depth and literary quality. As a result, Zuckmayer's works were uneasily relegated to the twilight of folk literature. Also, in the 1940s and early 1950s, there was still a reluctance in Germany to devote scholarship to living authors. American literary scholarship has never suffered from a kind of prejudice that recognized only "high" literature. It is therefore not surprising that serious Zuckmayer research began with several minor articles in the United States and that it approached Zuckmayer with a much more open mind than German scholarship did: examples of such articles are Cohn (1946), Steiner & Frenz (1947), Boeninger (1952), Peppard (1952), Loram (1954), Guder (1953–54), and Spahr (1954). Most of these articles addressed individual works only, whereas Loram's (1954) is a general introduction of an author being presented to the American public. During these and the following years, American Germanists took the lead in Zuckmayer research not only as far as scholarly articles are concerned but also with regard to the number of dissertations, some of which were written in German but almost all of which were less interested in form and aesthetics than they were in Zuckmayer's worldview as expressed in his writings. These dissertations include Jacobius (1955), Glade (1958), Engelsing-Malek (1960), Lehrer (1962), Barrick (1964), Maddox (1975), Balinkin (1976), Finke (1990), and Grange (1991). From the early 1970s on, a number of other more established American Germanists continued contributing extensively to Zuckmayer research, particularly Henry Glade (1974, 1981a and b, 1983, 1989); Siegfried Mews (1972, 1973a and b; [with English] 1974, 1977, 1981a and b, 1983), Hans Wagener (1983a, b, and c, 1984, 1985, 1986, 1987, 1988, 1989, 1995), and Blake Lee Spahr (1992). Although American researchers, like those in Germany, became interested in sociocritical and political aspects of literature — for example Lehrer (1962) and Kvam (1976) — it is amazing that, on the other hand, textimmanent methods remained viable in this country much longer than in Germany, as in the works of Balinkin (1976), Finke (1990), and Grange (1991).

The contribution of other countries was minor. Exceptions are the Finnish article by Keijo Holsti (1984), the important Norwegian one by Brynhildsvoll (1976), the French one by Marie-Odile Blum (1993), and the British articles by H. F. Garten (1964), Sheila Rooke (1964), and Jennifer Taylor (1981).

Zuckmayer research in Germany did not begin until Teelen wrote his dissertation in 1952. In accordance with the ruling textimmanent school in German-speaking countries, German research first followed this approach almost entirely, focusing on aspects of aesthetic form: Teelen (1952), Pfeiffer (1953, 1965), Meinherz (1960), Vandenrath (1960, written at the University of Liège), and many others. Zuckmayer's popularity as required reading in West German schools is evident in a number of pedagogical articles — Benicke (1960), Riegel (1960), Keller (1978) — and commentaries on *Der Hauptmann von Köpenick* and *Des Teufels General* that, because of their nonscholarly nature, were not included in this study.

With the waning of Zuckmayer's popularity and appreciation after 1955, following the new demand that literature be sociocritical and that the writer help bring about social and political change, German scholarship became increasingly critical of the author. This tendency was aided by the failure of his new dramas, beginning with *Das kalte Licht* (1955), to win over the critics. Following Rilla's famous East German attack (1950), Adling's (1959) Marxist study is probably the most critical one of its kind, filled with the determined intent to misunderstand Zuckmayer. Adling looked at Zuckmayer's work as a political phenomenon, embodying his development into his time. The only other major East German contribution was Lüder's dissertation of 1987, which traced the reception of *Des Teufels General* in relation to the changing political agendas of the occupying powers in the West. But in the West other critical or at least cautious voices were heard, too: Kesting (1969), Wehdeking (1973), Huyssen (1976), and Ayck (1977). The leftist student revolt of 1968 left its mark on Zuckmayer scholarship (Ayck 1977), as did the leftist studies of German literature that dominated many German departments at American universities during the 1970s and 1980s (Huyssen 1976). Zuckmayer was taken most seriously by those scholars who paid attention to him as a renewer of the folk play during the Weimar Republic, notably Greiner (1958) and Rotermund (1970), and by those who documented the amazing impact he had on the German stage, above all Barbara Glauert (1977).

The rise of exile research in the 1960s also brought an interest in positivistic studies. In the United States, Glade (1981a and b, 1983) first traced Zuckmayer's life and activities in exile. This work was continued in Germany by Becker (1986a) and particularly Albrecht (1988, 1989), who provided stimuli for new biographical research. A great deal of correspondence was published, not only that with Carl Barth (Stoevesandt 1977) but correspondence with many others that appeared in the *Blätter der Carl-Zuckmayer-Gesellschaft*. A complete edition of all of Zuckmayer's letters, a considerable number of which are at the Deutsches Literaturarchiv Marbach, is a desideratum of Zuckmayer research.

Zuckmayer's popularity led to the publication of a number of biographies and monographs, most of them sympathetic toward the author and his colorful life and introductory by nature: Reindl (1962), Lange (1969), Bauer (1970), Ayck (1977), Mews (1981a), Wagener (1983a), and Becker (1984).

It is interesting that the modern critical methods developed during the past twenty years have so far hardly touched Zuckmayer research. One can only conjecture about the reasons: possibly the fact that the humanist Zuckmayer in turn attracted like-minded researchers who were mainly interested in the author's humanist ideas rather than in deconstructing his message. Only Luise Rinser, in her short portrait (1950), applied a psychoanalytical approach. In the meantime, at least, women's studies have finally discovered Zuckmayer. Whereas Balinkin's (1976) dissertation was textimmanent, Czech's (1985) thesis was stimulated by Kafitz's (1983) article, the latter of whom evaluated *Salware* in terms of Zuckmayer's vitalistic thinking, dispassionately considering the role of women *and* men. Although not feminist, Czech's M.A. thesis was based on criteria deduced from the history of the women's movement and applying at least some tenets of modern critical theory to Zuckmayer's work, whereas Lindner's (1986) investigation was more or less textimmanent. Apart from Wagener's (1995) critical article on *Ein Sommer in Österreich*, which applies contemporary theories of literary evaluation, and Blum's (1993) interdisciplinary essay, Zimmermann (1989) is so far the only critic who has applied a modern critical approach to Zuckmayer — with debatable results.

There is no doubt that Zuckmayer research in Germany received a great impetus from the founding of the *Blätter der Carl-Zuckmayer-Gesellschaft* in 1975. Under the able editorship of Gerald P. Martin, this periodical paid homage to its author, printing more or less scholarly articles, letters, reviews of Zuckmayer performances, testimonials, and reminiscences. After Martin resigned from the editorship in 1985, publication of the *Blätter* was interrupted. It is to be hoped that the editorial committee headed by Jochen Becker will be able to continue Martin's meritorious work. There is no doubt that in many of the society's publications there was a tendency to idealize their author and to look with distrust and annoyance at all who dared to criticize him, but it also has to be conceded that they managed to keep Zuckmayer's memory alive. These tributes to the author began with his first *Festschrift*, *Fülle der Zeit* (1956), and were continued in the *Festschriften* of

1976 (Glauert, Martin, and Heist 1976), the commemorative *Abschied von Carl Zuckmayer* (Glauert and Roland 1977), and the obituaries. *Carl Zuckmayer '78. Ein Jahrbuch* (1978) could have continued and become a forum for Zuckmayer research, but no follow-up volume ever appeared. Harro Kieser's (1986) collection of some of the most important research articles makes these available to a wide audience, but it is a retrospective of past investigations and is no substitute for a series with an ongoing scholarly dialogue.

Kieser's edition of Jacobius's bibliography (1971) almost gives the wrong impression — as if the end of Zuckmayer research had been reached. To be sure, during the past years there has been a considerable decline in the number of studies on Zuckmayer, but a lot remains to be done, particularly in the area of prose and poetry and in Zuckmayer's work for the film industry. There can be no doubt that the man and his work constitute a continuing challenge and opportunity for future Germanists.

Works Consulted

(In Chronological Order Within Subheadings)

Works by Carl Zuckmayer

1921. *Kreuzweg: Drama.* Munich: Wolff.

1925. *Der fröhliche Weinberg: Lustspiel in drei Akten.* Berlin: Propyläen.

1926. *Der Baum: Gedichte.* Berlin: Propyläen.

1927. *Ein Bauer aus dem Taunus und andere Geschichten.* Berlin: Propyläen.

1927. *Schinderhannes: Schauspiel in vier Akten.* Berlin: Propyläen.

1929. *Kakadu-Kakada: Ein Kinderstück.* Berlin: Propyläen.

1929. *Katharina Knie: Ein Seiltänzerstück in vier Akten.* Berlin: Propyläen.

1929. *Rivalen (What Price Glory?): Ein Stück in drei Akten (nach dem amerikanischen Schauspiel von Maxwell Anderson und Laurence Stalling. Frei bearbeitet von Carl Zuckmayer.)* Berlin: Arcadia.

1930. *Der Hauptmann von Köpenick: Ein deutsches Märchen in drei Akten.* Berlin: Propyläen. Translated by David Portman as *The Captain of Köpenick: A Modern Fairy Tale in Three Acts.* London: Bles, 1932; retranslated by Carl Richard Mueller as *The Captain of Köpenick,* in *German Drama Between the Wars,* ed. George E. Wellwarth. New York: Dutton, 1974. 179–296.

1932. *Die Affenhochzeit: Novelle.* Berlin: Propyläen. Translated by F. A. Beaumont as "Monkey Wedding." *Argosy* 23, 142 (1938): 53–69.

1932. *Gerhart Hauptmann: Rede zu seinem siebzigsten Geburtstag, gehalten bei der offiziellen Feier der Stadt Berlin.* N.p., published privately.

1934. *Eine Liebesgeschichte.* Berlin: Fischer. Translated by F. A. Beaumont as "A Love Story." *Argosy* 22, 138 (1937): 11–28.

1934. *Der Schelm von Bergen: Ein Schauspiel.* Berlin: Propyläen.

1935. *Salwàre oder Die Magdalena von Bozen: Roman.* Berlin: S. Fischer. (The edition was confiscated before shipment to the booksellers). Translated by Morey Firth as *The Moon in the South.* London: Secker & Warburg, 1937; translation republished as *The Moons Ride Over.* New York: Viking, 1937.

1936. *Salwàre oder Die Magdalena von Bozen. Roman.* Vienna: Bermann-Fischer.

1937. *Ein Sommer in Österreich: Erzählung.* Vienna: Bermann-Fischer.

1938. *Herr über Leben und Tod.* Stockholm: Bermann-Fischer.

1938. *Pro domo.* Stockholm: Bermann-Fischer. (Schriftenreihe Ausblicke).

1940. *Second Wind.* With an introduction by Dorothy Thompson. Trans. Elizabeth Reynolds Hapgood. New York: Doubleday, Doran, 1940; republished London: Harrap, 1941.

1944. (Coauthor). *Carlo Mierendorff: Porträt eines deutschen Sozialisten. Gedächtnisreden gesprochen am 12. 3. 1944 in New York von P. Hertz, A. Vagts, Carl Zuckmayer.* New York: published privately.

1945. *Der Seelenbräu: Erzählung.* Stockholm: Bermann-Fischer.

1946. (Coauthor). *Deutsche innere Emigration. Antinationalsozialistische Zeugnisse aus Deutschland. Gesammelt und erläutert von Karl O. Paetel. Mit Originalbeiträgen von Carl Zuckmayer und Dorothy Thompson.* New York: F. Krause. (Dokumente des anderen Deutschlands 4).

1946. *Des Teufels General: Drama in drei Akten.* Stockholm: Bermann-Fischer. Translated by Ingrid G. and William F. Gilbert as *The Devil's General,* in *Masters of German Drama,* ed. H. M. Block and R. G. Shedd. New York: Random House, 1962. 911–58.

1947–1952. *Gesammelte Werke,* 4 volumes.

Includes:

1947. *Die deutschen Dramen: Schinderhannes, Der Hauptmann von Köpenick, Des Teufels General.* Stockholm: Bermann-Fischer.

1948. *Gedichte: 1916–1948.* Amsterdam: Bermann-Fischer.

1950. *Komödie und Volksstück: Der fröhliche Weinberg, Katharina Knie, Der Schelm von Bergen.* Frankfurt am Main, Berlin: Fischer.

1952. *Die Erzählungen.* Frankfurt am Main, Berlin: Fischer.

1947. *Carlo Mierendorff. Porträt eines deutschen Sozialisten. Gedächtnisrede, gesprochen am 12. 3. 1944 in New York.* Berlin: Suhrkamp. (Beiträge zur Humanität). First edition of the above, 1944, that appeared in Germany.

1947. *Der Seelenbräu. Erzählung.* Berlin: Suhrkamp. First edition of the above, 1945, that appeared in Germany.

1947. *Des Teufels General. Drama in drei Akten.* Berlin: Suhrkamp. First edition of the above, 1946, that appeared in Germany.

1948. *Die Brüder Grimm: Ein deutscher Beitrag zur Humanität.* Frankfurt am Main: Suhrkamp. (Beiträge zur Humanität).

1949. *Barbara Blomberg: Ein Stück in drei Akten mit Vorspiel und Epilog.* Amsterdam, Vienna: Bermann-Fischer.

1950. *Der Gesang im Feuerofen: Drama in drei Akten*. Frankfurt am Main, Berlin: Fischer.

1950. *Salwàre oder Die Magdalena von Bozen: Roman*. Berlin, Frankfurt am Main: Suhrkamp. First edition of the above, 1936, that appeared in Germany.

1951. *Ödön von Horváth. Ein Kind unserer Zeit*, commemorative speech by Zuckmayer, preface by Franz Werfel. Vienna: Bergland.

1952. (Coauthor). Gerhart Hauptmann, *Herbert Engelmann: Drama in vier Akten*, completed by Zuckmayer. Munich: Beck. Includes Hauptmann's and Zuckmayer's versions.

1952. *Herr über Leben und Tod: Roman*. Frankfurt am Main: Fischer. (Fischer-Bücherei 6). First edition of the above, 1938, that appeared in Germany.

1952. *Die langen Wege; Ein Stück Rechenschaft: Rede*. Frankfurt am Main: Fischer.

1953. *Ulla Winblad oder Musik und Leben des Carl Michael Bellman*. Frankfurt am Main, Berlin: Fischer.

1955. *Engele von Loewen: Erzählungen*. Zurich: Classen. Selection from 1947–1952. *Gesammelte Werke*: 1952. *Die Erzählungen*.

1955. *Fünfzig Jahre Düsseldorfer Schauspielhaus, 1905–1955*. Ed. Düsseldorfer Schauspielhaus. Düsseldorf: published privately.

1955. *Das kalte Licht: Drama in drei Akten*. Frankfurt am Main: Fischer.

1957. *Ein Blick auf den Rhein: Rede, gehalten bei der feierlichen Verleihung der Würde eines Doktor honoris causa der Philosophischen Fakultät der Universität Bonn am 10. Mai 1957. Mit einer Einführung von Benno von Wiese und Kaiserswaldau*. Bonn: Hanstein. (Bonner akademische Reden 18).

1958. (Introduction). Werner Kraus: *Das Schauspiel meines Lebens. Einem Freund erzählt*. Stuttgart: Goverts.

1959. *Die Fastnachtsbeichte: Eine Erzählung*. Frankfurt am Main: Fischer. Translated by John and Necke Mander as *Carnival Confession*. London: Methuen, 1961.

1959. *Die Magdalena von Bozen: Roman*. Frankfurt am Main, Hamburg: Fischer. (Fischer-Bücherei 282). First edition of the above, 1936, that appeared in Germany.

1959. *Ein Sommer in Österreich: Roman*. Gütersloh: Bertelsmann-Lesering. First German edition of the above, 1938, that appeared in Germany.

1959. *Ein Weg zu Schiller*. Frankfurt am Main: Fischer.

1960. *Gedichte*. Frankfurt am Main: Fischer.

1960. *Gesammelte Werke*, 4 volumes. Berlin, Frankfurt am Main: Fischer.

1960. (Preface). Ingeborg Engelsing-Malek: *"Amor Fati" in Zuckmayers Dramen*. Constance: Rosgarten; Berkeley, Los Angeles: University of California Press. (University of California Publications in Modern Philology 61).

1961. . . . *hinein ins volle Menschenleben. Ausgew. u. eingel. von F. Th. Csokor*. Graz, Vienna: Stiasny. (Stiasny-Bücherei 88).

1961. *Die Uhr schlägt eins: Ein historisches Drama aus der Gegenwart*. Frankfurt am Main: Fischer.

1962. (Preface). Erhard Buschbeck: *Mimus Austriacus. Aus dem nachgelassenen Werk*, ed. Lotte von Tobisch. Salzburg, Stuttgart: Das Bergland-Buch. (Österreich-Bibliothek).

1962. (Coauthor). *Mainz: Gesicht einer Stadt. Fotos: Wolfgang Haut. Texte von Carl Zuckmayer, Adam Gottfron, Vilma Sturm*. Mainz: Mathias-Grünewald. Text partially in German, English, and French.

1962. With Paul Hindemith, *Mainzer Umzug für Singstimmen, gemischten Chor und Orchester*. Mainz: Schott.

1962. *Ein voller Erdentag: Zu Gerhart Hauptmanns 100. Geburtstag*. Frankfurt am Main: Fischer.

1962. *Eine Weihnachtsgeschichte*. Zürich: Arche. (Die kleinen Bücher der Arche 366/67).

1962. *Das Ziel der Klasse: Festrede zum vierhundertjährigen Bestehen des Humanistischen Gymnasiums in Mainz am 27. Mai 1962*. Mainz: von Zabern.

1963. (Preface). *Der Büchner-Preis: Die Reden der Preisträger 1950–1962*. Heidelberg, Darmstadt: Schneider. (Veröffentlichung der deutschen Akademie für Sprache und Dichtung, Darmstadt).

1963. *Geschichten aus vierzig Jahren*. Frankfurt am Main: Fischer.

1963. *Three Stories*, ed. Derrick Barlow. London: Oxford University Press. Comprises "Die Geschichte eines Bauern aus dem Taunus," "Die Affenhochzeit," and "Die wandernden Hütten."

1963. (Preface). *Das Werk des Nicolaus Cusanus: Eine bibliophile Einführung*, ed. Gerd Heinz-Mohr and Willebald Paul Eckert. Cologne: Wienand. (Zeugnisse der Buchkunst 3).

1964. *Das Leben des Horace A. W. Tabor: Ein Stück aus den Tagen der letzten Könige*. Frankfurt am Main: Fischer.

1965. *Engele von Loewen und andere Erzählungen*. Frankfurt am Main, Hamburg. (Fischer-Bücherei 654). Expanded new edition of 1955, *Engele von Loewen*.

1966. *Als wär's ein Stück von mir: Horen der Freundschaft*. Frankfurt am Main: Fischer. Translated by Richard and Clara Winston as *A Part of Myself* (abbreviated version). London: Secker & Warburg; New York: Harcourt Brace Jovanovich, 1970.

1966. *Für Gertrud von Le Fort: 11. Oktober 1966*. Published privately.

1966. *Meisterdramen*. Frankfurt am Main: Fischer

1967. *Dramen*. Afterword: Wilfried Adling. Berlin: Aufbau.

1967. *Meistererzählungen*. Frankfurt am Main: Fischer. New edition of 1963. *Geschichten aus vierzig Jahren*.

1967. *Scholar zwischen gestern und morgen: Ein Vortrag gehalten in der Universität Heidelberg anläßlich seiner Ernennung zum Ehrenbürger am 23. November 1967*. Heidelberg: Brausdruck.

1967. (Preface). Siegwart Sprotte: *Aquarelle auf Sylt. Einleitung von Herbert Read. Geleitwort von Carl Zuckmayer*. Berlin: Rembrandt.

1967. *Des Teufels General. Drama in drei Akten. Neue Fassung 1966*. Frankfurt: Fischer. (S. Fischer Schulausgaben).

1968. (Preface). Alfred A. Häsler: *Knie — Die Geschichte einer Circus-Dynastie*. Bern: Benteli.

1968. *Eine Auslese*, ed. Wolfgang Mertz. Vienna, Heidelberg: Ueberreuter.

1969. *Memento zum 20. Juli 1969*. Frankfurt am Main: Fischer.

1970. *Auf einem Weg im Frühling: Erzählung; Wiedersehen mit einer Stadt: Aus dem Stegreif erzählt*. Salzburg: Residenz.

1970. (Preface). Salka Viertel: *Das unbelehrbare Herz: Ein Leben in der Welt des Theaters, der Literatur und des Films*. Hamburg, Düsseldorf: Claassen.

1970. *Über die musische Bestimmung des Menschen: Rede zur Eröffnung der Salzburger Festspiele 1970*, ed. Max Kaindl-Hönig, with English translation by Richard Rickett and French translation by Martha Eissler. Salzburg: Festungsverlag.

1971. *Stücke meines Lebens: Mit persönlichen Einleitungen des Autors*. Frankfurt am Main: Büchergilde Gutenberg.

1972. *Heinrich Heine und der liebe Gott und ich. Rede zur Verleihung des Heinrich-Heine-Preises in Düsseldorf, 13. Dezember 1972*. St. Gallen: Zollikofer.

1972. *Henndorfer Pastorale*. Salzburg: Residenz.

1975. *Der Rattenfänger: Eine Fabel*. Frankfurt am Main: Fischer Taschenbuch Verlag. (Fischer-Taschenbuch 7023).

1975. (Preface). *Zirkus Knie: eine Zirkus-Dynastie*. Lausanne: Marguerat.

1976. *Aufruf zum Leben: Porträts und Zeugnisse aus bewegten Zeiten.* Frankfurt am Main: Fischer.

1976. (Preface). Peter Bamm, *Sämtliche Werke.* 5 volumes. Munich, Zurich: Knaur. (Knaur-Taschenbücher 451).

1976. *Werkausgabe in zehn Bänden, 1920–1975,* 10 volumes. Frankfurt am Main: Fischer Taschenbuch Verlag.

1976. *Zuckmayer-Lesebuch.* Frankfurt am Main: Fischer.

1977. *Gedichte.* Frankfurt am Main: Fischer.

1977. (Coauthor). *Späte Freundschaft in Briefen: Carl Zuckmayer — Karl Barth.* Zurich: Theologischer Verlag. Translated by Geoffrey W. Bromiley as *A Late Friendship. The Letters of Carl Barth and Carl Zuckmayer.* Preface by Hinrich Stoevesandt. Grand Rapids, Mich.: Eerdmans, 1982.

1980. *Rembrandt: Ein Film.* Frankfurt am Main: Fischer Taschenbuch Verlag. (Fischer-Taschenbuch 2296).

1981. *Einmal, wenn alles vorüber ist: Briefe an Kurt Grell, Gedichte, Dramen, Prosa aus den Jahren 1914–1920.* Frankfurt am Main: Fischer.

Bibliographies

Vandenrath, J. 1961. "Der Stand der Zuckmayerforschung: Beitrag zu einer kritischen Bibliographie." *Modern Language Notes* 76: 829–39.

Jacobius, Arnold John. 1971. *Carl Zuckmayer: Eine Bibliographie 1917–1971.* Continued from 1955 and updated by Harro Kieser. Frankfurt am Main: Fischer.

Mews, Siegfried. 1972. "Die Zuckmayer-Forschung der sechziger Jahre." *Modern Language Notes* 87: 465–93.

Kieser, Harro. 1976. "Carl Zuckmayer: Bibliographie 1971–1976." In *Festschrift für Carl Zuckmayer zu seinem 80. Geburtstag am 27. Dezember 1976,* ed. Barbara Glauert, Gerald P. Martin, and Walter Heist. Mainz: Krach. 116–20.

Mews, Siegfried. 1977. "Carl Zuckmayer (27 December 1896–18 January 1977) (Special Report)". *German Quarterly* 50: 298–308.

Mews, Siegfried. 1978. "Die Zuckmayerforschung 1961–1977." In *Carl Zuckmayer '78. Ein Jahrbuch.* Frankfurt am Main: Fischer. 228–72. Expanded version of Mews's above report of 1972.

Glauert, Barbara. 1978. "Carl Zuckmayer 1971–1977: Eine Bibliographie." In *Carl Zuckmayer '78. Ein Jahrbuch.* Frankfurt am Main: Fischer. 305–83.

Kieser, Harro. 1985. "Carl Zuckmayer: Bibliographie (I)." *Blätter der Carl-Zuckmayer-Gesellschaft* 11: 221–23.

Kieser, Harro. 1993. "Carl Zuckmayer: Bibliographie (II)." *Blätter der Carl-Zuckmayer-Gesellschaft* 14: 38–42.

Works about Carl Zuckmayer

Factor, Emil. 1920. [Review of *Kreuzweg*]. *Berliner Börsen-Courier.* 11 December 1920. Reprinted in Rühle, *Theater für die Republik*, 1967, 273–74.

Ihering, Herbert. 1920. [Review of *Kreuzweg*]. *Der Tag* (Berlin). 12 December 1920. Reprinted in Rühle, *Theater für die Republik*, 1967, 276–78.

Kanehl, Oskar. 1920. [Review of *Kreuzweg*]. *Die Aktion* 10: 718.

Kerr, Alfred. 1920. [Review of *Kreuzweg*]. *Berliner Tageblatt.* 11 December 1920. Reprinted in Rühle, *Theater für die Republik*, 1967, 275–76.

Kerr, Alfred. [Review of *Der fröhliche Weinberg*]. *Berliner Tageblatt.* 23 December 1925. Reprinted in Rühle, *Theater für die Republik*, 1967, 669–75; and in Glauert, *Carl Zuckmayer*, 1977, 35–39.

Loerke, Oskar. 1926. "Gedichte von Zuckmayer." *Berliner Börsen-Courier*, 26 July 1926. Reprinted in Loerke, *Der Bücherkarren*, ed. Hermann Kasack in collaboration with Reinhard Tgahrt. Heidelberg and Darmstadt: Lambert Schneider 1965. 346–48.

Lissauer, Ernst. 1926–27. "Zuckmayers Gedichte." *Die Literatur: Monatsschrift* 29: 21–23.

Bab, Julius. 1927. "Loerke, O. — Zuckmayer, C.: Neue deutsche Lyrik." *Hannoverscher Kurier.* 4 February 1927. Reprinted in Bab, *Über den Tag hinaus. Kritische Betrachtungen*, ed. Harry Bergholz. Heidelberg, Darmstadt: Lambert Schneider, 1960. 115–18.

Fechter, Paul. 1927. "Carl Zuckmayer: 'Schinderhannes.'" *Deutsche Allgemeine Zeitung.* 16 October 1927. Reprinted in Rühle, *Theater für die Republik*, 1967, 800–2; in Glauert, *Carl Zuckmayer*, 1977, 105–8; and in Kieser, *Carl Zuckmayer*, 1986, 40–43.

Franzen, Erich. 1927. "Novellen." *Die literarische Welt* 3 (28): 5.

Kästner, Erich. 1927. "Zuckmayers Schinderhannes." *Neue Leipziger Zeitung.* 16 October 1927. Reprinted in Glauert, *Carl Zuckmayer*, 1977, 108–10.

Kerr, Alfred. 1927. "Carl Zuckmayer: Schinderhannes." *Berliner Tageblatt.* 15 October 1927. Reprinted in Rühle, *Theater für die Republik*, 1967, 802–4.

Schwabach, Erik-Ernst. 1927. "Karl Zuckmayers Bauer aus dem Taunus." *Zeitschrift für Bücherfreunde.* N.F. 19: 246.

Fechter, Paul. 1928. "Carl Zuckmayer: 'Katharina Knie.' " *Deutsche Allgemeine Zeitung.* Berlin. 22 December 1928. Reprinted in Glauert, *Carl Zuckmayer* 1977, 118–22.

Kerr, Alfred. 1928. "Zuckmayer: 'Katharina Knie.' " *Berliner Tageblatt.* 22 December 1928. Reprinted in Rühle, *Theater für die Republik,* 1967, 911–12; in Glauert, *Carl Zuckmayer,* 1977, 122–25; and in Kieser, *Carl Zuckmayer,* 1986, 44–46.

Diebold, Bernhard. 1931. [Review of *Der Hauptmann von Köpenick*]. *Frankfurter Zeitung.* 8 March 1931. Reprinted in Rühle, *Theater für die Republik,* 1967, 1079–82.

Ihering, Herbert. 1931. [Review of *Der Hauptmann von Köpenick*]. *Berliner Börsen-Courier.* 6 March 1931. Reprinted in Rühle, *Theater für die Republik,* 1967. 1077–79.

Holländer, Felix. 1932. "Zuckmayer: Schinderhannes." In Holländer, *Lebendes Theater: Eine Berliner Dramaturgie.* Berlin: Fischer. 165–67.

Polgar, Alfred. 1939. "Carl Zuckmayer: 'Pro Domo.' " *Das Neue Tage-Buch* 7 (6) (2 April 1939): 141. Reprinted in Polgar, *Taschenspiegel,* ed. Ulrich Weinzierl. Vienna: Löcker, 1979. 85ff.; and in Polgar, *Kleine Schriften,* vol. 4: *Literatur,* ed. Marcel Reich-Ranicki in collaboration with Ulrich Weinzierl. Reinbek b. Hamburg: Rowohlt, 1984. 146–49.

Cohn, Hilde. 1946. "Carl Zuckmayer: Der Seelenbräu." *Monatshefte für deutschen Unterricht* 38: 360–62.

Eggebrecht, Axel. 1947. "Carl Zuckmayer." *Nordwestdeutsche Hefte* (Berlin) 2 (1): 39–41. Reprinted in 1985 in *Blätter der Carl-Zuckmayer-Gesellschaft* 11: 210–12.

Seyffarth, Ursula. 1947. "Zuckmayer, Carl: Der Seelenbräu." *Welt und Wort* H. 8 (August): 241.

Steiner, Pauline, and Frenz, Horst. 1947. "Anderson and Stalling's 'What Price Glory' and Carl Zuckmayer's 'Rivalen.' " *The German Quarterly* 20: 239–51.

Braun, Hanns. 1948. "Glosse zu 'Des Teufels General.' " *Hochland* 40: 498–500.

Weltmann, Lutz. 1948–49. "Two Recent German Plays." *German Life and Letters* 2: 1958–63.

Herdan-Zuckmayer, Alice. 1949. *Die Farm in den grünen Bergen.* Reworked edition Vienna: Salzer, 1968.

Rilla, Paul. 1950. "Zuckmayer und die Uniform." In Rilla, *Literatur, Kritik und Polemik*. Berlin: Henschelverlag. 7–27. Reprinted in Rilla, *Vom bürgerlichen zum sozialen Realismus: Aufsätze*. Leipzig: Reclam, 1967. 83–102; and in *Das deutsche Drama vom Expressionismus bis zur Gegenwart: Interpretationen*, ed. Manfred Brauneck. Bamberg: Buchner, 1970. 99–107; 3rd edition 1977. 103–11.

Rinser, Luise. 1950. [Review of *Salwàre oder Die Magdalena von Bozen*]. *Neue Zeitung* (Munich). June 12. Reprinted in 1983 under the title "Der Mond und sein Eigentum: Zu dem Roman *Salwàre* von Carl Zuckmayer." *Blätter der Carl-Zuckmayer-Gesellschaft* 9: 9–11.

Behl, C. F. W. 1952. "Zuckmayers Hauptmann-Drama." *Deutsche Rundschau* 78: 609–11.

Boeninger, Helmut. 1952. "A Play and Two Authors: Zuckmayer's Version of Hauptmann's 'Herbert Engelmann.' " *Monatshefte für deutschen Unterricht* 44: 341–48.

Peppard, Murray B. 1952. "Moment of Moral Decision: Carl Zuckmayer's Latest Plays." *Monatshefte für deutschen Unterricht* 44: 349–56.

Teelen, Wolfgang. 1952. "Die Gestaltungsgesetze im Bühnenwerk Carl Zuckmayers." Diss. Marburg.

Pfeiffer, Johannes. 1953. "Carl Zuckmayer: Der Seelenbräu." In Pfeiffer, *Wege zur Erzählkunst*. Hamburg: Wittig. 145–55. Reprinted in Kieser, *Carl Zuckmayer*, 1986, 165–175.

Guder, G. 1953–54. "Carl Zuckmayer's Postwar Plays." *Modern Languages* 35 (2): 54–56.

Loram, Ian C. 1954. "Carl Zuckmayer: An Introduction." *German Quarterly* 27: 137–149.

Spahr, Blake Lee. 1954. "A Note on 'Herbert Engelmann.' " *Monatshefte für deutschen Unterricht* 46: 339–45.

Erpenbeck, Fritz. 1955. "Old Shatterhand im Kalten Krieg: Zu Carl Zuckmayers neuem Drama." *Theater der Zeit* 10 (12): 1–5.

Jacobius, Arnold John. 1955. "Das Schauspiel Carl Zuckmayers: Wesen, Gehalt, Beziehung zum Gesamtwerk; mit einer Bibliographie des von und über Carl Zuckmayer veröffentlichten Schrifttums (1920–1954)." Diss. New York University. First part printed as *Motive und Dramaturgie im Schauspiel Carl Zuckmayers: Versuch einer Deutung im Rahmen des zwischen 1920 und 1955 entstandenen Gesamtwerkes*. Frankfurt am Main: Athenäum, 1971. All references in the text are to this version. Second part (bibliography) listed under **Bibliographies** as Jacobius, John Arnold. 1971.

Jaesrich, Hellmut. 1955. "Verwirrung des Menschen: Zu Carl Zuckmayers Zeitdrama 'Das kalte Licht.' " *Der Monat* (Frankfurt am Main) 7 (85): 79–82. Reprinted in Kieser, *Carl Zuckmayer*, 1986, 122–28.

Kaiser, Joachim. 1955. "Über 30 Bühnen? Carl Zuckmayer: Das kalte Licht" *Frankfurter Hefte* 10: 820–23.

Lederer, Moritz. 1955. "Zuckmayers kaltes Licht." *Deutsche Rundschau* 81: 1313–15.

Loram, Ian C. 1955. "Ulla Winblad: Words and Music by Zuckmayer and Bellman." *Monatshefte für deutschen Unterricht* 47: 11–18.

1956. *Fülle der Zeit: Carl Zuckmayer und sein Werk*. Frankfurt am Main: Fischer.

Includes, among others:

Happ, Alfred. 1956. "Dichterisches Theater." 31–60.

Rinser, Luise. 1956. "Porträtskizze." 13–30. Reprinted as "Carl Zuck- mayer" in Rinser, *Der Schwerpunkt*. Frankfurt am Main: Fischer, 1960. 45–70, and in 1981 under the title "Seine Helden sind seine Wunschbilder: Über Carl Zuckmayer." *Blätter der Carl-Zuckmayer- Gesellschaft* 7: 23–34.

Peppard, Murray B. 1957. "Carl Zuckmayer: Cold Light in a Divided World." *Monatshefte für deutschen Unterricht* 49: 121–29.

Vandenrath, J. 1957. "Carl Zuckmayers expressionistischer Erstling 'Kreuzweg.' " *Revue des langues vivantes* 23: 37–59.

Glade, Henry. 1958. "The Concept of *Humanität* in the Life and Works of Carl Zuckmayer, with Emphasis on the Later Period (1933–1956)." Diss. University of Pennsylvania, University Park, Penn.

Greiner, Martin. 1958. "Carl Zuckmayer als Volksdichter. *Hessische Blätter für Volkskunde* 49/50: 28–43; shortened version in *Theater und Ge- sellschaft: Das Volksstück im 19. und 20. Jahrhundert*, ed. Jürgen Hein. Düsseldorf: Bertelsmann Universitätsverlag, 1973. 161–73. All references in the text are to this version.

Adling, Wilfried. 1959. "Die Entwicklung des Dramatikers Carl Zuckmayer. Diss. Leipzig 1957." In *Schriften zur Theaterwissenschaft*. Vol. 1. Berlin: Henschelverlag. 9–289.

Lennartz, Franz. 1959. "Carl Zuckmayer." In Lennartz, *Deutsche Dichter und Schriftsteller unserer Zeit*. Stuttgart: Kröner, 8th edition 1959. 825– 30. 10th edition 1960. 769–76.

Sieburg, Friedrich. 1959. "Der Mord vor dem Dom." *Frankfurter Allge- meine Zeitung*. October 10. Reprinted in Sieburg, *Zur Literatur: 1957– 1963*, ed. Fritz J. Raddatz. Stuttgart: Deutsche Verlags-Anstalt, 1981. 155–58; and in Kieser, *Carl Zuckmayer*, 1986, 176–79.

Basil, Otto. 1960. "Umriß von Carl Zuckmayer." *Wort in der Zeit.* 6 (6): 11–19.

Benicke, Wolf. 1960. "Carl Zuckmayer: Des Teufels General: Eine grundsätzliche Betrachtung, wie und wie weit Spielfilme in die Dramenlektüre sinnvoll einbezogen werden können." *Der Deutschunterricht* 12 (6): 36–43.

Engelsing-Malek, Ingeborg. 1960. *"Amor Fati" in Zuckmayers Dramen.* Constance: Rosgarten; Berkeley and Los Angeles: University of California Press.

Glade, Henry. 1960. "Carl Zuckmayer's Theory of Aesthetics." *Monatshefte für deutschen Unterricht* 52: 163–70.

Lernet-Holenia, Alexander. 1960. "Die schöne Disharmonie: Anmerkungen zu Carl Zuckmayers 'Die Fastnachtsbeichte.' " *Forum* (Vienna) 7 (1960) 1174: 66–67.

Loram, Ian C. 1960. "The Resistance Movement in the Recent German Drama." *German Quarterly* 10: 183–90.

Meinherz, Paul. 1960. *Carl Zuckmayer: Sein Weg zu einem modernen Schauspiel.* Berne: Francke. Zurich: Renggli & Schwarzenbach.

Riegel, Paul. 1960. "Carl Zuckmayer, *Der Hauptmann von Köpenick.*" In *Das europäische Drama von Ibsen bis Zuckmayer: Dargestellt an Einzelinterpretationen,* ed. Ludwig Büttner. Berlin, Bonn: Diesterweg. 195–208.

Vandenrath, J. 1960. "Drama und Theater in Zuckmayers Bühnendichtung." Diss. Liège.

[Anonymous]. 1961. "Zuckmayer: Schlägt dreizehn." *Der Spiegel* 15 (44): 86–89.

Vandenrath, J. 1961. "Zuckmayers Bearbeitung von Gerhart Hauptmanns 'Herbert Engelmann.' " *Revue des langues vivantes* 27: 216–31.

Bienek, Horst. 1962. *Werkstattgespräche mit Schriftstellern.* Munich: Hanser. 164–78, 224. Reprinted Munich: Deutscher Taschenbuch Verlag, 1965. 200–218.

Hodgson, Helen. 1962. "Die Uhr schlägt eins: Ein historisches Drama aus der Gegenwart." *German Life and Letters* 15: 332–33.

Lehrer, Robert Kafka. 1962. "Social Awareness in the Folk Plays of Carl Zuckmayer." Diss. Stanford University, Palo Alto, Calif.

Moser, Josef. 1962. "Carl Zuckmayer, 'Der Seelenbräu.' " *Der Deutschunterricht* 14 (5): 55–64.

Muller, Siegfried. 1962. "Another Note on 'Herbert Engelmann.' " *Monatshefte für deutschen Unterricht* 54: 291–96.

Pankow, Gisela. 1962. "Die 'Welt des Spiegels' in zwei modernen Novellen." *Literaturwissenschaftliches Jahrbuch* 3: 345–51.

Reindl, Ludwig Emanuel. 1962. *Zuckmayer: Eine Bildbiographie.* Munich: Kindler.

Glade, Henry. 1963. "The Motif of Encounter in Zuckmayer's Dramas." *Kentucky Foreign Language Quarterly* 10: 183–90; German version 1978. "Das Begegnungsmotiv in Carl Zuckmayers Dramen." *Blätter der Carl-Zuckmayer-Gesellschaft* 4: 153–60.

[Anonymous]. 1964. "Zuckmayer-Premiere: König Tabor." *Der Spiegel* 18 (48): 140–42.

Barrick, Raymond Erford. 1964. "A Characterization of the Mystical Philosophy of Carl Zuckmayer as Revealed in his Life and Works." Diss. Tulane University, New Orleans, La.

Butzlaff, Wolfgang. 1964. "Die Schlüsselwort-Methode — Grundlagen und Beispiele." *Der Deutschunterricht* 16: 93–120.

Garten, H. F. 1964. "Carl Zuckmayer." In *Modern German Drama.* London: Methuen. Second edition. 192–200.

Rooke, Sheila. 1964. "Carl Zuckmayer." In *German Men of Letters,* ed. Alex Natan. Vol. 3: *Twelve Literary Essays.* London: Oswald Wolff. 209–33.

Maßberg, Uwe. 1965. "Der gespaltene Mensch: Vergleichende Interpretation der Physiker-Dramen von Brecht, Dürrenmatt, Zuckmayer und Kipphardt auf der Oberstufe." *Der Deutschunterricht* 17 (6): 56–74.

Pfeiffer, Johannes. 1965. "Carl Zuckmayer: *Eine Liebesgeschichte.*" In Pfeiffer, *Was haben wir an einer Erzählung: Betrachtungen und Erläuterungen.* Hamburg: Wittig. 49–55.

Rischbieter, Henning. 1965. "Zuckmayers *Des Teufels General.*" In Rischbieter, *Deutsche Dramatik in West und Ost.* Velber b. Hannover: Friedrich. 45–46.

Drewitz, Ingeborg. 1966. "Im Leben zu Hause. Carl Zuckmayer — Versuch eines Porträts." *Merkur* 20: 1195–99. Reprinted in Drewitz. *Zeitverdichtung, Essays, Kritiken, Porträts: Gesammelt aus zwei Jahrzehnten.* Vienna, Munich, Zurich: Europaverlag, 1980, 207–12; and in Kieser, *Carl Zuckmayer,* 1986, 15–21.

Glade, Henry. 1966. "Carl Zuckmayer's *The Devil's General* as Autobiography." *Modern Drama* (Lawrence, Kans.) 9 (1): 54–61.

Michael, Friedrich. 1966. " 'Als wär's ein Stück von mir': Carl Zuckmayers Erinnerungen." *Wiesbadener Kurier.* December 10. Reprinted in Michael, *Der Leser als Entdecker: Betrachtungen, Aufsätze und Erinnerungen eines Verlegers.* Selected and compiled together with the author by Volker Michels. Sigmaringen: Thorbecke, 1983. 188–90; also reprinted in Kieser, *Carl Zuckmayer,* 1986, 180–83.

Weimar, Karl S. 1966. "The Scientist and Society: A Study of Three Modern Plays." *Modern Language Quarterly* (Seattle) 27: 431–48.

Paulsen, Wolfgang. 1967. "Carl Zuckmayer." In *Deutsche Literatur im 20. Jahrhundert,* ed. Otto Mann and Wolfgang Rothe. 5th edition. Berne and Munich: Francke. 332–61, 441–42.

Rühle, Günther (ed.). 1967. *Theater für die Republik. 1917–1933: Im Spiegel der Kritik.* Frankfurt am Main: Fischer.

Speidel, E. 1968. "The Stage as Metaphysical Institution: Zuckmayer's Dramas 'Schinderhannes' and 'Der Hauptmann von Köpenick.' " *Modern Language Review* 63: 425–36.

Kesting, Marianne. 1969. "Carl Zuckmayer. Zwischen Volksstück und Kolportage." In Kesting, *Panorama des zeitgenössischen Theaters: 58 literarische Porträts.* Revised and expanded edition. Munich: Piper. 278–83.

Lange, Rudolf. 1969. *Carl Zuckmayer.* Velber b. Hannover: Friedrich.

Witter, Ben. 1969. "Mit Zuckmayer in schwindelnder Höhe: 'Obwohl mir alles Theoretische fremd ist, bin ich ständig mit Zeitfragen beschäftigt.' " In Witter, *Spaziergänge mit Prominenten.* Zurich: Diogenes. 39–47. Reprinted in Witter, *Prominentenporträts: 25 Porträts prominenter Zeitgenossen.* Frankfurt am Main: Fischer Taschenbuchverlag, 1977. 7–12.

Bauer, Arnold. 1970. *Carl Zuckmayer.* Berlin: Colloquium. 2nd supplemented edition. 1977. (All references in the text are to this edition). American edition: trans. Edith Simmons. New York: Ungar, 1976.

Heist, Walter (ed.). 1970. *Carl Zuckmayer in Mainz.* Mainz: Krach.

Koester, Rudolf. 1970. "The Ascent of the Criminal in German Comedy." *German Quarterly* 43: 376–93.

Rotermund, Erwin. 1970. "Zur Erneuerung des Volksstücks in der Weimarer Republik: Zuckmayer und Horváth." In *Volkskultur und Geschichte. Festgabe für Josef Dünninger zum 65. Geburtstag.* Berlin: Erich Schmidt. 612–33. Reprinted in *Über Ödön von Horváth,* ed. Dieter Hildebrandt and Traugott Krischke. Frankfurt am Main, 1972. 18–45.

[Larese, Dino]. 1972. *Der helle Klang: Zu Carl Zuckmayers 75. Geburtstag in Amriswil.* Amriswil: Amriswiler Bücherei.

Mews, Siegfried. 1972. "*Der Hauptmann von Köpenick*: 'Ein deutsches Märchen' oder Kleider machen Leute." *Germanic Notes* 3 (6): 42–46. Reworked version reprinted in 1978 in *Blätter der Carl-Zuckmayer-Gesellschaft* 4: 20–26.

Geiger, Heinz. 1973. *Widerstand und Mitschuld: Zum deutschen Drama von Brecht bis Weiss.* Düsseldorf: Bertelsmann Universitätsverlag.

Mews, Siegfried. 1973a. *Carl Zuckmayer, Des Teufels General.* Frankfurt am Main: Diesterweg, 2nd supplemented edition 1979; 3rd edition 1987.

Mews, Siegfried. 1973b. "From Karl May to Horace A. W. Tabor: Carl Zuckmayer's View of America." *Mosaic: A Journal for the Comparative Study of Literature and Ideas* 6 (2): 125–142. Reprinted in *Deutschlands literarisches Amerikabild: Neuere Forschungen zur Amerikarezeption der deutschen Literatur*, ed. Alexander Ritter. Hildesheim: Olms, 1977. 476–94. All references in the text are to this reprint.

Sudhof, Siegfried. 1973. "Carl Zuckmayer." In *Deutsche Dichter der Gegenwart: Ihr Leben und Werk*, ed. Benno von Wiese. Berlin: Erich Schmidt. 64–82.

Wehdeking, Volker. 1973. "Mythologisches Ungewitter: Carl Zuckmayers problematisches Exildrama 'Des Teufels General.' " In *Die deutsche Exilliteratur 1933–1945*, ed. Manfred Durzak. Stuttgart: Reclam. 509–19. Reprinted in Kieser, *Carl Zuckmayer*, 1986, 86–102.

Charbon, Remy. 1974. "Zweimal Krise des Vertrauens: Carl Zuckmayer: 'Das kalte Licht.' " In Charbon, *Die Naturwissenschaften im modernen deutschen Drama.* Zurich: Artemis. 70–76.

Glade, Henry. 1974. "*Der Gesang im Feuerofen*: Quintessential Zuckmayer." In *Views and Reviews of Modern German Literature. Festschrift für Adolf D. Klarmann*, ed. Karl S. Weimar. Munich: Delp. 163–70. Reprinted in 1980 as " 'Der Gesang im Feuerofen: Zuckmayers Humanitätsideal" in *Blätter der Carl-Zuckmayer-Gesellschaft* 6: 88–97; and in Kieser, *Carl Zuckmayer*, 1986, 103–116.

Mews, Siegfried, and Raymond English. 1974. "The 'Jungle' Transcended: Brecht and Zuckmayer." In *Essays on Brecht: Theater and Politics*, ed. Mews and Herbert Knust. Chapel Hill, N. C.: University of North Carolina. 79–98. Reprinted in 1978 in German translation as "Im amerikanischen Dickicht: Brecht und Zuckmayer" in *Zuckmayer '78. Ein Jahrbuch.* 181–207.

Heist, Walter. 1975. "Unzusammenhängende Bemerkungen zu 'Der Rattenfänger.' " *Blätter der Carl-Zuckmayer-Gesellschaft* 1: 17–19.

Maddox, Marvin Robert. 1975. "Carl Zuckmayer's Relation to Gerhart Hauptmann: 'Meisterschaft, Vorbild, Verpflichtung.' " Diss. University of North Carolina at Chapel Hill. Short version in *Germanistische Dissertationen in Kurzfassung.* Berne, Frankfurt am Main, Las Vegas: Peter Lang, 1979. 242–48.

Krättli, Anton. 1975–76. "Zuckmayers 'Rattenfänger': Nach der Uraufführung im Schauspielhaus Zürich." *Schweizer Monatshefte* 55 (10): 16–19.

Bäcker, Paul. 1976. "Notizen zur Blomberg." *Blätter der Carl-Zuckmayer-Gesellschaft* 2: 8–16.

Balinkin, Ausma. 1976. "The Central Women Figures in Carl Zuckmayer's Dramas." Diss. University of Cincinnati. Published 1978. Berne, Frankfurt am Main, Las Vegas: Peter Lang.

Brynhildsvoll, Knut. 1976. "Leben und Weltverständnis in der frühen Lyrik Carl Zuckmayers." *Blätter der Carl-Zuckmayer-Gesellschaft* 2: 45–75. Reprinted in Kieser, *Carl Zuckmayer*, 1986, 187–229.

Cowen, Roy C. 1976. "Type-Casting in Carl Zuckmayer's *The Devil's General.*" *University of Dayton Review* 13 (1): 81–94.

Elliott, Jim, Bruce Little, and Carol Poore. 1976. "Naturwissenschaftlerdramen und kalter Krieg." In *Geschichte im Gegenwartsdrama*, ed. Reinhold Grimm and Jost Hermand. Stuttgart: Kohlhammer. 54–65.

Glauert, Barbara (ed.). 1976a. *Carl Zuckmayer auf der Bühne: eine Ausstellung zum 80. Geburtstag des Dichters am 27. 12. 1976, Foyer des Rathauses zu Mainz, 17. 12. 1976 - 27. 2. 77.* Mainz: Landeshauptstadt.

Glauert, Barbara, Gerald P. Martin, and Walter Heist (eds.). 1976. *Festschrift für Carl Zuckmayer: Zu seinem 80. Geburtstag.* Mainz: Krach.

Includes, among others:

Korlén, Gustav. "Carl Zuckmayer in Schweden." 62–66.

Glauert, Barbara 1976b. "Carl Zuckmayer auf der Bühne: Bericht über die Fundorte." 102–15.

Kieser, Harro. "Carl Zuckmayer: Bibliographie 1971–1976." 116–20.

Heist, Walter (ed.). "Der Dichter und der Politiker: Ein Briefwechsel." 121–51.

Hildebrand, Alexander. 1976. "Fülle des Daseins, Fülle des Augenblicks: Marginalien zum lyrischen Werk Carl Zuckmayers." *Blätter der Carl-Zuckmayer-Gesellschaft* 2: 32–44.

Huyssen, Andreas. 1976. "Unbewältigte Vergangenheit — Unbewältigte Gegenwart." In *Geschichte im Gegenwartsdrama*, ed. Reinhold Grimm and Jost Hermand. Stuttgart, Berlin, Cologne, Mainz: Kohlhammer. 39–53.

Imseng, Werner. 1976. *Carl Zuckmayer in Saas-Fee: Ein Album.* Frankfurt am Main: Fischer.

Kvam, Wayne. 1976. "Zuckmayer, Hilpert, and Hemingway." *Publications of the Modern Language Association of America* 91: 194–205.

Mews, Siegfried. 1976. "Von Karl May zu Karl Marx: Zuckmayers Bonanza-Millionär Tabor." In *Die USA und Deutschland: Wechselseitige Spiegelungen in der Literatur der Gegenwart,* ed. Wolfgang Paulsen. Berne and Munich: Francke. 84–91.

Rotermund, Erwin. 1976. "Zur Vergangenheitsbewältigung im deutschen Nachkriegsdrama: Zuckmayer, Borchert, Frisch." *Blätter der Carl-Zuckmayer-Gesellschaft* 2: 76–85.

Ayck, Thomas. 1977. *Carl Zuckmayer in Selbstzeugnissen und Bilddokumenten.* Reinbek b. Hamburg.

Glauert, Barbara, and Bertold Roland (eds.). 1977. *Abschied von Carl Zuckmayer: Ehrung, Dank und Freundschaft. Eine Dokumentation.* Mainz: Krach.

Glauert, Barbara (ed.). 1977. *Carl Zuckmayer: Das Bühnenwerk im Spiegel der Kritik.* Frankfurt am Main: Fischer.

Grothe, Heinz. 1977. "Zwischen Berlin und Hollywood: Carl Zuckmayer und der Film." *Blätter der Carl-Zuckmayer-Gesellschaft* 3: 27–29.

Hein, Jürgen. 1977. "Zuckmayer: Der Hauptmann von Köpenick." In *Die deutsche Komödie: Vom Mittelalter bis zur Gegenwart,* ed. Walter Hinck. Düsseldorf: Bagel. 269–86, 399–401. Reprinted in Kieser, *Carl Zuckmayer,* 1986, 47–70.

Martin, Gerald P. 1977. "Eine verspätete, aber geglückte Zuckmayer-Premiere: Zur deutschen Erstaufführung des 'Kranichtanz' am 19. 2. 1977 im Deutschen Theater in Göttingen." *Blätter der Carl-Zuckmayer-Gesellschaft* 3: 20–26.

Mews, Siegfried. 1977. "Die unpolitischen Exildramen Carl Zuckmayers." In *Jahrbuch für internationale Germanistik.* Series A, vol. 3: *Deutsches Exildrama und Exiltheater: Akten des Exilliteratur-Symposiums der University of South Carolina 1976,* ed. Wolfgang Elfe, James Hardin, and Günther Holst. Berne, Frankfurt am Main, Las Vegas: Peter Lang. 139–48. Reprinted in Kieser, *Carl Zuckmayer,* 1986, 71–85.

Reif, Adelbert. 1977. "Der Mensch ist das Maß: Ein Gespräch mit Carl Zuckmayer." *Blätter der Carl-Zuckmayer-Gesellschaft* 3: 4–14.

Stoevesandt, Hinrich (ed.). 1977. See **Works by Carl Zuckmayer.** 1977. *Späte Freundschaft in Briefen.*

Carl Zuckmayer '78: Ein Jahrbuch, ed. Barbara Glauert in collaboration with Siegfried Mews and Siegfried Sudhof. Frankfurt am Main: Fischer.

Includes, among others:

Glauert, Barbara. 1978. "Pankraz erwacht: Entstehung — Materialien — Wirkung — Editionshinweise." 47–51.

Mews, Siegfried. 1978. "Die Zuckmayerforschung 1961–1977." 228–72.

Mews, Siegfried and English, Raymond. 1974. "Im amerikanischen Dickicht: Brecht und Zuckmayer." 181–207.

Keller, Bernhard. 1978. "Die Auseinandersetzung mit dem Nationalsozialismus im Drama: Vergleichende Analyse von Zuckmayers 'Des Teufels General' und Brechts 'Arturi Ui.' " *Sammlung: Jahrbuch für antifaschistische Literatur und Kunst.* 1: 147–58. Reprinted in *Antifaschistische Literatur im Unterricht,* ed. Uwe Naumann. Frankfurt am Main: Röderberg, 1980. 6–12.

Mathy, Helmut. 1978. " 'Austunken muß es das Volk . . . ': Carl Zuckmayers Urteil über den rheinhessischen Separatismus und die französische Rheinlandbesetzung von 1918 bis 1930." *Blätter der Carl-Zuckmayer-Gesellschaft* 4: 26–37.

Poser, Hans. 1978. "Komödie als Volksstück: Zuckmayer, Horváth, Brecht." *Neophilologus* 62: 584–97.

Riewoldt, Otto F. 1978. *Von Zuckmayer bis Kroetz: Die Rezeption westdeutscher Theaterstücke durch Kritik und Wissenschaft in der DDR.* Berlin: Erich Schmidt.

Badenhausen, Rolf (ed.). 1979. "Carl Zuckmayer und Gustav Gründgens." *Blätter der Carl-Zuckmayer-Gesellschaft* 5: 214–43.

Fleckenstein, Günther. 1979. "Carl Zuckmayer: Das Makabre in seinen Gedichten." In Fleckenstein, *Personen und Wirkungen,* ed. Landesbank Rheinland-Pfalz. Mainz: Krach. Reprinted in 1980 in *Blätter der Carl-Zuckmayer-Gesellschaft* 6: 68–76.

Mews, Siegfried. 1979. " 'Somewhere in France': Ein antifaschistisches Exildrama von Carl Zuckmayer und Fritz Kortner." In *Deutsche Exilliteratur: Literatur im Dritten Reich,* ed. Wolfgang Elfe, James Hardin, and Günther Holst. Berne, Frankfurt am Main, Las Vegas: Peter Lang. 122–31.

Swediuk-Cheyne, Helen. 1979. "Der Rattenfänger Bunting: Ein gesteigerter Schinderhannes." *Blätter der Carl-Zuckmayer-Gesellschaft* 5: 246–50. Reprinted in Kieser, *Carl Zuckmayer,* 1986, 129–35.

Heiskanen, Christine and Piltti. 1980. *Die Sterne sind geblieben: Porträt einer Freundschaft mit Alice und Carl Zuckmayer.* Zurich and Stuttgart: Classen.

Lederer, Herbert. 1980. "The Drama of Ernst Udet: A Nazi General in Eastern and Western Perspective." In *Theatrum Mundi: Essays on German Drama and German Literature Dedicated to Harold Lenz on his 70th Birthday, September 11, 1978*, ed. Edward R. Haymes. Munich: Fink. 175–80.

Martin, Gerald P. R. (ed.). 1980. "Carl Zuckmayer und sein Bibliograph: Aus dem Briefwechsel mit Arnold J. Jacobius (1953–1976)." *Blätter der Carl-Zuckmayer-Gesellschaft* 6: 117–57.

Swediuk-Cheyne, Helen. 1980. "Das Thema 'Von vorne wieder anfangen' als Leitmotiv in den Werken von Carl Zuckmayer." *Blätter der Carl-Zuckmayer-Gesellschaft* 6: 161–70.

Glade, Henry. 1981a. "Carl Zuckmayers Exiljahre: Die europäische Etappe. 1933–1939." *Arbeitskreis Heinrich Mann: Mitteilungsblatt. Sonderheft* 10: 77–86.

Glade, Henry. 1981b. In collaboration with Andreas Strenger. "Carl Zuckmayers Exiljahre. 1933–1941." *Blätter der Carl-Zuckmayer-Gesellschaft* 7: 151–62. The first half of this article is identical with Glade, Henry, 1981a. Glade 1981a and b were later published together as one essay, Glade, Henry. 1989.

Grell, Kurt. 1981. See **Works by Carl Zuckmayer.** 1981. *Einmal, wenn alles vorüber ist.*

Grimm, Reinhold. 1981. "Harras in Dallas." *Brecht-Jahrbuch* 1980. 201–105. Reprinted in 1981 in *Blätter der Carl-Zuckmayer-Gesellschaft* 7: 176–79.

Mews, Siegfried. 1981a. *Carl Zuckmayer.* Boston: Twayne.

Mews, Siegfried. 1981b. "Who is Carl Zuckmayer? Zur Rezeption Zuckmayers in den Vereinigten Staaten." *Blätter der Carl-Zuckmayer-Gesellschaft* 7: 3–22.

Taylor, Jennifer. 1981. "The Dilemma of Patriotism in German Plays of the Second World War." *New German Studies* 9: 181–92.

Martin, Gerald P. 1982a. " 'Ganz neu aus meiner Phantasie.' Der Weg zum 'Rattenfänger' dargestellt an Carl Zuckmayers Briefwechsel mit Günther Niemeyer in den Jahren 1964–1975." *Blätter der Carl-Zuckmayer-Gesellschaft* 8: 173–211.

Martin, Gerald P. (ed.). 1982b. "Carl Zuckmayer und Gottfried von Einem." *Blätter der Carl-Zuckmayer-Gesellschaft* 8: 212–22.

Martin, Gerald P. (ed.). 1982c. "Irrationale Lust am Fabulieren: Die Uraufführung des *Rattenfänger* in der Kritik." *Blätter der Carl Zuckmayer-Gesellschaft* 8: 223–37.

Meiszies, Winrich. 1982. "Carl Zuckmayer und die Lindemanns: Aus seiner Korrespondenz mit Louise Dumont und Gustav Lindemann." *Blätter der Carl Zuckmayer-Gesellschaft* 8: 34–48.

[Zuckmayer, Carl]. 1982a. "Fünf Briefe an Boleslaw Barlog." *Blätter der Carl-Zuckmayer-Gesellschaft* 8: 14–19.

[Zuckmayer, Carl]. 1982b. "Fünf Briefe an Henry Goverts." *Blätter der Carl-Zuckmayer-Gesellschaft* 8: 20–26.

Glade, Henry. 1983. In collaboration with Andreas Strenger. "Carl Zuckmayer in Vermont." *Blätter der Carl-Zuckmayer-Gesellschaft* 9: 112–24.

Kafitz, Dieter. 1983. "Überlegungen zu den Frauengestalten in Carl Zuckmayers Roman 'Salwàre oder Die Magdalena von Bozen." *Blätter der Carl-Zuckmayer-Gesellschaft* 9: 12–30.

Martin, Gerald P. (ed.). 1983. " 'Eine hinreißende Dichtung: Carl Zuckmayers Salwàre oder Die Magdalena von Bozen in den Augen der Kritik." *Blätter der Carl-Zuckmayer-Gesellschaft* 9: 41–63.

Mews, Siegfried. 1983. " 'Edler Fatalismus': Zuckmayers Exilroman 'Salwàre.' " *Blätter der Carl-Zuckmayer-Gesellschaft* 9: 162–71. Reprinted in Kieser, *Carl Zuckmayer*, 1986, 149–64.

Uthmann, Jörg von. 1983. "Nachwort." In Carl Zuckmayer, *Austreibung 1934–39.*" Stuttgart: Reclam. 127–33.

Wagener, Hans. 1983a. *Carl Zuckmayer*. Munich: C. H. Beck.

Wagener, Hans. 1983b. "Stationen der Selbstbesinnung: Zu Carl Zuckmayers Autobiographien." *Blätter der Carl-Zuckmayer-Gesellschaft* 9: 77–88.

Wagener, Hans. 1983c. "Vom Rampenlicht zum 'kalten Licht': Zur Dramatik Carl Zuckmayers nach 1945." In *Nachkriegsliteratur in Westdeutschland*, ed. Jost Hermand, Helmut Peitsch, and Klaus R. Scherpe. Vol. 2: *Autoren, Sprache, Traditionen*. Berlin (West): Argument. 73–88.

Albrecht, Richard. 1984. "Persönliche Freundschaft und politisches Engagement: Carl Zuckmayer und Erich Maria Remarques 'Im Westen nichts Neues' 1929/30." *Blätter der Carl-Zuckmayer-Gesellschaft* 10: 75–86.

[Anonymous]. 1984. "Die 'Affäre' von Köpenick — heute auf der Bühne: Kritiker äußern sich zu Aufführungen in Berlin, München und Mainz." *Blätter der Carl-Zuckmayer-Gesellschaft* 10: 145–68.

Becker, Jochen. 1984. *Carl Zuckmayer und seine Heimaten*. Mainz: Krach; revised edition Mainz: Schmidt, 1989. All references in the text are to this edition.

Gobert, Boy, and Engeroff, Claus. 1984. "Zur Konzeption: 'Der Hauptmann von Köpenick.' " *Blätter der Carl-Zuckmayer-Gesellschaft* 10: 138–40.

Holsti, Keijo. 1984. "Der Teufelspakt: Einige Anmerkungen zu Carl Zuckmayers Drama 'Des Teufels General.' " In *Festschrift für Lauri Seppänen zum 60. Geburtstag*, ed. Ahti Jäntti and Olli Salminen. Tampere: University of Tampere. 265–71.

Martin, Gerald P. (ed.). 1984. " 'Wir sind noch dem Wunder begegnet . . . ': Der Briefwechsel [mit Fritz Usinger]." *Blätter der Carl-Zuckmayer-Gesellschaft* 10: 7–58.

Wagener, Hans. 1984. "Geschichten von einer Geburt: Zum Bedeutungswandel eines Motivs in der Prosa Zuckmayers." *Seminar* 20: 116–26. Reprinted in 1984 in *Blätter der Carl-Zuckmayer-Gesellschaft* 10: 194–202.

Czech, Sonja. 1985. "Das Bild der Frau in Carl Zuckmayers Dramen." *Blätter der Carl-Zuckmayer-Gesellschaft* 11: 121–90.

Erné, Nino. 1985. "Vier Begegnungen mit Carl Zuckmayer." *Blätter der Carl-Zuckmayer-Gesellschaft* 11: 201–9.

Hain, Bruno. 1985. "Der Lyriker Carl Zuckmayer in England." *Blätter der Carl-Zuckmayer-Gesellschaft* 11: 225–27.

Martin, Gerald P. 1985. "Carl Zuckmayer und Hans Cleres." *Blätter der Carl-Zuckmayer-Gesellschaft* 11: 212–17.

Robertshaw, Alan. 1985. "The downfall of General Harras: Carl Zuckmayer's *Des Teufels General* and its critical reception." *Modern Languages* 66: 242–47.

Wagener, Hans. 1985. "Zwischen Elegie und Zeitstück: Zum Exilwerk Carl Zuckmayers." In *Schreiben im Exil: Zur Ästhetik der deutschen Exilliteratur 1933–1945*, ed. Alexander Stephan and Hans Wagener. Bonn: Bouvier. 161–77.

Albrecht, Richard. 1986 [1989]. "Literarische Prominenz in der Weimarer Republik: Carl Zuckmayer. Zwei Hinweise auf einen Zusammenhang." *Blätter der Carl-Zuckmayer-Gesellschaft* 12: 127–33.

[Anonymous]. 1986 [1989] "Zuckmayers Werk zwischen Volkstümlichkeit und Realismus: Eine Podiumsdiskussion." *Blätter der Carl-Zuckmayer-Gesellschaft* 12: 5–28.

Becker, Jochen. 1986a. "Zuckmayer im Exil." In *Exil und Rückkehr: Emigration und Heimkehr*, ed. Anton Maria Keim. Mainz: H. Schmidt. 137–53.

Becker, Jochen. 1986b. [1989] "Ein Sommer in Österreich: Eine Korrektur." *Blätter der Carl-Zuckmayer-Gesellschaft* 12: 34–36.

Fleckenstein, Günther. 1986. "Zuckmayer überzeitlich: Arbeit an seinem dramatischen Werk." In *Exil und Rückkehr: Emigration und Heimkehr*, ed. Anton Maria Keim. Mainz: H. Schmidt. 159–70.

Frizen, Werner. 1986. *Carl Zuckmayer, "Der Hauptmann von Köpenick": Interpretation*. 2nd reworked and supplemented edition. Munich: Oldenbourg, 1988.

Kieser, Harro (ed.). 1986. *Carl Zuckmayer: Materialien zu Leben und Werk*. Frankfurt am Main: Fischer Taschenbuch Verlag.

Includes, among others, the following previously published articles and excerpts from books:

Drewitz, Ingeborg. 1966. "Im Leben zu Hause: Carl Zuckmayer — Versuch eines Porträts." 15–21.

Fechter, Paul. 1927. "Carl Zuckmayer: 'Schinderhannes.' " 40–43.

Kerr, Alfred. 1928. "Zuckmayer: 'Katharina Knie.' " 44–46.

Hein, Jürgen. 1977. "Zuckmayer: 'Der Hauptmann von Köpenick.' " 47–70.

Mews, Siegfried. 1976. "Die unpolitischen Exildramen Carl Zuckmayers." 71–85.

Wehdeking, Volker. 1973. "Mythologisches Ungewitter: Carl Zuckmayers problematisches Exildrama 'Des Teufels General.' " 86–102.

Glade, Henry. 1974. " 'Der Gesang im Feuerofen': Zuckmayers Humanitätsideal." 103–16.

Jaesrich, Hellmut. 1955. "Verwirrung des Menschen. Zu Carl Zuckmayers Zeitdrama 'Das kalte Licht.' " 122–28.

Swediuk-Cheyne, Helen. 1979. "Der Rattenfänger Bunting, ein gesteigerter Schinderhannes." 129–35.

Wagener, Hans. 1983. "Von metaphysischem und dichterischem Theater: Zuckmayers Dramentheorie." 136–46. Chapter from Wagener, *Carl Zuckmayer*, 1983. 162–71.

Mews, Siegfried. 1983. " 'Edler Fatalismus': Zuckmayers Exilroman 'Salwàre.' " 149–64.

Pfeiffer, Johannes. 1955. "Carl Zuckmayer: 'Der Seelenbräu.' " 165–75.

Sieburg, Friedrich. 1959. "Der Mord vor dem Dom." 176–79.

Michael, Friedrich. 1966. " 'Als wär's ein Stück von mir': Carl Zuckmayers Erinnerungen." 180–83.

Brynhildsvoll, Knut. 1976. "Leben und Weltverständnis in der frühen Lyrik Carl Zuckmayers." 187–229.

Lindner, Gabriele. 1986 [1989]. "Die Frauengestalten im Werk Carl Zuck-mayers, dargestellt anhand der weiblichen Titelfiguren Katharina Knie, Ulla Winblad und Barbara Blomberg." *Blätter der Carl-Zuckmayer-Gesellschaft* 12: 49–126.

Wagener, Hans. 1986. "Carl Zuckmayers *Rembrandt*: Drehbuch und Drama." *Michigan Germanic Studies* 12: 151–63.

Lüder, Werner. 1987. "Carl Zuckmayer's antifaschistisches Drama 'Des Teufels General' — Das Werk im Kontext des Gesamtschaffens des Autors und seine Wirkung als Modellfall von Rezeptionsbesonderheiten in Nach-kriegsdeutschland." Diss. Humboldt-Universität, Berlin (East).

Wagener, Hans. 1987. "Carl Zuckmayer (1896–1977)." In *Dictionary of Literary Biography*. Vol. 56: *German Fiction Writers, 1914–1945*, ed. James Hardin. Detroit: Gale Research. 307–317.

Albrecht, Richard. 1988. "The Journey of No Return: Carl Zuckmayer im Exil." In *Albrecht: Exil-Forschung: Studien zur deutschsprachigen Emigration nach 1933*. Frankfurt am Main, Berne, New York, Paris: Peter Lang. 265–314. Reprinted in 1989 as "Carl Zuckmayer im Exil, 1933–1946: Ein dokumentarischer Essay." *Internationales Archiv für Sozialgeschichte der deutschen Literatur* 14: 165–202.

Berlin, Jeffrey B. (ed.) 1988. "Carl Zuckmayer and Ben Huebsch: Unpub-lished Letters about Stefan Zweig's Suicide." *Germanisch-Romanische Monatsschrift* 38: 196–99.

Wagener, Hans. 1988. "Mensch und Menschenordnung: Carl Zuckmayers 'deutsches Märchen' 'Der Hauptmann von Köpenick.' " In *Deutsche Komödien: Vom Barock bis zur Gegenwart*, ed. Winfried Freund. Munich: Fink. 226–40.

Albrecht, Richard. 1989. "Das FBI-Dossier Carl Zuckmayer." *Zeitschrift für Literaturwissenschaft und Linguistik*. 19 (73): 114–21.

Glade, Henry. 1989. In collaboration with Andreas Strenger. "Carl Zuck-mayer." In *Deutschsprachige Exilliteratur seit 1933*, ed. John M. Spalek and Joseph Strelka. Vol. 2: *New York*. Part 2. 1033–56. Identical with Glade, Henry, 1981b, followed by Glade, Henry, 1983.

Karalus, Wolfgang. 1989. "Wilhelm Voigt: Versuch über einen Unsterbli-chen." *Sinn und Form* 41: 830–41.

Wagener, Hans. 1989. "Carl Zuckmayer." In *Deutsche Dichter: Leben und Werk deutschsprachiger Autoren*, ed. Gunther E. Grimm and Frank Rainer Max. Vol. 7: *Vom Beginn bis zur Mitte des 20. Jahrhunderts*. Stuttgart: Reclam. 473–82. Reprinted in *Deutsche Dichter: Leben und Werk deutschsprachiger Autoren vom Mittelalter bis zur Gegenwart*, ed. Grimm and Max. Stuttgart: Reclam, 1993. 695–98.

Zimmermann, Rainer. 1989. *Das dramatische Bewußtsein: Studien zum bewußtseinsgeschichtlichen Ort der 30er Jahre in Deutschland.* Munich: Aschendorff.

Finke, Margot. 1990. *Carl Zuckmayer's Germany.* Frankfurt am Main: Haag & Herchen.

Grange, William. 1991. *Partnership in the German Theater: Zuckmayer and Hilpert, 1925–1961.* New York, Berne, Frankfurt am Main, Paris: Peter Lang.

Mettenberger, Wolfgang. 1992. "Das Volksstück Carl Zuckmayers — eine Untersuchung über Wesen und Wirkung seines Werkes." *Blätter der Carl-Zuckmayer-Gesellschaft* 13: 36–52.

Spahr, Blake Lee. 1992. "Carl Zuckmayer." In *Dictionary of Literary Biography.* Vol. 124: *Twentieth-Century German Dramatists, 1919–1992,* ed. Wolfgang D. Elfe and James Hardin. Detroit, London: Gale Research. 457–69.

Blum, Marie-Odile. 1993. "Expérience et réflexion dans *Katharina Knie* de Carl Zuckmayer." In *Etudes Allemandes. Recueil dedié à Joël Levèbvre.* Vol. 6 (Lyon). 259–69.

Frankmölle, Michaela. 1993. "Die schuldhafte Verwicklung des Menschen, aufgezeigt an den Figuren der 'Fastnachtsbeichte.'" *Blätter der Carl-Zuckmayer-Gesellschaft* 14: 23–37.

Wagener, Hans. 1995. "Carl Zuckmayers Ein Sommer in Österreich: Hymne mit Mißtönen." In *Moderne österreichische Literatur,* ed. Karlheinz F. Auckenthaler. Bonn: Böhlau.

Index